# THE SHOULDERS
# WE STAND ON

# THE SHOULDERS WE STAND ON

*How Black and Brown people fought for change in the United Kingdom*

## PREETI DHILLON

dialogue
books

DIALOGUE BOOKS

First published in Great Britain in 2023 by Dialogue Books

10 9 8 7 6 5 4 3 2 1

A CIP catalogue record for this book
is available from the British Library.

ISBN 978-0-349-70282-7

Typeset in Berling by M Rules
Printed and bound in Great Britain by
Clays Ltd, Elcograf S.p.A

Papers used by Dialogue Books are from well-managed forests
and other responsible sources.

Dialogue Books
Carmelite House
50 Victoria Embankment
London EC4Y 0DZ

www.dialoguebooks.co.uk

Dialogue Books, part of Little, Brown, Book Group Limited,
an Hachette UK company.

To those who fought, and those who fight.

# Contents

# Introduction

I grew up in Southall, near Heathrow Airport in west London. Dubbed 'Little Punjab' for the thousands of northern Indian families that live there, as you pull into the train station the 'Southall' sign greets you in both English and Gurmukhi.* I hated Southall growing up; the traffic, the catcalls, the noise. The pungent smell of cooking seeped into my hair, clothes and skin. I could never wash it off. Walking along the Broadway on my way to school (big up Dormers Wells!) I would groan a little and imagine leaving Southall. I fantasised about where else I would live and what it might smell like; ideally like fresh laundry, straight out of the dryer. I knew very little about Southall except where to get the tastiest samosas, the best value for money salwar kameezes, and which ethnicities and nationalities lived in which areas, and what that supposedly meant in terms of safety.

I vaguely knew that there had been racism 'back in the day'. My dad told me about truanting from school to avoid racism in the classroom, and the casual racism he'd face walking on the streets or hanging out with his friends in the park. But I

---

* Punjabi script.

certainly didn't know that Southall was the site of so much heartbreak from the 1960s to 1980s, with the menace of the National Front, racially motivated killings, police brutality and even death at the hands of the police. I didn't know that Southall birthed crucial anti-racism campaigns and movements of the era, like the Southall Youth Movement that patrolled the streets to defend the community against fascists and police harassment. No one in my family talked about that history when I was growing up as the memories are painful, and besides, 'good immigrants' don't complain.

Like many of us in childhood, I first learned what was going on in society from glimpses of the news. I remember hearing about Stephen Lawrence but didn't really understand what it all meant. As I started to engage more with the world around me, in sauntered Tony Blair; his shiny smile and thick hair – luscious from all the promise it carried – beamed down at me from the TV. I grew up with the notion that 'Britain is a multiracial and multicultural society' and that there would be 'prosperity for all', as the 1997 Labour manifesto said.[1]

I had no reason not to believe it. I hadn't been on the receiving end of any open racial abuse, the government invested heavily in public services, and for the blink of an eye it was even cool to be Asian. We were on TV, and *funny*, in *Goodness Gracious Me*. We were good at sports other than cricket, at least in *Bend It Like Beckham*. Missy Elliott used bhangra beats in 'Get Ur Freak On'. Madonna dressed in saris and wore a bindi. I didn't know the word 'appropriation' then – I was just excited that one of the world's biggest stars wanted to dress like me.

To my young, uninformed, impressionable mind, events

like the murder of Stephen Lawrence and the Iraq War were anomalies, remnants of a bygone era, nothing but small bumps on the smooth path of progress. I thought everything would be OK. Now, as a historian, I am embarrassed at how little I knew of the history of the UK and the society into which I was born.

I stumbled upon the rich history of Southall after I was inspired by the Black American political activist Angela Davis to do some digging around. Seeing her speak at the Southbank Centre for International Women's Day in 2019 was the closest an 'In conversation with' can come to a stadium concert. The crowd was absolutely buzzing, Davis could barely get out a sentence without whooping and cheering drowning her out. As she mentioned groups and movements I had never heard of that were involved in US civil rights action, such as the Black female maids behind the Montgomery Bus Boycott, it got me thinking that there must have been movements in the UK too. *Surely?* A few internet searches and library-book reservations later and suddenly I learned about dozens of campaigns, strikes and movements led by Black and Brown people, men and women alike, all right here in the UK, including in Southall.*

I decided that I wanted to know everything. The hardship, the heartache and, more than that, the fight back. I wanted

---

* In this book I am capitalising Black and Brown. This is to emphasise that there is community among Black and Brown people through a shared history of oppression, and a solidarity through movements such as those detailed in this book. There is an ongoing debate about capitalisation and whether to also capitalise white. Language is imperfect and subjective and it may be that in a few years I would not make the same decision, but, for now, the capitalisation I have chosen seems appropriate given the subject matter.

to know everything that happened in parts of London outside of Southall that we never visited as they were deemed
'too dangerous'. And outside of London: how did Black and
Brown people live in Bristol, in Bradford and beyond? Did
they experience racism and in what forms? How did they fight
back? Did they fight at all? These questions and many more
evolved to make this book.

Spoiler alert: people did fight back, and in spectacular ways.

This book tells the stories of ten remarkable movements,
campaigns and organisations led by Black and Brown people
in the 1960s to 1980s, that fought against racism and capitalism, and impacted the way we live in the UK. It looks at the
fight in all areas of life including education, work, healthcare,
housing and on the streets, drawing on secondary literature,
local history projects, archival material and oral history.

It focuses on the 1960s to 1980s as I wanted to understand
the UK that my parents grew up in and that I was born into
as a racialised person. We know about the miners' strikes,
deep recession and the rise of Margaret Thatcher. We know
about the one and only England football World Cup victory,
the Beatles and dodgy fashion choices. But there is so much
more. Learning about that era helps us understand the society
that we live in today, and inspires us to continue fighting for
change where it's needed.

And, oh boy, is it needed.

The 1960s to early 1980s were a tempestuous time in UK
history. Neoliberalism hadn't taken hold quite yet, though
heady capitalism continued to whip Britain's sails as it nav-
igated the decline of the Empire. Black and Brown arrivals

from the Commonwealth brought with them the experience and knowledge of imperialism and anti-imperialism and real, radical desire for a different existence; one which didn't rely on the exploitation of people. They didn't find the same desire for change among all the people of the UK, especially the middle and upper classes who benefitted from the status quo of exploitation. They were greeted with a hostile environment, overt racism in the streets, at school and at work, and a home was a hard place to find when it was still legal and socially acceptable to refuse to rent to someone Black or Brown. Some of the Black and Brown arrivals weren't content with being 'good immigrants' and decided to do something about the racism they experienced.

Fundamentally, the movements all fought for the same thing: freedom from the multiple shackles of oppression for themselves and others. The fight was not just for themselves in the UK but for oppressed peoples the world over. For many, this wasn't a fight for equality, an equal footing with white people, but for deep, systemic change. As Tariq Mehmood, an activist of the era, put it, they weren't fighting for a piece of the pie, they didn't even want the crumbs, they wanted the whole bakery.[2]

The struggle took different forms. There were protests and marches, armed with placards and slogans such as 'come what may, we're here to stay'. These heavily policed marches meant arrests, which meant fighting battles in a courtroom. You might also have ended up in court as a target of unwarranted police attention (read: racial profiling). In other situations, resistance meant withholding the one thing you had that white people wanted: your labour. The year 1981 saw the last-ditch form of resistance: an uprising. How people resisted differed depending on the exact circumstances they found themselves in but it was almost always accompanied by Black and Brown solidarity to an extent that seems almost unthinkable now in our divided society.

Today, our challenges look different and yet eerily similar to those of the 1960s to 1980s. Luckily it is no longer a national sport to beat up Brown people and we're not likely to see a 'no blacks, no dogs, no Irish' sign in the window of an apartment building. Racial discrimination is actually illegal now. But after the Brexit vote, racial violence and hate speech made a comeback even stronger than all the recent thirst for nineties nostalgia.[3] And now the bread and butter of racism is the systemic, institutional racism that permeates our lives through policy, legislation and cultural norms. It leads to tragedies like Grenfell, rampant Islamophobia, stripping British citizens of their citizenship, deaths in police custody and unequal treatment in the healthcare system, to name just a few manifestations.

Change in the 1960s to 1980s was not inevitable, and it did not occur through happenstance or divine intervention. It occurred through the collective action, the rugged determination and the sheer audacity of the communities that pushed for change.

As then, resistance today also takes many forms. There is not one 'right' way to resist, though a lot of public opinion (and laws) would beg to differ. Resistance includes signing petitions, writing to your MP, following and amplifying organisations doing the work, calling for public inquiries and taking to the streets. It includes using your voice, a pen, your fists. In many instances, mere existence is an act of resistance. And when people would see you suffer, joy and laughter are the most powerful forms of resistance.

Like many, however, I feel like individual action is often pointless. I do like signing petitions, and I enjoyed writing to my MP asking him to vote against Boris Johnson's no-deal Brexit, to which he responded, 'I need no persuading!' which made me chuckle and then sigh. I had influenced nothing. Penning a pithy tweet can take a whole evening, but solitary actions all seem to reinforce one thing: it's not enough. It's easy to believe that resistance is futile, but we know that collective action is the one thing that works. That's why I choose to focus on movements. I do, however, include the role of individuals within those movements – these are people whose names are rarely or never mentioned and they need to be put back into the story.

'If this history is so important,' I hear you say, 'then why don't we already know about it?' Good question, dear reader. There are two reasons. The first is that Britain likes to pretend it is not a racist country. We look to the era of fascist groups such as the National Front and the time when it was legal to refuse to serve someone to say, 'Look, we don't have racism like that any more, ergo, we're not racist.' And no matter how racist we are, there is always someone 'more racist' than we are. We compare ourselves to the USA to justify our actions, and without the manifestations of white supremacy similar to our transatlantic cousins – like a mob storming the Houses of Parliament – we are sold the lie that Britain is fine and therefore what is the point of discussing the sordid past? But Britain is in fact so racist that it doesn't think it's racist. Just see what's in the news on any given day, such as 2021's propaganda-esque Commission on Race and Ethnic Disparities' report (the *Sewell Report*), or the police officers who took selfies with the bodies of murdered Black sisters Nicole Smallman and Bibaa Henry, and how '(almost) straight outta Compton' Meghan Markle is discussed.[4] Or look at the UN report that says that Black people in the UK are subject to the use of excessive force by the police, which leads to deaths in custody.[5] Britain's motto should be 'I'm not racist, but . . .'

The second reason we don't know this history ties into the first: this is history that has been deliberately kept from us. The study of history is central to creating the type of society we want, and the type of people we want in that society, to ensure we toe the party line and play nice. In the UK, that means that we mostly discuss victories in the World Wars and how the slave trade was abolished by a solitary, white, British man. Only 11 per cent of GCSE students learn anything about the contribution of Black people in Britain, and in 2020 the government turned down a request to review the curriculum in England to include more Black and Brown history.[6] The version of history we learn also helpfully assists the promotion of capitalism with its focus on individualism rather than communities.

If we were to learn about Black and Brown people in the UK then we'd need to have uncomfortable conversations about what life was like and why, and learning about those who fought against injustice and disrupted the status quo might just give us ideas above our station. It's the same reason why we don't learn about the Haitian Revolution, the uprising of enslaved people in 1791 who freed themselves from French colonial rule, or the Indian Uprising of 1857. And how can all the stories fit in the one month a year that we're allowed to discuss 'Black' history? And the first South Asian Heritage Month in the UK was only in 2020.

What would happen if we knew about the epic, two-year long strike at the Grunwick factory, led by Brown women, that rallied the nation's working class? Or the classification of Black children as 'educationally subnormal' and the tireless fight of the Black Education Movement against it? For starters, it would be a lot harder to convince us that the current policies and practices we see aren't racist, classist and misogynistic.

I selected the ten movements, campaigns and organisations in this book because they are the ones that impacted me the most when I learned about them. They are the ones that made me stop what I was reading and text a friend to ask, 'Did you know about this?!' They are the movements that brought tears to my eyes, made me feel powerful, and helped me the most to understand the UK I was born into and as it is today.

This book starts by setting the scene of UK life in the 1960s, 1970s and the beginning of the 1980s. It sweeps through the highs and lows of the decades to show what directly provoked the social movements. The rest of the book is dedicated to those movements, and tells the stories of their emergence, what they did, and the impact they had. It ends by taking stock of where we are now, how far we've come and how far we still have to go.

This book unapologetically (and sometimes apologetically, I am British after all) centres movements formed and led by

Black and Brown people. 'Brown' here refers to people of South Asian descent. The movements they led were pioneering and it is time for them to become common knowledge. They also provide important lessons for us today, though this is not intended to be a 'how-to' guide.

Some of what you read here will shock you. Some of it will upset you. If you're anything like me, it might even give you nightmares. Be warned that what you learn cannot be unlearned. I will never see Britain in the same way but I sure am glad I know. I understand Britain more now: learning what happened makes me facepalm and say, 'Ohhhh! That's why we left the EU!' or 'Ohhhh! Now I get why the police have a race problem.' Nothing happens in a vacuum, especially with a political system like ours that replicates itself generation after generation.

Despite the shock and upset, absorbing these stories has made me feel stronger than I ever thought possible. It's akin to the tingly feeling I get when I see kickass women in books or films, and how I imagine many white, cis, hetero, able-bodied men feel every day. Seeing people just like me represented in history helps me believe that I can create change too.

It is not always an easy read – racism and state-supported violence are rarely light material – but it is ultimately a book of hope. Hope that together we can make a difference, that together we are powerful, and that we don't have to tackle this alone. There is a long and deep history of activism by people who look like us, and they can inspire us to make a difference, just like they did. We are in the midst of a racial reckoning, and this book aims to show us that change is possible. It will stoke the fire of hope, and show us that together we are the architects of the future.

I now have a new appreciation for Southall. I moved out of Southall long ago (disappointingly not to a place that smells like fresh laundry), but when I visit the Broadway it is no longer such a nuisance. Its continued existence is a symbol of determination, the noise an act of defiance against those who wanted to silence us.

*Before we go on, please know that there is a trigger warning on this entire book. It records the use of racial slurs and there is frequent reference to physical and mental harm. I have not censored what happened and have therefore not edited use of the N word or the P word, or other imagery or phrases.*

# Chapter One

## So, What Happened?

'We are here because you were there.'[1]

AMBALAVANER SIVANANDAN,
Director of the Institute of Race
Relations 1973–2013

Fires had blazed for hours. An inferno of shops, offices and houses had blurred the skyline. Flames had licked overturned cars, both police and private. Chunks of brick and pavement, shards of glass and abandoned riot gear littered the streets. Hundreds of people had been arrested. Hundreds had been injured, possibly thousands if you counted the protestors, though no one did. Millions of pounds worth of damage had been done. Residents staggered among the ruins, the stench of petrol filling their nostrils, looking for something recognisable amid the wreckage, and wondered, 'What now?'

This scene was repeated to varying degrees across Britain in the spring and summer of 1981. In twenty-nine towns and cities nationwide, Black, Brown and white people, mostly young men, rose up against police brutality, high unemployment and the spectre of fascism. All symptoms of the endemic disease of racism. Protestors were met by walls of police and tear gas. It was the first time tear gas had ever been used on the mainland, and it was the first time police were offered armoured vehicles and water cannons.[2] New methods of control for a new perceived threat to public order.

The uprisings were met with surprise from the British public and politicians alike, but they shouldn't have been a surprise. For decades, Black and Brown people had been defending themselves against the effects of racism on the streets, at work, in schools and in the courtroom. Nineteen eighty-one was simply an extension of that resistance.

Uprisings of the kind seen in 1981 are the last resort of people who haven't been listened to, who have been deliberately marginalised and are left with few other options. After all, no one destroys their own home unless they have to, right? Especially if they have nowhere else to go. So how did it come to this in 1981? Where did it all begin? How did Black and Brown people end up in the UK anyway, in a country where it seemed the white majority did not want them? To understand this, we must go back centuries, to how Black and Brown people came to be on the isles and what happened afterwards, to see why by 1981 they had finally had enough.

The people of the UK have never been homogenous, not in skin colour, language or religion. Black and Brown people have been in the UK for centuries – the earliest records of Black people in the UK date back to Roman times. Later, the seemingly never-ending colonial period and industrial age ushered in the first large increase in Black people on the isles, mostly in positions that quite literally served white people. People from Africa and the Caribbean were brought or came to the UK during the transatlantic slave trade. It is estimated that at any given time, around 10,000 Black people lived in the UK in the 1700s, out of a total population of over 10 million by the end of the century.[3]

As long as there has been racism, or oppression of any kind, there has been resistance to it. London in the 1760s has been described by scholar Peter Fryer as 'a centre of black resistance', and in a show of solidarity that may seem unusual today, white, working-class people joined with the Black working class against a common enemy: the rich ruling class. They joined together to protect the liberty of Black people in the UK and protest for the freedom of Black people in the USA.[4] Racism was a supporting pillar of the Empire, and resistance to it started to tremble the foundations of Empire Headquarters.

Records for South Asians in the UK date back as early as the 1600s. The East India Company hired men from the Indian subcontinent as lascars (sailors) on their voyages. They did not have many opportunities to travel back after their work was done and often settled in Britain's port cities.[5] British families also brought over women as ayahs (nannies) and servants for the summer holidays, or as cheap help when their stint in the colony ended.

These early settlers made their mark on the cultural landscape of Britain. In 1810, a former soldier called Sake Dean Mahomed opened the Hindoostane Coffee House in George Street in London, the country's first Indian restaurant, thus pioneering the trend that for many has become the most appreciated cultural contribution of South Asians to the UK.[6]

Fast forward to the 1900s and despite the horrors unleashed in the name of Empire – no, the railway still does not justify colonisation – many people from South Asia and the Caribbean believed in the UK's expansionist project and the 'mother country'.[7] One and a half million South Asians and at least 15,000 West Indians contributed to the First World War, both in supporting roles as well as on the front lines.[8] Unlike in Europe, this was without conscription, though it was not always by choice either.

Predictably, Black and Brown people were not always warmly welcomed. The War Office did not want to arm Black people to fight against white.[9] And there were disputes about where to station Indian troops in the war. Should they be in Egypt, where they would be among people who looked like them, or on the Western Front? After the war ended, the UK's Black and Brown population increased to around 20,000, many of whom had been part of the war effort and decided to stay in the UK, or else were stranded after being demobilised and not given options for onward travel.[10]

The interwar period was not peaceful in the UK, proving the old adage that the absence of war is not the same as peace. Job scarcity, the increase in interracial relationships and just good ol' fashioned white supremacy led to clashes that often ended in displacement, injuries or death.[11] That the white folks had won the war thanks to Black and Brown support didn't stop them turning on that support, like winning a game of dodgeball then throwing the balls at your own team members.

Unlike a game of dodgeball, this had life-or-death consequences. Charles Wootton, a twenty-four-year-old Black Bermudan sailor who had served Britain in the war, was chased down the streets of Liverpool by a group of white people as he fled a police raid on his house. He ended up in the Queen's Dock, eventually drowning as up to 2,000 people, including the police, looked on.[12] No arrests were made. The year 1919 saw attacks on Black, Chinese and Arab communities as many of the discontents towards post-war Britain were taken out on Black and Brown people. There were clashes across the nations, including in Cardiff, Glasgow and Hull.[13]

Antisemitism was also rife. It wasn't a particularly new phenomenon in the UK: the 1905 Aliens Act intended to limit the number of Jewish people entering the country.[14] This continued in the interwar period, with the 1932 establishment of the British Union of Fascists by Oswald Mosley – sorry, *Sir* Oswald Mosley – and these 'Blackshirts' regularly attacked Jewish people. This led to one of the biggest anti-fascist events in British history, the Battle of Cable Street in 1936, where 20,000 anti-fascists, Jews, socialists and more clashed with the Blackshirts and police.

Another 2.5 million South Asians and 10,000 West Indians were involved in the war effort for the Second World War.[15] This included Noor Inayat Khan, a spy who became the first woman of South Asian descent to be recognised with a historical blue plaque in 2020. Unlike the First World War, the Second World War decimated the national supply of labour in the UK and soon there were more jobs than workers. The number of workers fell by a further 1.4 million after the war as married women and older people chose, or were coerced, to leave work for domestic duties or retirement.[16] At the same time, white Brits emigrated to New Zealand, Australia and Canada as those countries also needed labour. In short, the UK was desperate for workers; the National Health Service needed doctors and nurses after its creation in 1948, factories and foundries needed manual labourers, and cities needed to be literally rebuilt as they lay devastated from bombings.

Britain tried to fill these vacancies with Brits and other white citizens by creating the 1948 British Nationality Act. It codified what was already the reality: British subjects/ Commonwealth citizens could come and go as they pleased on a par with subjects living in Britain itself.* It was expected that the British Nationality Act would lure white immigrants from Australasia and Canada, but this didn't work as there was also a labour shortage in those areas. White Europeans were also encouraged to live and work in the UK, and thousands were allowed entry as refugees. By the end of the 1950s, more than 250,000 Eastern Europeans had migrated to the UK, and there were 680,000 Irish migrants in the UK by 1961.[17]

The British government had, however, not foreseen that the British Nationality Act would encourage migration of Black and Brown people from the colonies. In the same year as the Act was passed in 1948, the now infamous HMT *Empire*

---

* Everyone who lived within the realm of the British Empire had always been considered 'British subjects', but some countries, such as Canada, were now introducing their own citizenship, so the new title of 'Commonwealth citizen' was introduced to indicate the ongoing equality of everyone within the Commonwealth, regardless of whether the country was independent or not. Confused? Yeah, immigration legislation has never exactly been logical or user-friendly.

*Windrush* carried 1,027 passengers to the UK, around half of whom were from Jamaica and wanted to find work in the 'motherland'. This event for many people marks the beginning of the post-war immigration period. Black and Brown people from the West Indies, South Asia and West, East and Southern Africa moved to the UK to contribute to the flailing economy and in the search of better opportunities. Better than those that could be found at home, where the damage wrought by colonisation and the aftermath of independence, or natural disasters, made for a hard life. Despite the labour shortage, the new arrivals weren't always warmly welcomed; Liverpool witnessed three days of racist attacks in 1948, the same year that the *Windrush* landed, echoing the violence that had taken place there in 1919 in the aftermath of the First World War.

By the mid-1950s, as recruitment drives in the UK had proven unsuccessful, London Transport, British Rail, the British Hotel and Restaurant Association and the NHS actively recruited in the Caribbean, even paying transatlantic travel costs for some new recruits. In his role as health minister, Enoch Powell actively recruited West Indian nurses (if the irony of that is not obvious yet, wait until later in the chapter when Powell will come up again).[18] Migrants found work across the country, from factories in west London to the textile mills of Yorkshire. They found jobs in transport, health, hospitality, construction and manufacturing.

Many migrants came alone, leaving their families behind as they didn't plan to stay in the UK. The plan was to save money to take back home. 'My idea – and the other fellows' as well,' said Carl Hoyte, a bus driver born in Barbados, 'was to come here for five years, get as much money as you can and go back . . . I'm still here after 44 years and I still ain't got the money!'[19] The inflated hopes of making it big were soon popped when it became clear that Black and Brown workers did not have access to the same opportunities as the white ones. Black female nurses in the NHS were hired as State Enrolled Nurses rather than State Registered Nurses, which was a lower position with a qualification not even recognised by countries in the Caribbean.[20] And without money to save, or even enough money for the return journey, the temporary migrants became permanent settlers.

Harold Macmillan, the Conservative Party Prime Minister, said in 1957, 'most of our people have never had it so good', but this wasn't true for all of Britain's people. Long-term settlement of Black and Brown people did not always go down well with the white population. The 1950s ended with acts of racial violence that foreshadowed the violence that was to become a prominent feature of life in the 1960s to 1980s.

In 1958, a week after racist attacks had shaken Nottingham, a riot broke out in Notting Hill in London after a white woman was seen arguing with her Black husband in public, playing on one of the biggest bugbears of white supremacy: interracial relationships. This prompted five days of attacks on the West Indian population in the neighbourhood by Teddy boys armed with iron bars and butcher's knives, many of whom supported Mosley and his new Union Movement, or the White Defence League, or one of the other extreme, right-wing groups.

Safety couldn't be guaranteed inside either, as petrol bombs were thrown into houses and businesses frequented by the Caribbean community. A first group of Teddy boys would pass by and mark the houses where Black people lived, so the following group knew which houses to attack.[21] A police officer reported at the time that he saw a mob of a few hundred white people shouting, 'We will kill all black bastards. Why don't you send them home?'[22] One of the Black men arrested for possession of weapons, George Lawrence, said in his defence that 'they will kill us if we do not help ourselves'.[23] This proved prescient.

Not to be scared into submission, journalist and activist Claudia Jones and others organised a Caribbean carnival in early 1959 to bring the community together in an expression of joy. This was the first event in what was to later become the world-famous Notting Hill Carnival.

A few months later, Teddy boys murdered Antiguan-born Kelso Cochrane in Notting Hill. No one was charged with his murder. Cochrane was the Stephen Lawrence of his day.

Nineteen sixty. What would become fondly known as the 'Swinging Sixties' had just begun, and life in the UK was on the up and up. The fog of the Second World War had lifted and the whiff of prosperity was in the air. The economy grew by a whopping 6 per cent, a figure I've never seen in my lifetime.[24] British rock and roll was in its infancy, and Cliff Richard dominated the charts that year with three number-one hits (in case you don't know, he's the guy who sings 'Mistletoe and Wine' at you on a loop every December). Strides were made in television entertainment as the Grand National horse race was broadcast for the first time, and *Coronation Street* premiered to the joy of 7.7 million viewers.

The UK was still clinging on to numerous colonies, with territories and influence stretching from Australia to Jamaica.

As the 1960s went on, things seemingly got better and better for people in the UK. The death penalty was abolished (for murder at least), homosexuality was legalised (in two of the four nations of the UK), the contraceptive pill was launched and abortion legalised (under certain conditions). The miniskirt took over the fashion world and liberated young women from dressing like their mothers. 'Beatlemania' spread like wildfire around the world and the Rolling Stones sang about their lack of satisfaction.

Technological advances saw a huge rise in affordable consumer electronics. In just ten years, the proportion of UK households with a television rose from 58 per cent to over 90 per cent.[25] The UK developed the supersonic Concorde with France.

And no discussion of 1960s UK would be complete without mentioning England's football World Cup victory in 1966. What is perhaps most impressive by today's standards, however, is that even by the end of the decade you could buy a house for just £5,000 with change to spare, the equivalent of around £63,000 today.[26] There is widespread nostalgia for the 1960s. In 2016, Brits chose the 1960s as the decade in which Britain was at its 'greatest'.[27]

Despite being the 'greatest' decade, as skirts got shorter so did the patience of many white Brits as the perceived threat to their 'British' way of life grew. For the 415,000 Black, Brown and otherwise 'non-white' people in the UK in 1961, the 1960s was a tumultuous decade.[28] It became harder for Black and Brown British citizens to even enter the country, then finding work was difficult and then on top of that there was the constant police harassment with which to deal.

The fears of white Brits were stoked by the government as much as renegade figures such as Oswald Mosley. The Conservative government started to close the door that had been wedged open by the British Nationality Act, with the 1962 Commonwealth Immigrants Act that ended free movement for Commonwealth citizens. Now, citizens who wanted to live and work in the UK had to apply for a voucher based on their skills. The Commonwealth Immigrants Act fully unleashed the racism that had been clawing at the gate throughout the 1950s. The state had declared that people in the Commonwealth were different to people on the British Isles, in what was essentially state-sanctioned racism.

This racism could be seen in all areas of life, from housing to work to school. Going a day without open racism was unusual, and 'no blacks, no dogs, no Irish' signs were as de rigueur as the miniskirt. And there was little legal recourse to be had: racial discrimination was not illegal in the early 1960s. To rephrase: racial discrimination was *legal* in the early 1960s.

Trying to find housing was particularly difficult.

To let: decent single bed-sitting room with facilities to cook in basement kitchen. Suit a working gentleman or woman. Only respectable people need apply. No coloured please.[29]

Adverts such as the one above were common, though perhaps some didn't say 'please'. Councils imposed residency requirements for council housing to exclude newly arrived migrants from eligibility. Meanwhile, private landlords that offered them accommodation weren't necessarily progressive, and many charged extortionate amounts for overcrowded housing. One of these slum landlords was Peter Rachman, who became so notorious that 'Rachmanism' is in the dictionary as a term synonymous with exploitative landlord practices. Really, it is, look it up. I'll wait.

Black and Brown people did not passively accept this discrimination. They actively fought against it. In response to Rachmanism and otherwise discriminatory housing practices, communities started informal savings and lending groups to help one another buy property. Mutual aid groups and welfare organisations sprang up. One such group was the Indian Workers' Association, discussed in Chapter Two. It was originally formed in the interwar period to campaign for Indian independence. It was revived in multiple cities and towns initially as a welfare organisation to help migrants navigate the tricky bureaucracy of life in the UK and soon became involved in anti-racist campaigns.

In the workplace, Black and Brown people were often faced with a 'colour bar', meaning they wouldn't be hired, or there were strict race-based quotas to limit the proportion of non-white workers in a company, usually to no more than 5 per cent. Companies were often supported in this by the white-dominated trade unions.[30] It even happened in industries, such as transport, that had solicited Black and Brown workers after the war. The second movement discussed, in Chapter Three, is the Bristol Bus Boycott of 1963, which exposed the use of the colour bar in the UK beyond a shadow of a doubt. The eight other movements discussed are from the 1970s onwards, but first let's look at what happened in the rest of the 1960s that led to the need for even more organising.

'I have come here,' said Malcolm X, 'because I am disturbed by reports that coloured people in Smethwick are being badly treated. I have heard they are being treated as the Jews under Hitler. I would not wait for the fascist element in Smethwick to erect gas ovens.'[31] On the invitation of the Indian Workers' Association, Malcolm X was speaking from Smethwick, a town west of Birmingham. That is, Birmingham, West Midlands, not Birmingham, Alabama.

By the 1964 general election, immigration was a hot-button issue, with 85 per cent of white Brits agreeing that too many immigrants had been let into the country.[32] A group of young white people launched a branch of the Ku Klux Klan. Known as 'Britain's racist election', it saw fierce competition as Labour sought to claw its way back into power after a thirteen-year hiatus.[33] The industrial town of Smethwick had been firmly held by Labour ever since 1945. But following the end of the war there had been factory closures and housing shortages, combined with an increase in immigration, and people were concerned for their way of life.

White constituents were angry and unconvinced by Labour's manifesto, which discussed the importance of peaceful race relations at the same time as reducing immigration. Conservative hopeful Peter Griffiths stoked and exploited this anger with the unofficial slogan 'If you want a nigger for a neighbour, vote Labour'.[34] It worked. Peter Griffiths won, booting out the incumbent Labour MP and shadow foreign secretary. Labour won the election nationwide with a slim majority, but it would soon become indistinguishable from the Conservatives in terms of immigration policy.

A glimmer of hope seemed to come the year after the tense election, with the passage of the Race Relations Act of 1965. For the first time, discrimination on the grounds of ethnicity, colour, race or nationality was illegal and incitement to racial hatred was now an offence. It also created the Race Relations Board to promote racial harmony and to oversee violations of the Act.

The Race Relations Act, though a piece of landmark legislation, did very little to help Black and Brown people. Key areas were noticeably absent from the legislation – employment, housing, shops, education and the police. So, nearly every major area of life. The 'incitement to racial hatred' provision of the Race Relations Act was even used to prosecute Black people, the very people it was created to protect, like Michael X who was jailed for a year for stoking racial hatred towards white people.[35] And the Race Relations Board was a lame duck from the outset; its remit was so specific that of the 327 complaints received in its first year of existence, 238 fell outside of its responsibilities, that's 73 per cent.[36]

In the same year as the Race Relations Act, the Labour government tightened immigration by reducing the number of vouchers available from 20,800 to 8,500 a year.[37] The state would give you crumbs with one hand as it slapped you with the other.

Omitting the police from the Race Relations Act was significant as the police themselves were often the instigators of racial violence. The first community review of police racism in 1966 stated: 'It has been confirmed from reliable sources that sergeants and constables do leave stations with the express purpose of going "nigger hunting", that is to say, they do not get orders from superiors to act in this way, but among themselves they decide to bring in a coloured person at all cost.'[38] While shocking, the report confirmed what Black people already knew and regularly experienced.

It is little surprise then that despite the Race Relations Act, the public felt they had free rein to express their racism. The UK edition of the Ku Klux Klan burned crosses and threatened death as they would 'never allow this place to become a dumping ground of Afro–Asian filth'.[39] Hitherto disparate anti-immigration and fascist organisations joined forces to create the National Front political party in 1967. Just two decades on from the Second World War, fascism was still very much alive; the leaders were self-proclaimed fans of Hitler and the Nazis. One of them, Martin Webster, was caught on tape calling the National Front a 'well-oiled Nazi machine'.[40] If it's not obvious, they stood on a racist and xenophobic manifesto. The National Front was not the first of its kind, nor the last.

In 1968 the government tightened immigration again, prompted by the increase in British Asian migrants arriving in the UK from countries such as Kenya, Zambia, Malawi and Tanzania following 'Africanisation' policies. The Labour government responded with the Commonwealth Immigrants Act of 1968. Now only Commonwealth citizens with a parent or grandparent born, naturalised, adopted or registered as a citizen of Britain could live in the UK. Up to 200,000 Asians, as well as other Black and Brown people from the ex-colonies, were now stranded, but it handily meant that many white people in Australia, New Zealand and Canada could still settle in the UK as their parents or grandparents had usually been born there.[41] Seventy-two per cent of the public supported the new Commonwealth Immigrants Act.[42]

The thin veil hiding the racist motives of immigration legislation had been dropped entirely. Where the previous Commonwealth Immigrants Act of 1962 had not been openly racist, instead discussing 'skills', the 1968 Act was now openly racially motivated. Even so, for some it didn't go far enough, as dependents of migrants already in the UK continued to arrive and the voucher system from 1962 was still in place. The government was under fire from all angles, facing opposition to the Immigrants Act because it didn't go far enough, and opposition because it went too far and stripped citizens of their rights.

Due to this immense pressure, the government was considering a second Race Relations Act. In the run-up to a reading of the Race Relations Bill, Conservative MP and member of the shadow cabinet, Enoch Powell, gave a speech:

It almost passes belief that at this moment twenty or thirty additional immigrant children are arriving from overseas in Wolverhampton alone every week – and that means fifteen or twenty additional families a decade or two hence. Those whom the gods wish to destroy, they first make mad. We must be mad, literally mad, as a nation to be permitting the annual inflow of some 50,000 dependants . . . It is like watching a nation busily engaged in heaping up its own funeral pyre.[43]

It didn't stop there. Quoting a constituent, he said 'in this country in fifteen or twenty years' time, the black man will have the whip hand over the white man'. This anti-immigration tirade is now infamously known as the 'Rivers of Blood' speech. Powell believed the Race Relations Act was a mistake and that non-white migrants would dominate the UK and its white citizens, with dire consequences. He wanted an end to immigration, and preferably a Ministry for Repatriation.[44] Bit of a change from just a few years prior when he was minister for health and actively recruited workers from the Caribbean. Powell was fired from his position in the shadow cabinet the day after the speech, the Race Relations Act 1968 became law, and discrimination in employment and housing (but notably still not the police) was officially made illegal. But the damage was done.

Never mind the impact of migration, the speech itself had dire consequences. It fanned the flames of racism and gave legitimacy to fascist groups such as the National Front. After Powell's speech, the National Front, Union Movement and other right-wing extremist groups joined with dockers and porters on the streets of east London, brandishing signs that read 'Back Britain, not Black Britain', 'Powell speaks for us', 'Forever white England' and 'Jobs and housing – Britons first'. The secretary of the Immigrants Control Association said, 'we are worried about the amount of double marriage and overbreeding among coloured immigrants which is leading to overcrowding'.[45] A new national sport of 'Paki-bashing' emerged, though it was not limited to people of Pakistani origin. Anyone who was a shade of brown could be 'Paki-bashed'.

The decade ended with the death of David Oluwale, a Nigerian-born Leeds resident who had been in and out of mental health institutions with issues possibly brought on by blows to the head in one of his frequent encounters with the police.[46] He died by drowning in 1969 while escaping the police.*

In the same year, the UK ratified the United Nations International Convention on the Elimination of All Forms of Racial Discrimination, which states that 'any doctrine of racial differentiation or superiority is scientifically false, morally condemnable, socially unjust and dangerous'.[47] It was dangerous indeed.

Nineteen seventy. A new decade. The headiness of the 1960s would soon dissipate as Paul McCartney left the Beatles, the first topless 'page three' model appeared in the newspapers, and the Conservative Party won a shock victory in the general election. The UK ended the sixties and started the new decade bopping to a Rolf Harris cover of a US Civil War song about helping others called 'Two Little Boys'. Incidentally, Margaret Thatcher counted this song among her favourites.[48] It wasn't all doom and gloom – the Gay Liberation Front had its first march, and the Equal Pay Act was signed. But the reputation of the 1970s as a distinctively less glamorous decade than the sixties or the eighties is well-earned.

The 'dark ages' of post-war Britain, the 1970s saw unemployment reach over a million for the first time since the

---

* In April 2022 the organisation Remember Oluwale mounted a blue plaque on the Leeds Bridge in his honour – it was almost immediately stolen.

1930s, the peak of the 'Troubles' in Northern Ireland, and rubbish piled up so high in the streets you could barely walk; not even the dawn of space hoppers and rise of flares could help Britain navigate them.[49] The Labour Party said that Britain faced 'the most dangerous crisis since the war'.[50] The sun was well and truly setting on the British Empire, finally forcing Britain to reconsider and reformulate its relationships with much of the world, and within its own borders.

As the early migrants realised they weren't going back any-time soon and immigration laws had made entering the UK more difficult, they had started to bring over family members. Other migrants were also still coming in smaller numbers to the UK and by 1971 there were an estimated 1.3 million Black and Brown people in the UK, more than double the number in 1961, and that number would reach over 2 million by the end of the decade.[51] In a now-familiar story, as the quality of life for the population of the UK declined and numbers of Black and Brown people increased, racism got worse.

In April 1970, Tosir Ali was walking home from work a little past midnight when he was attacked by two men with a knife, dying from stab wounds to his throat. His wallet was found with his body, including cash – he hadn't been robbed. Ali's murder was part of a growing trend; according to a survey by the Pakistani Student Federation in 1970, more than 25 per cent of its members had been physically assaulted in the previous year.[52] Despite the worrying pattern of racist attacks, the media often engaged in victim-blaming, with an *Observer* article noting 'any Asian careless enough to be walking the streets alone at night is a fool'.[53] Paki-bashing was the victims' fault.

A few months later, the Conservative government under Edward Heath came to power in a surprise victory. The attack on Black and Brown communities continued under his government. The 1971 Immigration Act formalised what the 1968 Commonwealth Immigrants Act had started, by getting rid of the idea of a 'Commonwealth citizen' and introducing the terms 'patrial' and 'non-patrial' instead. 'Patrials' were people with a parent or grandparent born or naturalised in the UK who therefore had the right to live and work, and 'non-patrials' were subject to work permits with time limits on how long they could stay. They weren't to settle. The 1971 Act also expanded the powers of the police, Home Office and immigration authorities. Although Powell's dream of a Ministry for Repatriation didn't come true, any migrant who wanted to be repatriated would be assisted by the government.[54]

The 1971 Immigration Act was put to the test in the summer of 1972. The Ugandan leader Idi Amin, who was in power thanks to support from the UK government, gave the country's Asian community ninety days to leave the country. Approximately 50,000 of the 80,000 Asians now looking for a place to go were British passport holders, which meant there was a decision to make: would the Brits accept the British citizens, as was their obligation under international law so they would not become stateless, or would they refuse entry using the patrial requirements under the 1971 Immigration Act?[55] The UK eventually admitted around 30,000 Asians, on the proviso that this was an exceptional case.[56] This proviso wasn't enough to assuage some people and local councils. Leicester City Council took it upon itself to deter potential Asian settlers with an advert in a Ugandan newspaper warning people that 'in your own interests and that of your family you should ... not come to Leicester'.[57]

Was restricted immigration really just about racism? There were two main arguments used for restricting the entry of Black and Brown people, not just in 1972 but through-out these decades. One was the idea of acting in the 'best interest' of both the settled and potential migrants. The Conservatives, the *Guardian* reported, 'were only thinking about the Uganda Asians' best interests, British passports or no British passports, they just wouldn't be happy here if they came in greater numbers'.[58] The impact on Asians already settled in the UK was also used as an argument for limiting numbers, as 'immigrants already settled here stand to suffer more than anyone else from a rate of new immigration greater than the social body of the host country can digest or than its prejudices can tolerate'. [59]

The second argument was that the island nation was too crowded, and controlling the number of (non-white) people entering would help to improve the quality of life for everyone, and assist racial harmony. In 1976 Labour Prime Minister (spoiler alert: Labour won the general election in 1974) James Callaghan said to his party, 'I have never wavered from the view that in a small and highly populated country there is a limit to the number of immigrants we can absorb. Therefore strict control over immigration is necessary.'[60] The Conservatives had the same stance. 'It is true,' said party leader Margaret Thatcher, 'that Conservatives are going to cut the number of new immigrants coming into this country, and cut it substantially, because racial harmony is inseparable from control of the numbers coming in.'[61]

'Too many immigrants' was a lie. From 1964 to 1983, there were more people emigrating from the UK than immigrating to it except in 1979.[62] In fact, this was the case overall for the twentieth century.[63] So, yes, restricted immigration was about racism. It was, and still is, state-led racism.

This was all happening under a tense economic climate for the whole country. The economic glory days of the 1960s screeched to a halt in the 1970s. A coal-miner strike in 1972 led to a three-day working week as businesses couldn't operate without their regular coal-powered electricity, and more than a million people lost their jobs.[64] A year later, the issues still largely unresolved, the three-day week was imposed again, unemployment skyrocketed, inflation was over 10 per cent and rising, and Britain plunged into a recession. The post-war economic boom was well and truly over.

The police continued to disproportionately target Black and Brown people, and especially young Black people. The so-called 'sus' law allowed police to stop and search anyone for simply looking 'suspicious' by drawing on the 1824 Vagrancy Act. In London in 1977, young Black people made up just 3 per cent of the population but they constituted 44 per cent of the arrests made under the 'sus' laws.[65] The police force was almost exclusively white; for obvious reasons, police officer wasn't regarded as a desirable job for Black and Brown people, and the informal colour bar meant that there were fewer than twenty-four Black officers across the whole country in the mid-1970s.[66]

The children of the first Black and Brown migrants were coming of age in the 1970s and didn't like what they saw. By the mid-1970s, 40 per cent of the Black population in Britain were British born and raised, and they wouldn't accept the same treatment as their migrant parents.[67]

The increase in state and street racism led to a proportionate increase in resistance. Inspired by their American cousins and drawing on liberation politics from around the world, Black people created Black Power groups in the UK, such as the British Black Panthers, the Black Liberation Front and the Fasimbas. Brown people also joined some of these groups. The rise of Black Power organisations was of concern to the government and police, who often cracked down harshly on any inkling of Black Power activity. One such crackdown of a small protest against police harassment in Notting Hill led to the epic trial of the Mangrove Nine in 1971, discussed in Chapter Four.

Soon after, the Fasimbas were embroiled in a legal case of their own. Four members of the Fasimbas were arrested outside Oval Underground Station in London on their way back from a meeting to discuss how they could support recently arrested Black Liberation Front leader, Tony Soares. The 'Oval Four' had the misfortune of running into Detective Sergeant Derek Ridgewell, notorious for frequent confrontations with Black men and his heavy-handed methods. 'Nigger-hunting' was still alive and thriving. The 1972 trial of the Oval Four is discussed in Chapter Five.

As we've seen, immigration control was closely accompanied by attempts to promote 'racial harmony'. Integration of migrants and buying into the 'British' way of life were a key part of this. Education has always been central to integration in society and civic participation, and this became even more important for policymakers in the 1970s as the number of Black and Brown children increased. The problem was, they didn't know how to do this so, instead, schools declared many children, especially Black children, to be 'educationally sub-normal' and dumped them in special schools. Chapter Six looks at the umbrella Black Education Movement, as migrant parents and communities took matters into their own hands to campaign against these policies, and Black communities provided their own education programmes.

Black and Brown women had specific experiences of racism to which others weren't subjected. For instance, the Home Office carried out 'virginity tests' on Brown women at Heathrow Airport as they entered the country to join their fiancés. Where anti-racist movements were dominated by men, which was most of them, the particular experience of being a Black or Brown woman was often overlooked. This was despite the fact that Black and Brown women were front and centre of campaigns in all areas of life, responsible as they were for carrying so many of the daily burdens. And the general Women's Liberation Movement was dominated by white women who didn't yet have 'intersectionality' in their vocabulary. Chapter Seven discusses the Brixton Black Women's Group and the Organisation of Women of Asian and African Descent (OWAAD), movements that centred issues affecting Black and Brown women as Black and Brown women.

Black and Brown women were particularly at risk of exploitation in the workplace. Asian women have even been called 'the worst off of all British workers'.[68] The unemployment rate among young Black people increased twice as quickly as the general population between 1973 and 1976.[69] Employers took advantage of the economic climate and stereotyping of women in particular and exploited workers with low pay and poor working conditions. This didn't stop Black and Brown workers from fighting back; strikes were frequent and often impactful – after all, factories needed their labour. In contrast to their reputation as submissive and docile, Brown women repeatedly resisted the low standards of working conditions, as happened in the strike at Grunwick, which we will see in Chapter Eight.

The government didn't deny the inequality for Black and Brown people, nor did it deny it could do something to solve that inequality. The Racial Discrimination White Paper of 1975 stated:

> Racial discrimination, and the remedial disadvantages experienced by sections of the community because of their colour or ethnic origins are not only morally unacceptable, not only individual injustices for which there must be remedies, but also a form of economic and social waste which we as a society cannot afford ... it is inconceivable that Britain, in the last quarter of the 20th Century, should confess herself unable to secure for a small minority of around a million and a half coloured citizens their full and equal rights as individual men and women.[70]

Yet the solution once again did not go far enough. The Race Relations Act was expanded in 1976, this time to include indirect discrimination. The new Race Relations Act went further than any legislation before it, but it still didn't include the police or the prison system in its scope.[71]

And despite the Race Relations Act, or maybe because of

it, the second half of the seventies was fraught with social tension and brutal racist violence.

Much of the violence of the era involved the National Front (and other white supremacist groups), their supporters and the police. While membership remained relatively low, for a time the National Front was Britain's fourth biggest party, and it impacted the daily public life of Black and Brown people in the UK.[72] Its members held meetings in areas with high numbers of Black and Brown people, like at the Southall Town Hall, and they sold their newspaper on the streets of east London, but not without protest. The National Front is synonymous with 1970s UK, in much the same way as the miners' strikes.

Racially motivated murders became more commonplace, and continued to be dismissed by police who insisted on downplaying the racial aspects. Altab Ali was one such victim, who was stabbed to death in an alleyway near Brick Lane. Police foot-dragging led the Bengali community to unite like never before to march on Downing Street and take back control of the streets. The 'Battle of Brick Lane' is discussed in Chapter Nine.

Racial violence wasn't limited to London; Mohan Dev Gautam died after being set alight outside her home in Leamington Spa. The police were unwilling and/or unable to protect Black and Brown people and white allies, so they had to take their safety into their own hands. The Asian Youth Movements were at the forefront of community protection, with the cry of 'self-defence is no offence'. Resistance spread and Asian Youth Movements appeared across the country like antibodies to the disease of racism. This inevitably led to arrests, and more than one court case. One such trial was that of the Bradford 12, which echoed the Mangrove Nine trial, and also set a ground-breaking precedent in UK legal history. The trial of the Bradford 12 and the Asian Youth Movements more widely are discussed in Chapter Ten.

By the end of the decade, the UK was in turmoil. The 1970s ended with the 'Winter of Discontent', the biggest strike action since 1926, which coincided with the coldest winter in sixteen years. In total, nearly 30 million working days were lost in 1979 due to strike action.[73] Workers from both the private and public sectors were not happy with the government's attempt to limit wage increases, and as refuse collectors and gravediggers went on strike, piles of rubbish lined the streets and bodies were stacked on top of each other in factories in heat-sealed plastic bags.[74]

The impact of this showed at the polling booths in May 1979. The Labour government lost its tenuous hold on power to the Conservative Party, under the leadership of one Margaret Thatcher. In the run-up to the election, Thatcher appeared on the popular ITV show *World in Action* to discuss the Conservatives' policies. When asked about immigration, Thatcher said, 'people are really rather afraid that this country might be rather swamped by people with a different culture'.[75] She went on to advocate zero immigration of Black and Brown people, apart from compassionate cases, and stated that, 'In my view, that is one thing that is driving some people to the National Front. They do not agree with the objectives of the National Front, but they say that at least they are talking about some of the problems. Now, we are a big political party. If we do not want people to go to extremes, and I do not, we ourselves must talk about this problem and we must show that we are prepared to deal with it.'

Thatcher advocated for the Conservatives to try and take the wind out of the National Front's sails by adopting even more extreme immigration policies. It wouldn't be the last time this argument was made. The public clearly agreed: the Conservatives won with a majority of forty-three seats. The Christmas number one in 1979 was Pink Floyd's 'Another Brick in the Wall (Part 2)'.

Nineteen eighty. The UK chugged, sputtered and creaked its way through the year. In good news, five gold medals were won at the controversial Moscow Olympics, and Alton Towers theme park opened its doors. In not so good news, John Lennon was shot and killed, and Thatcher's infamous economic policies began. The economy dropped into recession again and inflation reached over 20 per cent. Unemployment reached over 2 million, the highest figure since 1935, with young people bearing the brunt as over half of those affected were under twenty-four years old.[76] Thatcher dismissed claims her government was responsible for the current situation, calling the administration 'one of the truly radical ministries of post-war Britain'.[77] The rising income equality seen since the end of the war was about to be reversed.[78] The age of neoliberalism, which favours free trade, deregulation and reducing government spending, had begun.

Life was continually trying for many of the 2.1 million Black and Brown people living in the UK.[79] The Bristol police raided a café in St Pauls in Bristol, which led to a seven-hour violent clash between police and the local Black community.[80] Between 1976 and 1981, at least thirty-one Black and Brown people were murdered across Britain; they were stabbed, burned and bombed to death.[81]

It is no wonder then that in 1981 the rising tension came to a head, as we saw at the beginning of this chapter. January 1981 set the tone for the year with a house-party fire in New Cross, London that led to the deaths of thirteen Black teenagers and young adults. This was followed by a botched police investigation in which the families and communities of the dead suspected racially motivated arson and didn't believe the police were taking them seriously. After the racism that had built up over the 1970s and before, and the disproportionate impact of the tanking economy, enough was enough. Brixton rose up and soon, spurred by the discrimination and racism in their own hometowns, Black and Brown people across the country fought back, from Liverpool to Leeds, and Bristol to Bolton. The uprisings of 1981 are the last movement discussed, in Chapter Eleven.

Nineteen eighty-one was a turning point in race relations in the UK. Not a 180-degree turn from 'racist' to 'not-racist', but rather a small curve, from 'crudely and openly racist' to 'more subtly racist … for the most part'. Signs saying 'no blacks, no dogs, no Irish' faded, overt violence was less frequent, but prejudice and discrimination were rife. Racism morphed and assumed a new form to become the beast we know as 'institutionalised racism'. Reflections on the 1980s to the present day are included in the Conclusion.

But I'm getting ahead of myself. Let's go back and start at the beginning with one of the first organisations founded by and for Brown people, the Indian Workers' Association.

# Chapter Two

# Indian Workers' Association

'We are fighting for the light, and if I am
sacrificed, it doesn't matter; for there will be
others who will see the dawn.'[1]

JAGMOHAN JOSHI,
General Secretary IWA GB, 1964–79

Anant Ram arrived in the UK aged twenty-four, having
spent weeks on a trip that took him by train from his village
in Punjab to Bombay, via boat to Venice, to eventually end
up in Victoria, London.[2] The boat cost £31, the present-day
equivalent of around £1,700.[3] Ram had already been married
for around fifteen years (since he was nine) but he travelled
with a male friend, leaving his wife and four children behind.
He wasn't unusual in this: most people travelling from the
Indian subcontinent to the UK at the time were solo men.

Ram went to an address he had been given for a Varyam
Singh who lived behind Spitalfields Market. He had never
met Singh before, but he was taken in, given a place to stay
and help to get a vendor's licence application. It was 1936,

and being a pedlar, or travelling salesperson, was one of the few job options open for Brown immigrants. Ram walked door-to-door for six or seven miles a day selling women's clothes and men's ties, all the while enduring being eyed up suspiciously and frequent calls of 'Blackie'. He got letters from his father telling him news of home and his wife and children, but Ram could not afford to visit.

Ram wasn't happy in London and moved to Coventry, ending up at 38 Spring Road at the house of another contact. Ram heard about a group that the local Punjabis had formed, calling themselves the 'Indian Workers' Association' (IWA). The name was a bit of a misnomer: the main objective was Indian independence from the British Raj, which had ruled India for some eighty-odd years by that point, and for many years before that in other guises. The name did speak, however, to the secondary concern of life for Indian migrants in the UK. Coventry wasn't the only branch of the IWA; they soon popped up in all areas with high concentrations of Indian migrants, with eight branches around the country from London to Dundee by 1943.[4]

Ram joined the IWA and learned about concepts such as 'freedom' and 'slavery' through the regular guest speakers, he contributed to the paper *Azad Hind* (Free India), and by 1945 he was assistant secretary of his branch.

The IWA was a cause for concern for the British government, given the war and the pro-independence fervour among its many colonies. The India Office carefully monitored the IWA and its activities, stopping the entry of the *Hindustan Ghadr* paper from California, sent by a partner, pro-independence party.[5] The government was also concerned about potential post-war issues that could be caused by the increased settlement of Indians, especially as some had married 'or otherwise set up house with English women', as an India Office document puts it. This indicated the 'beginnings of a social problem ... which will not become fully apparent until after the end of the war when industrial conditions return to normal'.[6] While the government worked to disperse the IWA leadership, Indian workers participated in daily life in the UK, with around a hundred contributors to this 'social problem' taking part in Coventry's 1942 May Day celebrations, winning the trophy for 'best display'.[7]

The IWA faded soon after Indian independence in 1947. Not only had the original aim been achieved, but a lot of infighting caused the group to fracture and split. IWA 1.0 may have been over, but IWA 2.0 would soon emerge and would prove to have more staying power. It would come to be one of the most influential organisations led by Brown people that the UK has ever seen. This chapter will focus on two of the major issues the IWA Southall branch took on: bussing and virginity testing.

After the Second World War, as we saw in the previous chapter, there was a large increase in the number of Black and Brown people – often British citizens – migrating to the UK. Most were men coming alone who lived in shared accommodation, even sharing beds on a rotation system, known as 'hot bedding', depending on who had a day shift versus a night shift. Finding work was hard, due to, you guessed it, racism. The newbies were taught etiquette by those already accustomed to British practices, which led to some approaching factories wearing suits to appear respectable, and Sikh men cutting their head and facial hair and removing their turbans.[8] Following these rules didn't mean automatic entry into employment given the colour bar, and most newcomers found jobs at a limited number of places that were known to hire Brown people.

As well as racism, language was a real barrier to life in the UK. In Southall, an area with a high level of immigration from the Punjab, only 20 per cent of migrants were fluent in English, and 45 per cent didn't speak any English at all.[9] Across the country, those fluent in English helped others to fill in forms and get work, and provided in-person translation services at doctors' surgeries and the bank.

Helping the community took up a lot of time for people who already had full-time jobs, so there was a need for a formal system to help, and thus the Indian Workers' Association 2.0 was born. Manmohan Singh Basra set up the IWA South Staffordshire branch in 1956 for the purpose of helping migrants, and they soon had 150 members. In the same year, the IWA Southall was formed.

The new IWA branches shared very little with the pre-war organisation except the name, but the choice was deliberate. They named themselves after the original IWA in honour of one of its supposed members, Udham Singh, the man who assassinated Michael O'Dwyer, who had been the lieutenant general of Punjab during the Jallianwala Bagh massacre in 1919.[10] Udham Singh was hanged in the UK at age forty, a martyr for the cause of Indian independence, and rumoured to have been part of the IWA Coventry branch. Recognising his contribution to India was important to the diaspora.

The IWA accepted all Indians as members regardless of

background, and accepted Pakistanis as associate members (which, if you know anything about Indo-Pakistani relations, you will know is quite a show of solidarity we could do with more of). In reality, though, membership skewed heavily Punjabi. Membership was huge: it is estimated that in some areas over half of Punjabi men were members of the IWA.[11]

The focus of IWA branches to start with was welfare and cultural and social support, with a concentration on immigration policy in particular. They acted locally but cooperated nationally, and combined under the banner of 'IWA GB' in 1958. Combining efforts meant that they were better able to influence national policy. The first policy concern was regularisation of Indians who had travelled on forged documents to work around the stringent requirements set up by the Indian government, and were now stuck in the UK. As many as 70 per cent of Indians who arrived between 1957 and 1959 didn't have the right documents.[12] Thanks to the IWA's efforts, the Indian High Commission issued valid passports so Indians could now travel back to India, and it reduced the risk of exploitation at work.

Fractures soon started to appear between the IWA branches, reminiscent of the immediate post-war fissions. Factions formed based on divisions in Indian politics as well as the vision for the IWA in Britain. Should the IWA be primarily concerned with welfare and social assistance, or politics and policy? Should the IWA, as an independent organisation, accept state funds or not? Should the IWA work with the Labour Party or not? Was the 'Indian' part of IWA the most important focus, or the 'Workers' part? Were the problems faced by Indians caused by their own behaviour and attitudes, or the racist society in which they found themselves? Who sympathised with the Congress Party of India (the party in power in India) vs the Communist Party of India (and its own splinter groups)?

The IWA Southall soon separated itself from the IWA GB. Led by Vishnu Sharma, IWA Southall was pro-coordination with the government, pro-Labour Party and pro-assimilationist (its logo was a handshake between a Brown hand and a white hand), while IWA GB saw the problems faced by Indians as coming from racism in society and was determined to stay outside of racist government initiatives. The IWA Southall collaborated with and supported the Labour Party at election times, while under Avtar Jouhl's leadership the IWA GB invited Malcolm X to Smethwick in 1964, and advised members to abstain from voting in 'Britain's racist general election'.

Regardless of the differences, there were some common aims between the IWA factions. Opposition to the immigration bills and the fight for workers' rights were key activities of all IWAs. Brown workers were often kept apart from other workers through intermediaries, who acted as brokers between them and the foremen. The (Brown) brokers spoke English and knew how the system worked, and would negotiate working patterns, including allocation of overtime, as well as be in charge of finding new recruits. Many worked on a system of bribes and favours, and some would charge potential recruits to be hired.[13] To counter this, the IWA helped members to become shop stewards (the elected union representatives) in the workplace, thereby removing the need for separate brokers. Many IWA leaders themselves were shop stewards.[14] The segregation of toilet facilities (yes, that happened in the UK as well) and alternatives to redundancy such as job-sharing were also widespread issues that the IWA took up.[15]

By some accounts, the white-dominated unions didn't much care about the new arrivals at first; after all, with more migrant labour to do the menial jobs, white labour could take the management roles.[16] But other accounts discuss the open hostility from unions and their white membership from the beginning, threatening to withhold labour if workplaces hired Black and Brown staff. In Greenford, adjacent to Southall, the Transport and General Workers' Union even called for a ban on immigration.[17]

In at least one instance there was an accusation of reverse racism. At the Midland Motor Cylinder Company, the Brown workers refused to work with white worker William Marshall, claiming that Marshall had 'jumped a long queue of coloured men who were in line for this job'.[18] Marshall's response was 'I seem to be at the centre of a colour bar in reverse.'

IWA leadership encouraged members to join existing unions despite the hostility; there was little point in having separate organisations as that would undermine the similarities in the class struggle of workers of all races.

Some workplaces didn't allow unionisation and the IWAs took those on too, the most prominent example being the strike at the R. Woolf rubber factory. Woolf's was one of the main employers for Punjabi men in Southall in the 1950s. This factory was one of the few places to hire Punjabi men; legend has it that someone responsible for hiring had fought with the Punjabi Sikhs in the Second World War and was therefore open to taking them on. It also helped that migrant labour was cheaper than domestic labour. Woolf's was initially a lifeline; when it was hard for men to find work, they knew that Woolf's would take them on. By 1965, 90 per cent of Woolf's labour was Brown, and 40 per cent of the Sikh men in Southall worked there.[19]

It was unforgiving work. The factory supplied rubber parts for cars and prams; it was dirty, smelly and hot. Workers spent up to sixty hours a week in those conditions, even seventy-five hours with overtime. Regular pay was £11 a week, around £170 today.[20]*

Management didn't let workers unionise; it had been tried in 1960 but the union wasn't recognised. In 1963 another attempt by two workers was more successful. They spent their evenings canvassing people directly at their homes to encourage them to sign up, with the support of the IWA, and managed to enrol over 450 workers. The factory eventually recognised the Transport and General Workers' Union in 1964. There was little Woolf's could do without risking losing all of its staff.

But that didn't stop it trying.

In May 1965 the management fired ten workers, all active union members, an action the workers knew was backlash for unionising in the first place. After arbitration failed and the Transport and General Workers' Union dragged its heels, the workers went on an overtime ban to show their opposition to the firing, discrimination and working conditions. Eventually the union negotiated the reinstatement of some of the workers.

---

* This was more than fifty years before the introduction of minimum wage legislation in 1999.

Later the same year, Mukhtiar Singh was fired after he accused another worker of stealing. The workers went straight to industrial action rather than arbitration, which meant going on strike without union support. The management responded by bringing in Pakistani workers to stoke community division and conflict.

Since the strike wasn't official there wasn't strike pay from the union and many members had lapsed on their dues by this point anyway.[21] The community rallied together to support the strikers; landlords postponed rent payments, shopkeepers provided free food, and gurdwaras and the IWA Southall raised £1,500 for the strikers and their families. IWA GB provided support by trying to persuade Woolf's suppliers to block supplies. The community still remembers the support provided more than fifty years ago. Tejinder Singh, whose father Pritam Singh Sangha was a shopkeeper at the time, says that 'elderly people come up to me even now and tell me "we remember Pritam Singh Sangha"'.[22]

The strike lasted for around seven weeks, when some workers returned but the demands were not fulfilled. The strike may not have been successful but it showed the country the collective power of Brown workers.

As the main link between the newly arrived community and the so-called 'host' community, the IWA Southall got involved in all areas of life. The Shepherd's Bush gurdwara, which had once been the only place for Sikhs to worship in London, was joined by a gurdwara operating out of a house on Beaconsfield Road in Southall with support from the IWA.[23]

In the same year as the strike at Woolf's, the IWA Southall

was also busy securing a permanent cultural and entertainment space for the local community. The Dominion Cinema was an 1,800-seat theatre, perfect for showing the latest Bollywood films, and the restaurant next door, Sagoo and Thakar's, was the perfect spot for loading up with samosas and other snacks for the screenings. The centre also housed a boxing ring, used for the popular sport of Indian wrestling, and there was enough space for the IWA's offices.

The centre cost £75,000, a third of which was donated by the community, with many families donating £100 – no small feat considering the average wages were around £12 to £13 a week.[24] The Dominion Cinema was the 'beating heart' of the community, according to one local resident.[25] It was used not only by Punjabis (who were mostly Sikh) but the whole Asian community, including by Muslims for Eid prayers.[26]

A few minutes away from the 'beating heart' lies Beaconsfield Road. Terraced houses of different colours line the street, each with large bay windows. Boxes of fresh fruit and vegetables are piled up high outside convenience stores, and inconspicuously nestled among the houses and shops is a school, Beaconsfield Primary. It's a small and unassuming school, made up of Victorian-style buildings that blend in with the surroundings. But there was nothing small about what was set in motion there in 1963.

Sir Edward Boyle, the Conservative minister for education, visited Beaconsfield Primary school at the request of the local council in 1963. The council had received complaints from white parents about the number of 'immigrant children' (read: Black and Brown children) in the schools in

Southall. Four hundred local, predominantly white, parents turned out to hear Boyle speak. He warned of an 'educational danger point' and sympathised with the complaints of the parents.[27] The student body at Beaconsfield was around 60 per cent Black and Brown at the time, predominantly Indian, and Boyle recommended that the ideal number was no more than a third, or around 30 per cent, of the total number of students.

It wasn't good enough for some white parents; those in the British National Party contingent showed up that night demanding fully segregated schools.[28] These conversations were happening across the country where Black and Brown children were going to schools that had been up to that point almost exclusively attended by white children. A month after Boyle's appearance in Southall, 300 parents protested the creation of a reception class for immigrant children at Lady Margaret Primary School, claiming that their children in other classes would be 'contaminated with TB, head lice and other "immigrant diseases"'.[29] Charming.

You may be wondering where the figure of a maximum of 30 per cent immigrant children came from, what detailed research and solid scientific theoretical basis this was built on, expecting me to quote a number of prominent studies. Erm, well, there was no basis really. Studies and research abounded on how most effectively to 'integrate' immigrants, and under what conditions contact between immigrants and natives would lead to harmony, but there was no evidence of any of that actually informing policy. Denis Howell, a Labour MP and joint parliamentary under-secretary for education and science, admits as much in his autobiography, saying that one of his main sources of evidence for the 30 per cent was the head teacher at his children's school who said the proportion was definitely a maximum.[30]

To achieve the desired proportion of a third, Black and Brown children would be bussed out to schools in neighbouring areas, sometimes up to ten miles away.[31] This could mean up to two hours of travel a day. For example, bus route 44 would leave Featherstone Infants School at 8.10 a.m. and arrive at North Ealing School at 8.58 a.m., forty-eight minutes later.[32]

So bussing started after Sir Edward Boyle gave it impetus, and by 1965 it became an official government recommendation. The Department of Education and Science's circular entitled *The Education of Immigrants* read:

> Experience suggests [that] up to a fifth of immigrant children in any group fit in with reasonable ease, but that, if the proportion goes over about one third either in the school as a whole or in any one class, serious strains arise. It is therefore desirable that the catchment areas of schools should, wherever possible, be arranged to avoid undue concentrations of immigrant children. Where this proves impracticable ... every effort should be made to disperse the immigrant children round a greater number of schools ...[33]

The circular didn't say what exactly defined an 'immigrant child', nor did it explicitly lay out the need for English proficiency to be a criterion for the children to be dispersed. As it was a recommendation rather than mandatory, some education authorities, including those with high numbers of Black and Brown children such as Brent in London, refused to implement bussing (though it did set up a 'special language centre' for immigrant children). But many education authorities gladly took up bussing, including in Bradford, Bristol, Leicester and Wolverhampton. The Borough of Ealing, which includes Southall, bussed children for nearly twenty years, starting informally in 1963 and then officially in 1965.

In Southall, Brown children were the main target of bussing. Some Black children were bussed, but it was more likely that they would be victims of being labelled as 'troublemakers' or 'educationally subnormal'. We'll come back to that in Chapter Six. Brown children were the primary target as many did not speak English as a first language and were therefore bussed on the basis that it would help them learn English. But they were never tested for English proficiency. By 1967 up to 1,000 children were being bussed in Southall; by 1974 this had increased to 2,400 primary-school children with a further 1,200 secondary-school students having to use public transport for dispersal.[34] Schools in Southall, meanwhile, had empty places.[35]

You may recall that bussing was also a practice in the USA, and you'd be right, but it was different in one major way. Bussing was used in the USA after desegregation to encourage mixing between white and Black children. Both Black children and white children were therefore bussed, unlike in the UK where white children were not bussed.

In the UK, it was argued that bussing would reduce the potential for segregation as white parents would be less likely to remove their children from schools if the numbers of Black and Brown children were kept low. It led to another form of segregation: there was usually little trace of integration in the schools to which the students were bussed.

Bussed children were often taught in temporary, makeshift huts put up at the sidelines of the school premises, or at the ends of the corridors. Teachers fought for resources and felt isolated themselves and cut off from the rest of the faculty. Bussed children were abused by other children from their school or from neighbouring schools.

A group of children going to Watford Secondary School, just north of London, wrote a letter to the IWA Southall saying, 'every morning and evening we change buses ... because we are of Indian or Asian origin ... this gang of white boys from Vincent School beat every coloured boy they get hold of and spit on the girls'.[36] Zulfi Hussain, who was bussed, recalls 'essentially, we were like lambs to the slaughter. As early as the first few days, it was very tough.'[37] Name calling became so common that the children didn't even bother to complain about it. No government official thought there would be racism at the predominantly white schools to which the children were being sent.[38]

The most dangerous part of the day was waiting for the bus. Abdul Malik was killed in Greenford in an inter-school fight as he waited for the bus back home to Southall.[39] Children were bussed to white-dominated areas, some of which were National Front strongholds and therefore a real danger zone. White men on motorbikes – we're talking grown-ass, adult men – would hit children with their helmets. Someone who was bussed remembers: 'We also used to get a police escort to get to the bus back home. Especially when it came around holiday time, the tension was escalating. It wasn't necessarily the white kids at the school we were at, it was a bunch of skinheads, National Front activists and fascists who came deliberately to give us hell.'[40]

Even without the physical and verbal abuse, many students didn't have a great time. I don't know about you, but I went to primary school a grand total of ten minutes' walk from my house. My friends who went to school with me lived close by, most within walking or cycling distance. I even walked to school by myself from quite a young age. Students who were bussed didn't have such luxuries. Making and keeping friends was hard.[41] The bus would often break down and the children would get blamed for arriving late to school.[42] And forget about extra-curricular activities, as the children had to leave as soon as school ended and sometimes up to thirty minutes before the end of the school day, when previously they had been involved in all areas of school life.[43] As one local said, 'they go as outsiders, they stay as outsiders and they come back as outsiders'.[44]

At first, many parents didn't know about any of this. As many as 20 per cent of Brown parents didn't even know which school their child attended.[45] Parents were busy hustling, trying to make ends meet, and some children came from one-parent households. Parents were concerned about their children's education (they were still Brown and Black parents, after all), but most didn't have the time/language skills/understanding of the system to find out what was happening. For the parents who did know about it, some saw bussing as positive to start with as they thought it would lead to smaller classes and therefore better education.[46]

So where did the IWA stand on all of this? It also saw bussing as positive at first. But it soon became clear that it wasn't the educational boon that had been promised. As stories of student experiences emerged, and after the 1971 Immigration Act (which made it harder for Black and Brown people who would previously have been citizens to live and work permanently in the UK), it became clear that the government did not have the best interests of the children at heart. From 1972, the IWA went on the offensive. The president of IWA Southall at the time, Ajit Rai, said,

> When our children started going to school, the host community resented it. They said these black children are bringing down the standard of our children … Then the bussing started. Our children of five, six years old were packed into the buses and taken to places where they had no friends, no house nearabout. They were taken like slabs, human slabs, packing and bringing them back. It was so inhuman.[47]

The IWA, in conjunction with the Indian Students' Association and West Indian Student Association, went door-to-door explaining the bussing policy and its damage, and gathering statements from parents. They took the statements to the council and local Labour MP, Sydney Bidwell, and the Race Relations Board.

The campaign centred on two arguments: that bussed children were disadvantaged in their education and more vulnerable to racism, and that the practice was discriminatory based on the 1968 Race Relations Act. The discrimination argument was based on the fact that it was only Black and

Brown children who were bussed, and not white children.

It was also soon shown that the council was using bussing as a way to avoid building new schools in the area. The cost of bussing per year stood at more than £200,000 at its peak, for which one school per year could have been built instead.[48]

The campaign was successful; the Race Relations Board called for an independent assessment, and released a report in 1975 which declared that the practice was indeed discriminatory. The Local Education Authority now had two options: they could either bus white children too, or build more schools. They decided to build more schools.

Bussing didn't come to a complete stop, though. It was slowly phased out and stopped in Southall in 1981, after eighteen years of the practice. The Ealing Local Education Authority justified this on the basis of providing time to build new schools, and to allow students who were near the end of their education to finish in their current school. But it was a success for the IWA and the other organisations that had taken up the campaign. After nearly twenty years, Brown and Black children could go to school in the same town they lived in.

Children in some other towns were not so lucky. While in Bradford it was also phased out by 1982, in Halifax it continued until 1986.[49]

By now you may be wondering if the IWA was just full of middle-aged men or whether women had any role to play. Long story short: the members were mostly middle-aged men. This isn't because women weren't working; Brown women went to work in their droves, often in backroom operations, but also on the factory floor. Many women in my family also worked in the factories around Southall; one of my aunts brought home a steady supply of Tetley's paraphernalia, including magnets with Tetley's characters on them, and trays and tins in the signature Tetley's blue. Needless to say, I thought she had the coolest job in the world.

There were some successful attempts to encourage women's membership in the IWA, such as at the Forward Trading Company clothing factory in Coventry, but membership among women was rare. Women played a crucial role behind the scenes of organisations like the IWA, such as preparing meals for meetings that would often take place in their homes. In Southall they would also give English language classes (started by volunteer Kirpal Kaur Ruprah) and sewing classes, and provide welfare services for other women.[50] There was a position of female welfare officer to help women in particular, but on the whole 'women's issues' were dealt with largely by other organisations, such as Southall Black Sisters, Awaz or the Sahil Project. These organisations dealt with all areas of life for women.

There was at least one issue which affected women that the IWA Southall took up. Given the proximity of Southall to Heathrow Airport, the IWA and the Joint Council for the Welfare of Immigrants did a lot of immigration work directly at the airport. They would be called in to assist immigration officers when there was a language barrier with those seeking entry, or potential cases where people could be denied entry. One former member recalls that the immigration officers would wait until late in the evening to process these cases, hoping to deter the volunteers from showing up, but they would work until midnight if they had to.[51] Familiarity with the way Heathrow and the immigration system worked gave the IWA a prominent role for newly arrived migrants from South Asia. It was no surprise then that in 1979 a woman who had recently arrived from India went to the IWA to report a traumatic experience she had suffered at Heathrow Airport.

'He was wearing rubber gloves and took some medicine out of a tube and put it on some cotton and inserted it into me,' the thirty-five-year-old woman said. 'I asked for a dressing gown but it was not provided. I was most reluctant to have the examination, but I didn't know whether it was normal practice here.'[52] This quote, taken from an article on the front page of the *Guardian* on 1 February 1979, exposed the Home Office practice of virginity testing on migrant women coming from South Asia. The woman chose not to be named in the article, but we know she became Mrs Kakar when she married in the UK. After arriving in the UK on 24 January with that reception, she went to the IWA to tell them what she had experienced, who then alerted the *Guardian*.

The revelation sent shockwaves through some parts of the UK, but was already a well-known secret in other parts. Amrit Wilson discussed it in her book *Finding a Voice*, published in 1978, the year before the *Guardian* ran the story. President Vishnu Sharma said that the IWA and others knew about it as early as 1969, ten years prior to the story breaking, but every time it was brought it up with the government the claim would be denied as they had no evidence.[53] Mrs Kakar-to-be produced her consent form, which clearly stated: 'This is to certify that I . . . agree to a gynaecological examination which may be vaginal if necessary.' The letterhead showed it came from 'HM Immigration Office'. Bingo, there was the evidence.

The Home Office reacted by saying that a medical examination had been carried out as per the right of the immigration authorities but the examination was not internal. A 'cursory' examination was enough to establish that 'she was virgo intacto', and that the woman in question did not have to remove all of her clothes.[54] However, a report from the doctor to the Home Office on the same day as the article appeared in the *Guardian* says that there was indeed penetration, of about half an inch.[55] The Home Office kept the issue as hidden as possible; it didn't want it to be known that virginity testing was a widespread, accepted immigration practice. And Labour was in government at this time, in case you're wondering.

Testing was seen as a way to check whether a migrant woman was a legitimate fiancée or not. Wives needed to apply for a visa from their home country to enter the UK, but fiancées could apply for entry on arrival. The Home Office suspected that fiancées coming in were actually wives trying to 'cheat the system', and so used virginity testing in cases where they suspected foul play, to determine whether the woman was unmarried. In case it needs saying: you cannot determine someone's virginity through a vaginal examination, and even if you could, it certainly doesn't mean that you should. Oh, and being unmarried doesn't mean you're a virgin.

The IWA sent telegrams protesting the practice to the prime minister, home secretary, leader of the opposition Margaret Thatcher, the high commissioner of India and anyone else it thought should hear that this was unaccceptable and had to stop.[56] It contacted other organisations such as the Joint Council for the Welfare of Immigrants and National Council for Civil Liberties to put pressure on the government for an inquiry into immigration practices.

Within just a few days, the Home Office had to agree that invasive testing had taken place and admitted to three cases, including the brave woman who came forward.[57] The IWA took this as a victory for its campaign, but it was suspected that this wasn't the whole truth. Demands for numbers came regularly in Parliament, especially from local MP Sydney Bidwell and Jo Richardson, MP for Barking. The home secretary, Merlyn Rees, once responded, 'I regret that the information requested is not available,' and simply ignored a request for numbers of tests done on women coming from the 'Old' Commonwealth, that is, white women from Canada, New Zealand and Australia.[58] Bidwell and Richardson knew that the testing was likely only ever done to women from South Asia, but the government squirmed its way out of publicly admitting it.

Private correspondence from the time confirms the racist bias of the testing. F. S. Miles, the British high commissioner in Dhaka, wrote to the assistant under-secretary of the Foreign and Commonwealth Office Donald Murray: 'It would be difficult to maintain that "discrimination" does not exist between the treatment of people entering Britain from the old and new Commonwealth . . . let us not pretend we are not "discriminating".'[59]

With its attempts to lie its way out of the matter well and truly scuppered, the government officially put a stop to the practice. The scandal continued, though, as more details emerged over the following weeks. After the under-secretary of state said in the House of Commons that 'such tests are not carried out at British posts overseas on women applying to come to the United Kingdom for marriage', it soon became clear that the testing had indeed been carried out on more women than just fiancées trying to enter the country, as it had been carried out abroad in British high commissions in Islamabad, Bombay, Delhi and Dhaka. A former immigration minister admitted that he knew it happened 'fairly frequently' in Bangladesh, and that he had tried to put a stop to it.[60] A letter sent from the Foreign and Commonwealth Office to 10 Downing Street says that from 1975 to 1979 there had been at least seventy-three cases in Delhi and nine in Bombay.[61]

No official figures have ever been published by the government, but a confidential government document from the time suggests between 123 and 143 women were subjected to testing overseas, and that figure is higher when the cases in the UK are taken into account.[62]

Stopping the practice didn't put an end to campaigning from the likes of the IWA. It wanted the instructions issued to immigration officers to be published, which the home secretary had refused to do, and a full inquiry into immigration practices (which also included the dubious use of X-rays to determine age, something which may be reinstated under the Nationality and Borders Bill 2022). It organised a public lobby of the House of Commons, briefed MPs for parliamentary questions, and shared information with the Indian government to help it pressure the UK government. The Indian government did just that, and even submitted a resolution to a meeting of the UN Commission of Human Rights to publicly admonish the UK government for its immigration practices, which really pissed them off.[63]

The IWA wasn't the only organisation campaigning on this issue. The Joint Council for the Welfare of Immigrants took a central role. Women's group Awaz organised a demonstration outside Terminal 3 of Heathrow Airport, which around 200 people attended. Members of the Organisation of Women of Asian and African Descent were among the demonstrators (more on them in Chapter Seven), as were Southall Black Sisters. North London Women against Racism and Fascism campaigned, as did law centres.[64] People picketed the home secretary's office, and organised demonstrations outside the British High Commission in Delhi. Immigration law was at its strictest since the introduction of the 1971 Immigration Act and the reality of this over the course of the 1970s had incensed a lot of people.

Virginity testing revealed so much about the psyche and inner workings of the British immigration system. What led everyone involved or complicit in virginity testing to think that it was a reasonable thing to do? What motivated the immigration officers, doctors, nurses and politicians who had authorised it, or carried it out? They clearly knew it was wrong as they worked so hard to hide it. It revealed the prejudices held by white Brits about Brown women: that no Brown woman would possibly have sex before marriage and that Brown women in their thirties would already be married.

It revealed the power and discretion that immigration officers had, and still have, to take actions as they see fit to deem whether someone is a bona fide immigrant or not. This was not because of a high incidence of fiancées entering the country, or even a high level of unauthorised entries. In 1977, only 11 per cent of immigrants were fiancées, and in the same year only 125 people were deported for breaching entry requirements.[65] Eleven per cent was hardly a lot considering that by that point most migrants were family members, since the 1971 Immigration Act had all but closed the door on primary immigration.

The most sinister explanation for virginity testing is put forward by two Australian academics who have done the most thorough investigation of the testing. They say that it was a way of showing Brown migrant women their position in British society, that 'the humiliating processes undertaken in the "virginity testing" procedures served to reinforce subordination of the migrant women to their marginal position in British society'.[66] It is interesting that the most detailed analysis of this has been done by academics in Australia rather than Britain. It's an issue that can't be touched in the UK.

You may realise that this section hasn't been delivered with my trademark wit you've come to know. I don't feel like laughing right now. Where to even begin? During the course of research for this book there is a lot that has made my blood boil and the grey in my hair multiply, but this is probably the practice that makes me the angriest and greyest, so please forgive the serious tone.

Mrs Kakar returned to India shortly after she married, her flights funded by the Cadbury Trust, as she didn't want to stay in the UK after what had happened. After much discussion between ministries, the Home Office offered her a £500 payment for her 'distress'. This was an *ex gratia* payment; that is, it did not come with any acceptance of 'wrongdoing' but was a show of good faith. The Home Office had initially suggested £750 but the Treasury thought that £500 was 'a substantial sum' and would be less likely to be seen as compensation for the cost of the return flight to India.[67] The Treasury also emphasised that the Home Office 'should stress the exceptional nature of the payment' so as not to invite compensation claims from the other victims.[68]

Mr Kakar wanted to sue the government for the breakdown of his marriage, which prompted it to consider offering him compensation too. But after seeking legal advice the government established that Mr Kakar didn't have a case, so it didn't bother.[69] No disciplinary action was taken against anyone in the government or immigration service, and the government did not issue an apology.[70]

To this day, the British government has never apologised for violating hundreds of women.

The IWA got its inquiry into immigration practices, led by the Commission for Racial Equality, with much protest from the government, which thought the Commission was stepping out of its remit. The report was eventually published in 1985 and revealed what the *Guardian* called a 'raw deal for blacks' in the immigration system.[71] The struggle wasn't over, but there had been some success. As Vishnu Sharma said in 1982, 'the community had a great victory, they knew that they could move governments!'[72]

Virginity testing was made illegal in the UK in November 2021.

The IWA still operates in many towns and cities of the UK, including Southall. The link with the Labour Party grew even stronger over time. Piara Khabra, a former president of the IWA Southall, succeeded Sydney Bidwell to become the area's first Brown MP in 1992, and the first Sikh MP in the country. He held the seat until his death in 2007, when he was succeeded in Parliament by Virendra Sharma, who had also served on the IWA executive committee in the 1970s.

Jagmohan Joshi of the IWA GB, whose excellent quote opens this chapter, passed away while leading a 4,000-strong march against racism in 1979.

IWA leaders of days gone by were husbands, fathers, brothers, uncles, cousins, workers and activists, and some have since become politicians. Many were also artists and poets, seeing art and culture as an avenue for resistance. This tradition has been attributed to influencing musicians such as Asian Dub Foundation and Fun-Da-Mental in the UK, who combine activism with their artistry.[73] Anant Ram, who we met at the start of this chapter and who joined the first IWA in Coventry, wrote a poem for one of his first public speeches, part of which read: 'how long before our appeals for mercy be accepted, when would the shackles of slavery be broken?'[74] Even from its earliest days, the struggle has always been about both racism and capitalism, as Ram recognised.

The IWA, in all its factions, has been integral to welfare and justice in the UK, not just for Indians but many immigrants. It has helped loosen the shackles, end racist policies like bussing and virginity testing, and though some are trying to tighten the bonds once again, they are weaker thanks to the work of organisations such as the IWA and can't be so easily secured. Anant, it won't be long now.

# Chapter Three

## Bristol Bus Boycott

'Every man has a right to work.'[1]

Campaign slogan

Mural of Audley Evans in St Pauls, Bristol. One of the 'Seven Saints of St Pauls'.

© Lucy Fulford

On a spring morning in April 1963, eighteen-year-old Guy Reid-Bailey arrives at the offices of the Bristol

Omnibus Company for a job interview. He is looking forward to it. He arrived in Bristol from Jamaica in
1961 at just sixteen years old, and was now living with his
aunt as he studied. The adjustment to life in the UK had been
a bit tough as discrimination and racism were quite common
and 'there was always a gang somewhere likely to attack'.[2]
This would be a good job. The buses were still a novelty
for Reid-Bailey, and lots of Black men worked on the buses
around the UK, including just a few miles away in Bath.

After seeing the advert in the paper, a teacher of his, Paul
Stephenson, had called the company ahead of time to check
that they were indeed hiring, and they were. There were
always jobs going on the buses; in any given year around 30
per cent of the staff would leave so they were always looking
for new workers.[3] Reid-Bailey would surely be a shoo-in; he
regularly went to church and was even a former officer of the
Christian youth group, the Boy's Brigade. He was educated,
a cricketer and dapperly dressed in a grey suit. Everything
looked good for Guy.

He introduces himself to the receptionist and tells her he
is there for an interview.

'I don't think so,' she says.

Reid-Bailey insists that he had been told to come. 'The
name is Mr Bailey.' The receptionist shuffles to the manager's office.

'Your two o'clock appointment is here, and he's Black.'

'Tell him the vacancies are full,' the manager responds.

Reid-Bailey insists there must be some sort of mix-up,
the advert was just in the paper, and Stephenson had called
in advance.

'There's no point having an interview,' the manager continues, 'we don't employ black people.'

Things didn't look so good for Guy any more.[4*]

You might think that the next step for Guy Reid-Bailey would
be to report the incident to some government body somewhere
that dealt with discrimination, which would have been a good
idea, if one had existed at the time. The first Race Relations
Act was still two years away, so discrimination was absolutely
legal and the Bristol Omnibus Company was acting within its
rights, even if they were far outside moral boundaries. Instead,
Reid-Bailey told his teacher Paul Stephenson what had happened, and the only option was to take action themselves.

Bristol is one of the most progressive cities in the UK these
days. One calculation put it at number six in the country,
though after the un-plinthing of Edward Colston and leading
the way on the 'Kill the Bill' protests, I'd say that's an under-
calculation.[5] It's not always been the case though. As a port
city, Bristol was central in Britain's role in dominating the high
seas and the world; having a statue to the deputy-governor of
the Royal African Company in the first place demonstrates
Bristol's links to the slave trade. Around 500,000 Africans
were transported on Bristol's ships in total.[6]

The early Black population in Bristol consisted of enslaved
people, including domestic servants, formerly enslaved people

---

* There are a few versions of this story around. Another version of the event
says that Stephenson called the company and arranged the interview, then
called back and let them know that Reid-Bailey was Black, at which point
he was then told not to bother coming in as the company didn't hire Black
people. Yet another version says that this case was being used by Stephenson
to prove the existence of the colour bar in some sort of sting operation.

and the descendants of enslaved people who were born in the UK. Life was hard for most people, and enslaved servants could potentially be sent away to the West Indies once they had served their purpose.[7] Many enslaved people who escaped did everything they could to avoid being kidnapped and sold.

That was life for a few centuries. Black people were nearly always a visible minority and, like other cities, Bristol saw an increase in the population after the Second World War. Most of the new arrivals ended up in the St Pauls area of the city. Bombed during the war, it was then abandoned in favour of building new housing estates.[8] It was the one area where Black people could actually get housing, and where many of the few thousand Black people in Bristol lived. In the classic chicken-or-egg scenario, the long-term Bristolians attributed the decline of St Pauls to the new arrivals rather than seeing them as victims of the decline themselves: they were the chicken, not the egg. Or is that the egg, not the chicken?

City Road in St Pauls may have, in the words of academic Madge Dresser, 'conjured up fears and fantasies of violence, immorality and lawlessness' for some Bristolians, but it was home and a safe haven for those who couldn't get housing else-where.[9] Even if that meant that residents like Roy Hackett had to get up at 4 a.m. to get to work in Wales for 8 a.m. St Pauls was, and still is, home for many of Bristol's Black community.

Faced with discrimination in housing and the threat of attack from Teddy boys, one resident, Owen Henry, recalls that 'we couldn't walk the streets on our own ... 'cause of the Teddy boys and at night, I should say, they would always gang up on us. So every time we go out we have to go out in a file of six or so.'[10] With rampant racism like that, is it any wonder then that Reid-Bailey didn't get an interview at the Bristol Omnibus Company?

No, no it wasn't. The company didn't have any Black or Brown drivers or conductors on its buses at all. Not a single one. It was a common occupation in London – heck, Black bus drivers had even been directly recruited in Barbados – but in Bristol there was an open secret that Black and Brown people need not apply. This was the most extreme version of the 'colour bar'. Other iterations included quotas on the proportion of Black and Brown workers, usually around 5 per cent of the workforce. The existence of the 'colour bar' was about as secret as ~~racism in the Royal Family~~ the existence of Santa.

Today, it is incredible to think that there was a time that Black and Brown people could not be bus drivers in parts of the UK. It is so common to see Black and Brown faces, especially men, staring unimpressed when you attempt to make eye contact and smile as you board a bus. I jest. I don't try to make eye contact and smile – I'm a Londoner after all. Black and Brown folks are overrepresented in the sector: 19 per cent of all bus and coach drivers in the UK are Black, Asian or Minority Ethnic (sorry to use the dreaded 'BAME' term here, but it's what the government used at the time of the statistic), and that goes up to 54 per cent in London, compared to 11 per cent of the national workforce as a whole.[11]

Back to just a few decades ago, colour bars were not just implemented on the whim of individual businesses, but supported and endorsed by trade unions too. In 1955, drivers and conductors of the Transport and General Workers' Union voted against the hiring of Black and Brown workers in Bristol; 'the Transport and General Workers' Union in the city had said that if one black man steps on the platform as a conductor, every wheel will stop.'[12] The maintenance section of the union, however, voted in favour of hiring Black and Brown workers, a clear statement on the type of work that was seen as fitting for Black and Brown people. The irony was that many Black and Brown workers were actually members of the Transport and General Workers' Union themselves in order to access 'closed shop' workplaces; that is, where you had to be a union member to get a job. Assuming, of course, there wasn't a colour bar in place.

Bristol wasn't unique in this conversation; also in 1955 bus workers in Wolverhampton banned overtime to protest the increased numbers of Black workers, and the Transport and General Workers' Union limited the number of Black bus workers to 52 of 900, or 6 per cent. It refused to call it a colour bar.[13] Similar scenes were evident in West Bromwich, where bus workers went on strike against the hiring of one Brown conductor. The union's response? 'I do not think there is any racial antagonism behind this.'[14]

If it wasn't racism that led to industrial action and votes against the hiring of Black and Brown people, then what was it? White workers and trade unionists would defend the actions as being economically motivated. Bus workers' wages had suffered a decline since the war, and morale had declined alongside it. They relied on overtime to make ends meet, often working up to 100 hours a week.[15] They could double their wages with overtime, taking them up to £20 per week.[16] To do this, there actually needed to be a shortage of staff to provide the chance for overtime. This was the argument put forward by many workers: it was nothing personal, simply a matter of trying to survive. Sound familiar?

Some arguments against hiring Black workers were more obvious in their reasoning. Fears about Black men abounded, in particular when it came to white female workers. A white driver recalled the racist prejudices held in the company at the time: 'The worst were the conductresses, I have to say. They were terrible. They'd say a black conductor would eventually become a driver, therefore they'd have to work with a black driver, and the things they could do at the end of the journey, you know? It was terrible. They thought they were wide open to rape. They believed that.'[17] The chairperson of the Bristol Omnibus Company said in 1963 that 'if we did start employing coloured people while we can still get white people, a lot of these white females would be leaving the job to go and get other jobs in the city'.[18] This isn't the place to go into the long history of the fear and hyper-sexualisation of Black men, but this is it in all its glory.

A radio interview with a female Bristol resident was also quite revealing:

INTERVIEWER: what would you think about coloured people coming to work on the buses?

FEMALE RESPONDENT: I don't like the idea very much.

INTERVIEWER: why not?

FEMALE RESPONDENT: I wouldn't like to work with them at night ... they would cause too much trouble, no we don't want them.

INTERVIEWER: what sort of trouble do they cause?

FEMALE RESPONDENT: well I mean just say we'll all be out of work if they start and they'll be ruling the country before long wouldn't they?[19]

Some white bus workers thought Black people ate Kitekat cat food.[20] I'm going to go ahead and say that some of the actions were racially motivated.

New Bristol residents Roy Hackett (the man who was getting up at 4 a.m. to go to work in Wales) and Owen Henry had brought up the colour bar with the local council directly themselves, as well as through the chairperson of the West Indian Association, Bill Smith. It was an issue that was close to Roy Hackett's heart, as his wife, Ena, had applied to be a conductor and was told the vacancy was filled, only for it to be readvertised the next day.[21] But more than that, it was just wrong. The pleas didn't get them very far. The council knew about the issue, and when it heard from the bus company manager Ian Patey that he had 'evidence' from other cities that diversifying bus crews led to a downgrading of the job and walkouts of white staff, it didn't disagree with him.[22]

Lacking support, Hackett and Henry, along with Audley Evans and Prince Brown, formed a small group, the Commonwealth Coordinated Committee (CCC), to tackle the injustice. They decided to distinguish themselves from the West Indian Association as working through them wasn't getting anywhere. The CCC met on Sundays at the Speedy Bird café, drinking fish tea and Red Stripe beer and listening to calypso as they discussed the issues of the day.[23] That's when Owen Henry heard about the new man on the block, Paul Stephenson.

Paul Stephenson, British-born to a West African father and Black British mother, was raised mostly in the care system. Despite that, he had an idyllic, middle-class early childhood in Essex, and then less than idyllic late childhood and teenage years in London.[24] He joined the Royal Air Force just before his sixteenth birthday for seven years, before studying to become a youth worker in Birmingham. After qualifying, he relocated to Bristol in 1962 in his first post as a youth and community development worker and supply teacher.[25] At one point he was the only Black teacher in Bristol.[26] He taught Guy Reid-Bailey and encouraged him to apply for the job with the Bristol Omnibus Company.

Stephenson would be an obvious asset to the cause as a veteran with an acceptably British accent. Henry was a respected figure in the community, known colloquially as the 'mayor of St Pauls', but eyed with suspicion by the local authorities.[27] Stephenson for his part thought tackling the colour bar would be easy: 'I didn't for a minute think I was going to get much opposition. Oh no, I thought, once it's out, people will say "this is ridiculous".'[28]

The first step was to see for himself that the colour bar existed. That's where he enlisted the help of his student, Reid-Bailey, in a sting operation.* Stephenson had made the initial enquiry to the Bristol Omnibus Company rather than Reid-Bailey because his English accent allowed him more convincingly to masquerade as white. After Reid-Bailey was turned away, Stephenson sprang into action.

He went to speak with manager Patey himself to confirm, as a second witness, the reason that Reid-Bailey had been turned away. Patey had no shame in admitting the colour

---

* The accounts of Stephenson and Reid-Bailey differ here. Reid-Bailey says that he didn't know it was a sting operation, he thought it was a genuine job opportunity, while Stephenson maintains that the purpose of the application was clear from the start.

bar existed and his reaction to Stephenson declaring that the CCC would take action was 'go away with your campaign, we are not employing black people'.[29]

Nineteen sixty-three was a booming year for civil rights action across the pond. The movement in the USA was gaining momentum that would soon lead to the March on Washington. Previous actions included a year-long bus boycott that led to desegregation of the buses in Alabama, and Freedom Riders had traversed the American South to test the desegregation laws on interstate buses. Stephenson, like many others around the world, drew inspiration from the USA, and he now had all the proof he needed to call for a boycott.

He joined together with members of the CCC and they formed the West Indian Development Council to manage the campaign. The boycott was announced at a small press conference on 29 April 1963, and Owen Henry was photographed by the press standing at the back of a bus, echoing scenes from the USA's recent past.

The boycott had begun.

The basic premise was a call for Black Bristolians, and Brown and white allies, to stay off the buses; to use other forms of transport instead – walking, bikes, carshare, taxi – and take away their custom from the buses. However, despite being inspired by the civil rights movement in the USA, Bristol's Black population didn't have the numbers required to bring the company to its knees through the removal of their custom, as it had in Alabama. In the early 1960s, of around 430,000 Bristolians, only 7,000 were Black (1.6 per cent).[30] Other tactics were needed too.

Press attention was key to raise public awareness and gain support. Fortunately, the newspapers were happy to oblige. On 30 April, the *Bristol Evening Post* declared, 'W. Indians 100 p.c. for bus boycott'.[31] And the boycott's leadership was already calling on church leaders, community leaders and politicians to support the campaign. Just a day later, on 1 May, a hundred students from the University of Bristol joined the West Indian Development Council on a march from the bus garage to the home of the unions, Transport House. One of those students was law undergraduate Paul Boateng, who would go on to become the UK's first Black cabinet minister.[32] The students delivered a petition with more than 2,000 signatures calling for an end to the colour bar.

Although the local, national and international press attention was instrumental in moving the process along quickly, the newspapers didn't consistently back the boycotters as to do so would risk alienating a large part of their readership. The *Western Daily Press* stated that racism was an uncomfortable fact of life and suggested segregated crews of bus workers to get around that.[33]

But overall the tactics worked and the boycott moved at an astounding pace. In the following days, Roy Hackett led marches and sit-down protests to block roads in key areas, such as between the bus depot and the city centre, so no buses could enter or leave.[34] Passers-by would ask what he and the others were up to and join the cause. Owen Henry and Paul Stephenson made speeches, especially trying to win over newly arrived immigrants who didn't want to rock the boat.[35]

Stephenson was a savvy campaigner and made links with prominent leaders. He wrote letters to local Labour politician

Tony Benn, who quickly provided his support, saying, 'I shall stay off the buses, even if I have to find a bike!'[36] The support of Labour leader Harold Wilson was enlisted, who publicly declared, 'I'm glad that so many Bristolians are supporting the campaign to get it [the colour bar] abolished. We wish them every success.'[37] One MP tabled a motion to ask the government to stop racial discrimination by bus companies.[38] Another MP asked the Conservative minister of transport if he would introduce legislation so transport licences would only be issued to companies that have anti-discrimination employment policies. He was told: 'I do not think that the road transport licensing machinery would be appropriate for this purpose. I would, however, expect road transport operators to avoid racial discrimination in their employment policy.'[39] OK then.

Stephenson even alerted Sir Learie Constantine, a popular former cricketer turned high commissioner for Trinidad and Tobago, to the issue. For Constantine, it didn't matter that most of the affected people were Jamaican and not Trinidadian, racism was racism. His actions were par for the course (I can't think of a suitable cricket-related phrase): he was an avid anti-racism activist and had published a pamphlet nearly a decade before called 'Colour Bar'.[40] Constantine met with the lord mayor of Bristol, the parent company of the buses, and the national chairperson of the union.

The high commissioner for Jamaica, Laurence Lindo, also got involved after facing criticism that he wasn't doing enough. Lindo also went to the parent company, which was keen to state that it did not advocate for the colour bar. The company said that Lindo and his team 'asked for an assurance that racial discrimination was not part of our policy. We gave them that assurance.'[41] *The Times* and the *Guardian* went so far as to declare the colour bar over on 8 May, just over a week after the boycott and campaign had started.[42] This proved to be a few months too early.

For as much support as the boycott earned, a large contingent of the Black community wasn't happy with how Stephenson and the West Indian Development Council were handling the matter. Some newly arrived immigrants thought the actions of the boycott were stirring up unnecessary trouble in a majority white country, but Stephenson, born and brought up in the UK, 'felt differently, this had always been my country'.[43]

Even the chairperson from the West Indian Association, Bill Smith, was against the boycott. According to Stephenson he 'genuinely believed that the Bristol Bus Boycott campaign undermined racial harmony in the city'.[44] As well as Smith's imagined 'racial harmony' in the city, he had a good relationship with many of the local councillors, and he may have thought that the boycott threatened that.[45] But those relationships hadn't necessarily been of help to the wider community, as Hackett and Henry saw first-hand when they tried to channel their complaints via the West Indian Association in the years before the boycott.

Stephenson also wasn't successful in getting the public support of the West Indian cricket team who happened to be in Bristol at the time – you didn't mix sport and politics – but he got a photo taken with the captain, which appeared in the papers and gave the illusion of support. See, savvy.

Opposition, unsurprisingly, came from white people too,

but from some unlikely places, in Stephenson's view. The bishop of Bristol, who was a personal friend of Stephenson – they even had Christmas dinner together – came out against the boycott. Stephenson received a visit from the bishop, who warned him he was about to publicly voice his opinion against the boycott with the defence 'I hope you understand sometimes it's difficult being a bishop.'[46]

The bishop then released a statement saying 'moral indignation which rushes into public utterance, without great care to know the facts only inflames passion and makes settlement more difficult'.[47] The Bristol Council of Christian Churches also released a statement decrying what it saw as trouble caused by 'a group of unrepresentative West Indians' and blamed the West Indian Development Council for inciting racial conflict.[48] As an advisor on immigration to the Jamaican High Commission said, 'it was nonsense to describe a group of West Indians as unrepresentative when no representative West Indian body existed.'[49]

This wasn't the Christian ideal that Stephenson and others had expected to surface. Martin Luther King Jr had received support from the churches and Stephenson had somewhat expected the same, especially given his good relationship with the bishop.[50] In response to the church's disdain, a group of around a hundred boycotters picketed the St Mary Redcliffe Church during a Sunday service. Despite the disappointment, Stephenson continued on.

The Bristol Omnibus Company, its parent company, and the local and national union branches played a game of hot potato. The Bristol Omnibus Company's Ian Patey reportedly said that the company had nothing against Black workers, but that if there were no colour bar, then fewer white people would apply for a job and it would affect the bus services.[51] He was just doing the bidding of the workers and the union. Ron Nethercott, the regional secretary of the union, and the 'most powerful man in the West Country' according to the papers, said that the union absolutely did not have a colour bar and that if the company wanted to employ Black people the union would go along with it.[52] In other words, he was just doing the bidding of the company.

But Nethercott was one of the fiercest opponents of the boycott; he didn't appreciate the blame that the unions were getting and thought Stephenson had gone about the matter the wrong way. When Labour politician Tony Benn met with Nethercott to try and assist the boycotters, Nethercott called Stephenson a communist and also stated that he was unrepresentative of the West Indian community, and said the union had been working on the matter for years.[53] If that was the case, they didn't seem to be getting very far.

He didn't reserve his slander against Stephenson for private meetings either; Nethercott called him 'irresponsible and dishonest' in a newspaper.[54] Stephenson sued Nethercott for libel and won £500 in damages.[55] Both Nethercott and Stephenson received abusive mail for their actions during the boycott.[56]

Given the opposition of Bill Smith and the West Indian Association to the boycott, Nethercott thought he could rely on Smith's support. Nethercott met with Smith (his 'I have a Black friend' acquaintance) and got him to sign a statement with the union calling for 'sensible and quiet negotiations'.[57]

Nethercott declared Smith the 'official' representative of West Indians and promoted him so heavily that even though Smith was indeed against the boycott he was uncomfortable with all the politicking and called on Nethercott to stop using him as a pawn.[58]

Twenty years after the boycott, Nethercott said, 'I've always believed it and I honestly believe it and I'll believe it to my dying day, [it was taken] out of all proportion. I think it was a thing that we could have resolved very quickly in this city, but I think situation grew upon situation which, no doubt about it, the local press enjoyed.'[59]

Nethercott arguably added fuel to the fire when he refused to meet with the organisers of the boycott.[60] 'This dispute is symptomatic of the ostrich-like bewilderment with which so many people in Britain contemplate the colour problem in their midst,' *The Times* said, and that certainly resonates when considering the actions of Nethercott and many others who seemed to bury their heads in the sand when it came to race.[61]

The role of high commissioners Constantine and Lindo proved pivotal in the boycott. Shortly after hearing from them, the bus parent company sent senior officials to Bristol to mediate between the company and union. By 13 May 1963 negotiations were a-go-go, just two weeks after the action had started. They were closed-door negotiations between the company and the unions, but the boycott organiser West Indian Development Council didn't have a seat at the table. It looked like it should be a quick affair; surely it would be, since the colour bar was apparently against company policy and the union was apparently against it too?

*

The 28 August 1963 was a seminal day in US history as it was the day that Martin Luther King Jr delivered his 'I have a dream' speech at the March on Washington. On the same day, history was also being made thousands of miles away in Bristol. More than three months after negotiations started, manager Ian Patey of the Bristol Omnibus Company declared 'there will now be complete integration without regard to race, colour or creed. The only criterion will be the person's suitability for the job.'[62] Not quite as eloquent as King's speech, but there were thousands of people who had been waiting to hear those words. The day before Patey delivered that statement, on the 27 August, city bus workers had agreed to end the colour bar.

Stephenson said, 'Bristol's coloured immigrants are grateful to the many Bristolians who gave support and sympathy in their struggle against racial discrimination. Coloured people offer good will to bus crews and ask that the past be forgotten so that friendship and understanding will prevail.'[63]

Did 'friendship and understanding prevail'?

A couple of weeks later Raghbir Singh started his new job as a conductor with the Bristol Omnibus Company, the first non-white employee in that role. It was a blow to the boycott leaders that the first recruit wasn't Black, but as Hackett said, 'we felt like we were winning. Not on a grand scale, but it is better to have one foot on the ladder than have no foot on the ladder. And we said we'll take it from here.'[64]

The Bristol Omnibus Company was unknowingly making quite a progressive move, hiring not only a Brown employee, but a practising Sikh who wore a turban. This was huge; a Sikh man in Manchester had his job application for a conductor position rejected in 1958 after refusing to remove his turban, sparking a dispute that was still ongoing at the time of the Bristol Bus Boycott and only successfully resolved in 1966.[65] London Transport only allowed turbans from 1964 after a community campaign.[66] It would also be hotly disputed in 1967 in Wolverhampton when Tarsem Singh Sandhu was suspended for showing up to drive his bus with a turban and beard, a ban which took two years to overturn.[67]

A sidenote: turban sighting still provokes a lot of excitement in my community, as it is symbolic to see our people being *that* visible. It isn't uncommon to hear someone shout 'Singh!' at the TV when someone wearing a turban appears, no matter how faded into the background they are. It's as though we have a sixth sense, or Singh sense, perhaps? It's not just us it seems; the first guardsman to wear a turban during the Trooping the Colour parade in 2018 caused quite a national stir; one complaint received by the BBC claimed that it was 'disfiguring an institution'.[68] I can't help but give thanks to those who fought for the right for Sikhs to wear turbans at work, as their actions allowed my turban-wearing uncle to have a long career on London's Underground.

Soon after Raghbir Singh made history, four more men started work as conductors: Norman Samuels and Norris Edwards from Jamaica, and Mohammed Raschid and Abbas Ali from Pakistan. Samuels went on to become a driver in October 1964, and on his first day crowds gathered to see the first Black bus driver in Bristol.[69] His son, Vernon Samuels, was born the same day he became a bus driver, and went on to become an Olympic athlete, representing Great Britain in the triple jump. (Insert poignant line here about this being a perfect example of 'the shoulders we stand on'.)

There wasn't a massive recruitment drive of Black and Brown workers though. By 1965, two years after the boycott, there were only four drivers and thirty-nine conductors.[70] It isn't publicly known what occurred during those negotiations in The Room Where It Happened, and it has been claimed that the end to the boycott was actually the imposition of a quota.[71*]

Guy Reid-Bailey didn't apply again for a job, as the whole campaign had put him off wanting to work on the buses.

Relationships between Black, Brown and white workers were cordial, though not necessarily what we'd call 'friendship'. After Singh started working as a conductor, the driver he worked with said, 'he's all right, mate'.[72] Black and Brown workers would generally avoid the bus crew's club as they were eyed with suspicion for speaking languages other than English, and they didn't want to talk buses in their free time and sing and dance to 'Knees Up Mother Brown'.[73]

Labour leader Harold Wilson told Paul Stephenson himself that he would introduce anti-discrimination legislation given everything that had happened in Bristol. In 1965, the first Race Relations Act was born (cue fanfare). But the legislation didn't go far enough, as we know. It excluded discrimination in employment, housing and education, and it wasn't until 1968 that it would be outlawed in these areas too. So the bus boycott may not have entirely changed the face of race

---

* In case there's any doubt, 'The Room Where It Happened' is a reference to *Hamilton*, not to former Donald Trump advisor John Bolton's book of the same name . . .

relations in the UK, but baby steps are still steps. Stephenson 'wanted to move the debate on from clashes with the Teddy boys in the streets to the rights of black people in this country', and he certainly did that.[74] It sent a powerful message to the nation: racial discrimination won't be tolerated.

So what happened afterwards to our plucky band of resisters? Sir Learie Constantine was forced to resign from his position as high commissioner of Trinidad and Tobago shortly after the boycott as he was seen to have overstepped his duties by interfering in the domestic affairs of the UK. But a few years later he was made the first Black life peer in the UK, and was just one of the three members of the House of Lords on the Race Relations Board. He died soon after, in 1971. A blue plaque hangs on the wall outside 101 Lexham Gardens in Earl's Court, the house where he wrote 'Colour Bar'.[75]

The Commonwealth Coordinated Committee continued working for the Black people of Bristol, especially in St Pauls. Roy Hackett continued as chair of the CCC, which is still going today as the Bristol West Indian Parents and Friends Association. In 1968 it set up the St Pauls festival, which is still an annual fixture on the Bristol cultural calendar, bringing 100,000 people to the streets on the first Saturday of July to celebrate Caribbean culture.[76] Hackett passed away in 2022 at the grand age of ninety-three.

Owen Henry, the 'mayor of St Pauls' and the 'Daddy' of the group, became a member of the Racial Equality Council.[77] In keeping with his prominent role in the community, he was a Voluntary Police Liaison Committee member to try and improve relations between the police and community following the clash between police and residents of St Pauls in 1980 (more on that in Chapter Eleven). Henry was awarded an Order of Merit by the Jamaican prime minister in 1979, and died in 1989.[78] Audley Evans helped set up the St Pauls festival and then left the UK soon after. He ended up in Florida, and continued helping other immigrants there, this time Haitians and Cubans.[79] Evans passed away in 1991.

Guy Reid-Bailey may not have worked on the buses, but he too continued to serve the community. Finding it difficult to be accepted into the local cricket clubs, he set up the Bristol West Indies Cricket Club. Though some clubs refused to play against them, they were not short of support, with up to six coachloads of fans turning up for their matches.[80] He worked in all sorts of jobs, including as a mental health nurse, and building parts for Concorde, and got a social work degree for good measure. In the mid-1980s, Reid-Bailey was one of the founders, along with Owen Henry and other community greats Barbara Dettering and Dolores Campbell, of the United Housing Association to help Black people with housing issues.[81] He ran the United Housing Association for twenty years, and it is still going, now as Brighter Places.

Paul Stephenson also continued to fight the good fight for the rest of his career and beyond. In one of the most incredible moves, as governor of a school in Brixton he approached Muhammad Ali on a visit to London and persuaded him to speak to the students, free of charge. They even went on to set up a sports association together for inner-city children.

Stephenson has been honoured and his work remembered in so many ways: the University of West England named a student bursary after him, and in 2017 he won a Pride of

Britain award.[82] Though he wasn't always regarded as such a national treasure. The year following the boycott he was arrested by eight police officers for ordering a drink in the Bay Horse pub, which said it didn't serve Black people. The trial was eventually dismissed, but not before the police officers tried to claim he was aggressive.

Hostility was common in his workplace too; the Police Federation in Coventry held a vote of no confidence against him in his position as a community relations officer, and Thatcher regarded him as a 'terrorist sympathiser' for being anti-apartheid. It's hard to shake the reputation of being a 'troublemaker' once you have it. At the time of writing, he is still 'troublemaking' in his eighties.

In 2013, the union Unite (which had merged with the Transport and General Workers' Union) issued an apology for supporting the colour bar in 1963. Oh, what is that I see on the horizon? *Vindication* . . . ? It has also dedicated a room to Paul Stephenson, Roy Hackett and Guy Reid-Bailey in the regional office, what was called Transport House in 1963 and since 2012 has been called 'Tony Benn House'.

The leaders are also dripping in royal praise for their services to Bristol: Reid-Bailey was awarded an OBE in 2005, Stephenson received one in 2009, and Hackett received an MBE in 2020.

Perhaps the most beautiful tribute to some of the leaders – not least because it avoids the awkward Empire and Commonwealth conversation involved with awards – can be seen walking the streets of St Pauls. As you wander those streets you are greeted by the *Seven Saints of St Pauls*, house-height murals of the faces of seven Black leaders, symbolically integrated into the community for which they tirelessly worked. The faces watch over beloved St Pauls, still one of the most deprived areas of Bristol, and still a strong community.[83]

Bristolians are still avid users of the buses, among the highest users in England in fact, taking around eighty-seven journeys per person in a year (who knows, maybe it'll be useful for a pub quiz someday).[84] They also still occasionally have issues with staff shortages.[85]

Today, there are mixed feelings about the legacy of the boycott among the leaders, and they know there is still work to do to fulfil the rights of the 16 per cent of Bristol's population that are ethnic minorities.[86] Stephenson now feels like little has changed, while Hackett was convinced that they did change something. He told his daughters that 'unless they fight for their right as a human being, they'll never change culture'.[87] And speaking of the younger generations he said, 'they can make a change if they put their mind to it. Change can happen, but you must confront and talk to people.'[88]

Young Bristolians are heeding those words; they put their mind to removing Edward Colston from his pedestal, and tens of thousands signed petitions to adorn the empty plinth with a monument to a Black leader. Mayor Marvin Rees is the first elected Black mayor in the UK.* Maybe one day soon we'll put Paul Stephenson, Roy Hackett or Owen Henry on the pedestal they deserve.[89]

---

* The first elected Black mayor, though not the first Black mayor overall – that goes to John Archer in 1913 in Battersea, and Jim Williams became lord mayor of Bristol in 1990, though that was a ceremonial post.

# Chapter Four

## Black Power and the Mangrove Nine

'Black oppressed people all over the world
are one.'[1]

British Black Panthers slogan

Barbara Beese at the Black Power demonstration and march, Notting
Hill, London, 9 August 1970.    © Metropolitan Police Service. From The National
Archives, ref. MEPO31/21 (A23)

There is no such thing as the Negro problem. What we are
talking about is the white problem . . . Isolated, we are weak

and very often in the minority. But united, we are strong
and very much in the majority. But majority without action
is impotent. This Black impotency has been exploited by
Whitey for far too long, too often, too ruthlessly. What we
need is a revolutionary philosophy which will educate the
Black man to be not only reactional but also actional ...
This philosophy we call today BLACK POWER.[2]

Thus read the manifesto of the Universal Coloured People's
Association, the first Black Power group in the UK.

Black Power swept the world in the late 1960s and 1970s.
The phrase originated in the USA, where its most famous
manifestation was in the Black Panther Party, with its icon of
a panther with snarling teeth and bared claws still instantly
recognisable today. Black Power wasn't limited to the USA;
the roar could be heard in the Caribbean and South America,
in West Africa, East Africa, and in Europe and the UK. It
could even be heard as far as Israel. This chapter and the next
discuss some pivotal moments in the history of Black Power
in the UK.

Black Power in the UK wasn't just a copycat of the movement in the USA (pun intended). Black communities were
already resisting racism and the long arm of imperialism in
the UK, and they were closely linked to anti-colonial struggles and revolutionary politics worldwide. Many followers of
Black Power in the UK were from the Caribbean and sub-
Saharan Africa or spent time in the regions to learn from
and work with revolutionary struggles, and some even went
to the protests in France in 1968. The name Black Power
simply gave them a new way to express these sentiments,

and the likes of Malcolm X and American Black Power leader Stokely Carmichael gave legitimacy to alternative forms of resistance. It wasn't all about playing nice or being 'respectable' any more.

'America was on fire ... and here was this fire coming. And we got to meet the fire,' activist Jessica Huntley reflected on Stokely Carmichael's visit to London in 1967.[3] Though the first Black Power group was set up in early 1967 before Carmichael's visit, the Universal Coloured People's Association, his presence and powerful oratory lit a fire that led to the spread of many more Black Power groups in the UK and changed how the movement worked. After his visit, the Universal Coloured People's Association expelled its white members, and founder Obi Egbuna left the organisation in April 1968 to form the British Black Panthers.

Black Power from the USA also came with a new representation of Blackness and now it wasn't taboo to be proud of being Black. Nina Simone sang 'To Be Young, Gifted and Black', James Brown said it loud that he was Black and proud. The mantra of 'Black is beautiful' was spread and absorbed by many people who had needed to hear it. Afros and dashikis were the order of the day.

What were the British advocates of Black Power fighting for? Different groups formed with slightly different objectives, but on the whole they fought against oppression and for liberation. They wanted to free the world from colonialism and imperialism. As part of the global majority their future was tied up in the future of their brothers and sisters worldwide. In a 1971 march against the restrictive Immigration Bill, the Black Panthers had a banner that read 'Black Oppressed

People All over the World Are One'.[4] Because of this global thinking, groups protested against apartheid in South Africa and US actions in Vietnam.

Obi Egbuna wasn't around to lead the Black Panthers for long. Three months after founding the group he and two others were arrested, put on trial at the Old Bailey, and imprisoned for inciting murder. This was for an article called 'What to do if cops lay their hands on a black man at Speaker's Corner'. It read, 'The moment the cops lay their hands on a Black brother, it is the duty of [the] Black crowd [to] surge forward like one big Black steam roller to catch up with the cop … till the brother is rescued, freed and made to flee at once.'[5] The arrests were made the day before a controversial documentary was due to air on the BBC; it had already been pulled once and there were attempts to get it pulled again. The episode of the documentary series *Cause for Concern* was about police brutality and harassment of the Black community. It was no coincidence that the police arrested a 'cause for concern' Black Panther leader the day before the programme: they wanted to show that they were the victims in this relationship.

After a stint under the leadership of David Udah, biochemistry doctoral student Altheia Jones-LeCointe became the de facto leader of the British Black Panthers. Although the organisation technically had no hierarchy, Jones-LeCointe was the 'intellectual ballast' and was seen as the leader by many.[6] Jones-LeCointe was no stranger to activism as she came from a family of political organisers in Trinidad and had been involved herself. One of her sisters eventually paid with her life for her organising activities in Trinidad.[7]

Jones-LeCointe worked closely with core members of the Panthers, one of whom would become her husband, Eddie LeCointe, as well as Barbara Beese and Brown members including Farrukh Dhondy and Mala Sen, who joined the group from a period of activism working closely with the IWA in Leicester after they heard Jones-LeCointe speak about immigrant rights.[8]

Awareness raising, consciousness building and education were among the Black Panthers' and other Black Power groups' main activities, and some of the least publicised by the media, which instead liked to focus on protests and run-ins with the police. As the Universal Coloured People's Association's manifesto states, 'BLACK POWER simply reflects a NEW STAGE IN THE REVOLUTIONARY CONSCIOUSNESS OF THE BLACK MAN.'[9] (Those capitals are in the original by the way, I'm not shouting.) Groups published newspapers and pamphlets, such as the Universal Coloured People's Association's first paper aptly named *Black Power Speaks* and the Panthers' *Freedom News*. Libraries and bookshops-cum-community spaces such as the Unity Centre in Brixton sprang up, many hosting supplementary classes for Black students.[10] (More on the importance of bookshops and supplementary schools to come in other chapters.)

Weekly readings were open to the public, and there were history classes with young people, but the arts and culture were as important as learning history and theory. Black Power publications often carried poems as well as political commentary and news. This inspired one of the Black Panther's Youth League members, Linton Kwesi Johnson, to take up poetry. 'Poetry was a cultural weapon in the black liberation struggle,' Johnson has reflected.[11] Johnson is one of the UK's most formidable poets, and he might have become an accountant instead had it not been for the Panthers.[12]

Community self-help was another key activity. The Black People's Information Centre was set up in Notting Hill, and not only had a stock of books and literature about Black radicalism but offered legal advice and support.[13] They visited Black people in prisons and hospitals to offer support and solidarity, and started a legal aid fund.[14]

The Panthers had four offices in Black communities across London: Notting Hill, Brixton, Finsbury Park and Acton, which was key for grassroots organising.[15] But their focus was not just on London, they organised a national coalition of Black Power organisations that included members in towns and cities such as Birmingham, Bristol, Leeds, Handsworth and Nottingham.[16]

Being a Panther wasn't just a political act, it was a way of life. The Panthers had strict membership criteria and only Black or Brown people could be members. They were open to white allies but wanted to be free to discuss whatever they wanted and didn't want white membership co-opting the cause. The Central Core, made up of eight to ten people at any time, decided on campaigning priorities and the editorial direction of *Freedom News*.[17]

Recruits had to go through a rigorous initiation process before they could become full members; not a fraternity hazing, but an education to unlearn the social conditioning they had received and then learn the way of Black Power. Writings from the American Black Panther Party were on the reading list. The Black Panthers were a very secretive group and kept few written records – it will soon become obvious why that was – so we don't know exactly how many people were members but it is estimated to be around 300, and it is likely there were thousands more who were supporters, though not members.[18]

The Black Panthers were heavily involved in the life of west London, and they and other groups had their work cut out for them. Notting Hill had seen the Teddy boy riots in 1958 and the murder of Kelso Cochrane in 1959, and there was a palpable underlying tension between its predominantly Black residents and white law enforcement that roamed the area. There were so many confrontations between police officers and the Black community that the residents got to know the officers by name. One of the most notorious in the area was PC Frank Pulley. He would put on a Jamaican accent when he talked to Black residents, and earned the nickname 'Puller' for 'pulling' Black people into the police station.[19]

Police officers such as PC Pulley frequently raided the few establishments in the area run by and for West Indians, and kept a close eye on certain streets, such as All Saints Road, that were associated with criminal activities. They kept a particularly close eye on number 8 All Saints Road, the home of the Mangrove restaurant, just two minutes' walk from Portobello Road Market.

The Mangrove was described at the time as the 'nerve centre' of the community.[20] Do you miss West Indian food and want a home-cooked meal or to find out where to get ingredients to make your own? Go to the Mangrove. Just arrived and want to find a place to live? Go to the Mangrove. Need to vent about Caribbean politics? Go to the Mangrove. Not only could you get some of the best West Indian food in London (spring chicken with rice and peas, and banana fritters for afters, anyone?) but it was a safe space to talk politics, shoot the breeze and hang out all night long, from 6 p.m. to 6 a.m.[21] Following two Race Relations Acts, it was illegal for pubs to refuse entry to Black people but it didn't mean they had to welcome them with open arms either, so the Mangrove served that purpose.

It was also frequented by international superstars such as Jimi Hendrix, Diana Ross, Marvin Gaye, Sammy Davis Jr, Bob Marley and Nina Simone when recording at the nearby Island Records studio or passing through London.

Frank Crichlow opened the restaurant in 1968. He was already known in Notting Hill for his late-night café El Rio, which he closed after being constantly hounded by the police. He opened the Mangrove instead, but that didn't stop the police harassment. The first year was relatively quiet, but the new year brought new trouble. The first raid took place on Friday 24 January 1969 around 11 p.m.[22] The police showed up with what they said was a search warrant, but they wouldn't let the manager look at it or allow him to call Crichlow, who wasn't at the Mangrove at the time. The police didn't find anything. When Crichlow found out what had happened, he called the local police stations, first Notting Hill then Notting Dale, both of whom denied they had conducted the raid. Only through calling Scotland Yard did he find out that Notting Hill's Criminal Investigation Department had ordered the raid. This department investigated serious crimes and their detectives were often plain-clothes officers. No 'serious crime' was found.

Raid number two took place a few months later, in the

summer. Again, nothing was found. Then there was a lull for the better part of a year but, in the meantime, a petition had been submitted to the council to revoke Mangrove's all-night licence, one of the reasons being 'that people with criminal records, prostitutes and convicted persons use the premises'.[23] The petition worked: the Mangrove now had to stop selling food at 11 p.m., which meant it would lose a significant part of its business. Crichlow had endured enough. He wrote to the Race Relations Board, saying that: 'My restaurant is patronised by respectable people, has never had a case with the police before – although they have unlawfully raided the premises on two occasions . . . I object to the entire incident because I know it is because I am a black citizen of Britain that I am discriminated against.'[24]

The police used the licence ruling in their subsequent raids of the Mangrove. Raid number three was in May 1970, and Crichlow was charged with using the premises outside of the licence arrangement, and for assaulting a police officer.[25] After that, the Mangrove went through raid after raid, after raid . . . after raid . . . after raid. A further *nine* raids to be precise, in the course of six weeks. One and half raids per week, if that were possible. The police always came up empty-handed.

When the police weren't busy raiding the place, they sat outside and watched the Mangrove instead. It may sound a little paranoid – you may think I'm writing this wearing a tin-foil hat – but the British police were in fact surveilling Black people they thought might make trouble, especially Black Power kind of trouble. Let's take a moment away from the Mangrove to examine this.

*

'Special Branch' was the name, surveilling was the game. This was not the same as the 'Special Patrol Group' paramilitary group, which we'll come across in later chapters; there was just a tendency to attach the word 'Special' to state bodies that did questionable things. Special Branch was set up for the same reason as the Special Patrol Group: in response to the conflicts in Ireland. Originally called the Metropolitan Police Special Irish Branch, it was formed in 1883 with the purpose of collecting intelligence on 'extreme' political and terrorist activity in the UK, 'keeping track of those suspected of "subversion of the democratic process"'.[26] There were soon Special Branch units all over the UK, as it was the main organisation doing this work before MI5 took the lead in the 1930s. After MI5 took the reins, Special Branch acted as a wing of the agency.[27]

Though small in number and peaceful, the Black Power groups were seen as a threat. In the USA, there had been uprisings in Detroit, New Jersey and Newark, and the police were keen to prevent the same thing happening in the UK. Black Power started to emerge in the old colonies, too, and this threatened the UK's hopes to maintain a grip on the Commonwealth countries. Again, if this sounds conspiratorial and paranoid, the case of British Guiana (now Guyana) is a helpful illustration of this fear.

In 1953 the colony was given semi-autonomy under a new constitution; they could hold elections and govern, but ultimate power still lay with the British. When the People's Progressive Party (PPP) won a resounding victory in the Guyanese elections, the British got scared that the PPP was too sympathetic to communism, and Prime Minister Winston

Churchill ordered an intervention – the constitution was suspended, the legislature dissolved, and key leaders and members were arrested and separated.[28] Britain ruled again for the next four years.

This kind of thinking was still very much present a decade later in 1967 when Stokely Carmichael left the UK earlier than planned after a visit from Special Branch, and was subsequently banned from the UK and thirty other territories.[29]

As quickly as they could raise a fist in the air, the government had created an apparatus to surveil and control the Black Power groups. The Black Power Desk was an intelligence unit created with the sole purpose of surveilling movements led by Black and Brown people, especially the Black Power organisations. It had files on each of the main individuals, and was even able to infiltrate the Black Panthers.[30]

It was because of the actions of Special Branch and other state organisations that the British Black Panthers were so secretive. It's members knew what was being done in the USA, as well as in the UK, to Black Power groups, and without documents there was less to hold against them. Although documents were sparse, photos were encouraged. In the days before smartphones allowed for filming and documenting acts of police harassment and violence, cameras with rolls of film were the order of the day. Neil Kenlock was a member of the Black Panthers and its photographer. His photos were key to telling stories from the point of view of the Panthers, which was to prove essential in what was to come. 'The camera was there to protect us,' Kenlock has said.[31] This is still true today – if not to protect then to seek justice.

*

Now that you realise that it was in fact the police who were paranoid and not me, let's get back to the Mangrove. Mangrove staff member and activist Darcus Howe wanted to do something about the police raids. He had spent time under the tutelage of his great-uncle C. L. R. James, participated in the Trinidadian Black Power Revolution in his birthland early in 1970 and worked with an American Black Power group, and he wasn't convinced that tactics like writing to the Race Relations Board or connecting to local leaders would get Crichlow anywhere.

Howe and Crichlow formed an 'Action for the Defence of the Mangrove' committee, along with the activist and wife of C. L. R. James, Selma James, and the barrister Tony Mohipp. The Black Panthers confirmed their support for the Mangrove. After some meetings at the James's house, the committee decided to organise a protest. They distributed leaflets around the area urging people to 'demonstrate in support of our community'. The committee outlined the reasons for the demonstration in a statement sent to the Home Office, 10 Downing Street, the leader of the Labour Party and the high commissioners of Jamaica, Barbados, Guyana and Trinidad. It read:

> We, the Black People of London have called this demonstration in protest against constant police harassment which is being carried out against us, and which is condoned by the legal system. In particular, we are calling for an end to the persecution of the Mangrove Restaurant, of 8 All Saints Road, W.11., a Restaurant that serves the Black Community. These deliberate raids, harassments and

provocations have been reported to the Home Office on many occasions. So too has the mounting list of grievances such as raids on West Indians parties, Wedding Receptions, and other places where Black People lawfully gather. We feel this protest is necessary as all other methods have failed to bring about any change in the manner the police have chosen to deal with Black People. We shall continue to protest until the Black People are treated with justice by the Police and the Law Courts.[32]

The protest took place on Sunday 9 August 1970. The weather was cooperative and the placards were ready to be raised. Demonstrators started gathering outside the Mangrove from about 2 p.m., some donning the striking apparel of the US Black Panthers: black berets, sunglasses and leather jackets. The plan was to march past three police stations, Notting Hill, Notting Dale and Harrow Road. Around 150 protestors gathered in total, a small affair considering other marches which drew thousands of Black and Brown people. Frank Crichlow and Darcus Howe were there, of course, as was the leader of the British Black Panthers, Altheia Jones-LeCointe and members such as Barbara Beese. Locals, activists and frequenters of the Mangrove came, including Rothwell Kentish, who showed up with his ten-year-old daughter before he was due to speak at another protest in the area, and the founder of the nearby Black People's Information Centre, Rhodan Gordon.[33] Passers-by would have been forgiven for thinking it was a bigger crowd than it was as there were around 200 police officers to start with, outnumbering the protestors, and plain-clothes officers posing as protestors themselves.[34]

The small group made their way to the first police station, stopping to listen to speeches by Howe and Jones-LeCointe. Howe said: 'We've complained to the police about the police and nothing has been done. We've complained to judges about judges and nothing's been done. We've complained to magistrates about magistrates and nothing's been done. We have complained to the council about the council and nothing has been done. Now we have to do something ourselves.'[35]

Protestors cheered in agreement with Howe and pumped their placards bearing slogans such as 'this is the time', 'black unity now' and, my personal favourite, 'black power is going to get your mama'. A few were carrying actual pigs' heads.

The demonstration passed the first police station. On the way to the second station the police called for reinforcements; they were on edge.[36] At Notting Dale station the protestors listened to another speech from Howe, and then someone spotted PC Pulley's car and chants of 'we want Puller, we want Puller' started. En route to Harrow Road police station, the protestors found themselves up against a wall of police officers, five-deep, at the intersection of Portnall Road and Marban Road.[37]

What started the events of the next twenty minutes will never be known, but was central to the trial that would follow and the consequences would last years. Some say the police were just trying to let traffic pass and this was misconstrued by the protestors; others say that there was confusion about the protest route. Some say that the police started pulling down placards and pinning people to the floor; the police say the protestors first launched bricks and bottles at them.

'Chaos reigned,' Howe recalled, 'the demonstration

literally exploded. The violence was ferocious ... The police were moved to an orgy of violence and abuse. It was a street fight.'[38] The police dragged protestors away, Jones-LeCointe was hauled off with her arms and legs splayed as she tried to help a fellow protestor who was bleeding. The protestors meanwhile 'gave as good as we got ... whole building skips were emptied at [the police]'.[39] As well as the police fighting on the street, there were more in marked and unmarked vehicles watching from the sidelines.

Nineteen protestors were arrested, including Altheia Jones-LeCointe, Barbara Beese, Anthony Carlisle Inniss, and later Darcus Howe as he sat in the Mangrove restaurant.

It was front-page news the following day. '17 police hurt in race fight', reported the *Guardian*, '19 held in clash with police', said *The Times*.[40] The arrested protestors appeared at Marylebone Magistrates' Court the same day as those headlines, charged with a mixture of charges including affray (disorderly physical conduct), possession of an offensive weapon and assault on police. Seven people were found not guilty, and the police wanted more time to gather evidence for any potential additional charges against the other defendants. It wasn't a regular occurrence for a small protest to garner such attention and have so many charges thrown around. Leaders such as Howe and Jones-LeCointe were convinced that it was an attempt to make an example of this Black movement, to reinforce the dangerous myth that Black people, Black immigrants no less, were causing trouble.

The home secretary, Reginald Maudling, called for an urgent report on the full episode, which didn't necessarily clarify events as there was some confusion as to who was behind the protest. Senior Scotland Yard officers thought it could be outsiders, possibly right-wing extremists, and were 'satisfied that there has been no major breakdown in relations between the police and the coloured population'.[41] The most visible and publicly well-known Black activist at the time was Michael X, and it was thought by politicians that he and his Black House community centre were behind the protest.[42]

A quick sidenote on Michael X. He was widely regarded by the press as the leader of the Black Power movement. He was vocal and often incendiary and was the first person arrested under the 1965 Race Relations Act, but he was not regarded as the leader by others in the movement. Michael X was known as a conman by many; he worked with Peter Rachman, the exploitative landlord we heard about in Chapter One, to forcefully gather rent from Notting Hill residents. However, his community space, the Black House, was famously supported by John Lennon and Yoko Ono, who donated a bag of their hair to Michael X to auction off as a fundraiser. The Black House closed soon after the Mangrove protest, and burned down in mysterious circumstances. Michael X left for his birth country, Trinidad and Tobago, where another community Black House eventually burned down and bodies were found in the garden. Michael X was charged with murder and executed.

The home secretary was most likely aware of the potential repercussions of any actions brought against the protestors. Start deporting suspected leaders and there could be a backlash. Use the Race Relations Act against them, like they had done with Michael X and Obi Egbuna, and there could be a backlash. Instead, the home secretary met with Black moderates such as David Pitt, who was deputy chair of the Greater London Council and chair of the government's Campaign Against Racial Discrimination, and he suggested that more Black police officers would go a long way to solving the tensions. It wasn't the first time this topic had come up. Earlier in the year a government White Paper called for more Black and Brown police officers but noted that previous recruitment drives to do just that had failed.[43]

Meanwhile, the police pored over their photos and reports of the day of the protest, and brought a new charge of 'incitement to riot' against some of the people they had originally arrested. They also made some new arrests: Rupert Boyce, Frank Crichlow, Rhodan Gordon, Godfrey Millett and Rothwell Kentish.[44] It seemed to the leaders within the Black Power movement that they had targets on their back, as though the police were deliberately trying to make a case against certain influential individuals. Altheia Jones-LeCointe and the Black Panthers mobilised. They went on a speaking tour, held a solidarity march in October 1970 along the same route as the Mangrove protest, and formed Black Defence Committees to raise support from allies.[45]

A few months after the protest, around Christmas, the defendants found themselves back in Marylebone Magistrates' Court. The police brought the new charges of incitement to riot in front of magistrate David Wacher. The police couldn't get their story straight; some said that the clashes on 9 August had been spontaneous, others said they were planned. Wacher thought some of the evidence was patchy at best and even threw out more than twenty pages of police statements.[46]

The police tried to change the charge to just 'riot' (from 'incitement to riot') but Wacher wasn't having any of it. By the end, the other charges were allowed but the most serious one of incitement to riot was thrown out. This was a victory for the defendants because if the charge had been allowed and later at trial they were found guilty of incitement to riot, they could have faced up to ten years in prison.[47] Afterwards, at a press conference held at the Mangrove, Howe said, 'The result of the hearing today demonstrated once again the contempt with which the police hold black people. The police were prepared to go to any lengths to pin incitement and riot charges on us who have exercised our right to demonstrate. The streets are the only platform.'[48]

It was a little too early to celebrate, though, as the state had invested too much in this to give up that easily.

The police didn't let up on the Mangrove restaurant and Frank Crichlow. Crichlow went through a trial for a breach of licensing laws in which he was found guilty and fined £225.[49] The police raided the restaurant again in January 1971, to find some people sitting around eating sweetcorn and drinking tea. Crichlow was fined again.[50] The raids took a toll on the business, and at one point the number of customers a week fell from 1,000 to 300.[51]

Things weren't just bad for Frank Crichlow, they were soon looking bleak for the others: the director of public prosecutions had gone against magistrate David Wacher's ruling and reinstated the charge of incitement to riot against seven of the protestors. An unusual move, and a huge blow to all of the nine who were now going to trial at the Central Criminal Court, better known as the Old Bailey, reserved for the most serious of crimes. The Mangrove Nine were: Barbara Beese, Rupert Boyce, Frank Crichlow, Rhodan Gordon, Darcus Howe, Anthony Innis, Altheia Jones-LeCointe, Rothwell Kentish and Godfrey Millett. They all pleaded not guilty to the thirty-two charges levelled against them.

Day one of the trial on 5 October 1971 was nearly fourteen months since the protest. Lady Justice sat atop the Old Bailey, twelve-foot tall, wielding a sword and the scales of justice, surveying the area as the defence, prosecution and members of the public entered Court Number One. Court Number One is like Centre Court at Wimbledon, the place where the biggest trials happen. It is kitted out accordingly; oak-panelled walls match the oak benches, chairs and tables crammed into the space. It was 'male, pale and stale', says Barbara Beese.[52]

Both sides had a lot riding on this trial. The police wanted to take down the Black Power leadership by painting a picture of violence. Their aim was to put an end to the Mangrove restaurant, but more importantly strike a blow against Black communities nationwide by deterring any sort of defensive action against the police. For the Mangrove Nine, at stake was literal physical freedom for themselves and their kids; Beese and Howe had a young son together and Jones-LeCointe was pregnant. They also bore the weight of the struggle: would they be believed or would the lies of the police continue to be validated? It was more than just their lives they were defending in the courtroom. They were quite pessimistic going into the trial, emotionally preparing themselves to go to jail.[53]

This wasn't the first trial of people involved in the Black Power movement; Altheia Jones-LeCointe's husband, Eddie

LeCointe, had been on trial earlier the same year with two other Panthers and found guilty, and we've seen that Obi Egbuna was arrested years prior. But this was to be a case like no other that had come before.

There were two radical moves from the very beginning that indicated that this was to be a unique trial. Previous trials including Black Power affiliates usually saw little to no input from the defendants themselves. Even Obi Egbuna, who made the Universal Coloured People's Association an exclusively Black organisation under his leadership, had white lawyers to defend him.

The nine needed representation, but who would defend them? Ian Macdonald, a young, white lawyer Darcus Howe knew, represented Barbara Beese, and another white lawyer, Michael Mansfield, represented Frank Crichlow. This wouldn't be the last time Macdonald and Mansfield would defend Black and Brown people; they were bona fide allies. However, the lawyer that Darcus Howe had consulted for the case in the magistrates' court recommended he plead guilty, which he refused to do.[54]

In the first of the radical moves, Darcus Howe and Altheia Jones-LeCointe decided to forgo lawyers and represent themselves. Howe had been a law student, and Jones-LeCointe was a doctoral candidate in science, but in the end, their education didn't matter in the courtroom. Later during the trial, Rhodan Gordon would get rid of his lawyer and defend himself too. Without the restraints of traditional legal representation, Howe and Jones-LeCointe were free to play the game of the trial and highlight what it was really about: racism and politics.

The second of the radical moves was an idea Howe had thought about when observing previous trials: calling for an all-Black jury. How could a white jury be seen as fair when racism and prejudice were so widespread in the UK? Would a white jury even understand the Caribbean accents and dialect of the defendants? There was technically legal provision for this as the Magna Carta from 1215 first established trial by jury. You may also be familiar with the charter from creating your own version at school and using teabags and burning the edges to give it that authentic ol' timey look.

Calls for an all-Black jury started even before the trial did, the Black Panthers circulated a petition stating that:

We are forced to defend our human rights against the racial prejudice of white jurors who do not represent the backgrounds from which we come, who are completely out of touch with the issues that affect our daily lives, and who are committed to upholding the standards of white, middle-class Britain . . . we stand no chance of getting justice from an all-white jury.[55]

Using the same line of argument in the courtroom as the petition, Macdonald argued that 'you cannot guarantee, in a society in which prejudice is rife, that a jury will not have on it persons who start off with prejudice against the defendants because they are black'.[56] For two whole days the defence tried to convince Judge Edward Clarke to grant them an all-Black jury, calling both on the Magna Carta and a Welsh case where the defendants were granted the right to a Welsh jury.[57] They failed; Clarke refused the request.

They wouldn't be deterred. Instead, they studied the list of potential jurors and their occupations carefully. If they couldn't have an all-Black jury, they could at least try and have working-class representation. The defence started asking the 100 potential jurors about the newspapers they read and how they would define 'Black Power' before this was stopped by Clarke.[58] Each of the nine defendants used their right to dismiss seven jurors, dismissing sixty-three potential jurors in total. Eventually twelve were selected, including two Black men. That even two jurors were Black was quite a feat considering that of the previous five hundred jurors that had been called up for trials at the Old Bailey, only three were Black.[59] Most of the jury were working-class. The trial proper could now begin.

The prosecution was up first. Would the jury believe the police were the victims of an orchestrated, intentional attack on that fateful Sunday, or that the police were in fact using this trial to try and take down important Black leaders and community members? If prosecutor Michael Hill got his way, the jury would soon think that the protestors had deliberately intended to whip up violence against the police.

Most of the witnesses the prosecution called were police officers present on the day of the protest, as well as some civilians from the area. The party line was that the police did not provoke an attack, they were simply escorting the demonstrators and were on the receiving end of violent acts which members of the Mangrove Nine specifically called for.

This was the story described by Detective Chief Superintendent Joseph Donnelly on day five of the trial. He said that Altheia Jones-LeCointe had stood on the bonnet of a car and more or less said 'we must get rid of the pigs'.[60] This was also the story Police Constable Paul Phillips relayed on day eight of the trial when he said that there were shouts of 'kill the pigs' and he claimed that, even as the police were attacked by flying sticks and bottles and pieces of brick, he didn't draw his truncheon.[61] Howe was accused of standing on a wall shouting 'kill the white pigs', and jumping over a six-foot wall to escape. Godfrey Millett was accused of shouting at a woman carrying a biracial baby, 'You had better think black, baby, or you die with the white pigs when the time comes.'[62] Kentish, Crichlow and Gordon were also accused of shouting encouragement to members of the crowd to attack the police.

Tensions were high from the beginning. The defence suspected that Judge Clarke was on the side of the prosecution, and some of the defendants let him know as much. A few weeks in, Gordon's lawyer was cross-examining PC John Lewis and asking about his statement from August 1970 when Judge Clarke interjected to say it would be hard for PC Lewis to remember what he had said more than a year ago. Gordon interjected from the front of the dock, 'You are taking over the case for the prosecution, you have been doing it over and over again. And you have called the black counsel incompetent.'[63]

Judge Clarke did not take such interjections in his court lightly, 'If I have any further offensive observations of that sort addressed to anyone in this court I shall take other steps—'

'I don't care,' Gordon responded, 'I have nothing to lose. You can only send me to the cells.'

Gordon wasn't the only one who spoke up. Darcus Howe was storming out, after what he saw as Judge Clarke's bias in allowing unfair questioning of a witness, when he was pushed down the stairs by a guard and got into an altercation. He said that his treatment by the warders, 'people who are supposed to protect me while I am in the dock can only be described as an outright provocation and a racist attack.'[64]

The Black Panthers and Black Defence Committees were the organising force behind public support. Panther Farrukh Dhondy would go to the courthouse every day after work and talk to those who had witnessed the day's trial, write it all down and send the details out to organisations around the country every other day.[65] Supporters for the Mangrove Nine picketed outside holding placards with slogans such as 'Our crime was we dared to demonstrate'.[66] They packed the public gallery and interruptions coming from the gallery led Judge Clarke to threaten to clear it. He also threatened to cancel bail for defendants who laughed.[67] Laughter may seem out of place in a courtroom for a criminal trial, but when police officers defended PC Pulley with statements such as, 'I consider him to be a first-class officer', they were highly likely to be met with laughter.[68]

A couple of weeks into the trial and it was the turn of PC Frank Pulley on the stand. Of the Mangrove he said, 'the place is a haunt for criminals, prostitutes, ponces and the like. Anyone going there is likely to be corrupted if not corrupted already.'[69] He continued, 'I think it is a den of iniquity.'

One of the defence lawyers asked, 'Are you suggesting that it is a place where young persons are likely to be corrupted?'

'I would have thought they would have been corrupted already to finish up there.'

Don't mince your words, Pulley.

The prosecution called fifty witnesses in total.[70] A little over a month after the trial had started, on 9 November 1971, it was the time of the defence.

The defence was ready. Howe, Jones-LeCointe, Beese and Crichlow had been meeting every night after court adjourned to discuss the day's events and prepare themselves for the next.[71]

The defendants were finally able to tell their side of the story, which was one of overwhelming police harassment, brutality and lies. Anthony Inniss was the first defendant to take the stand. He told the court that when the violence broke out, he decided to leave the demonstration, but as he did so a group of plain-clothed men got out of a car and came towards him in a 'hostile manner . . . I thought they were going to grab me, so I turned and ran. When they caught up with me I was punched in the ribs and pushed in the back.'[72]

By the time Rhodan Gordon was to take the stand, he was done with what he saw as a farcical trial. He refused to take the oath on the Bible, declaring, 'I used to have religious beliefs but I have seen so many policemen go into the witness box, take the oath on the Bible, and then tell a string of lies.'[73] Gordon maintained he had not plotted to attack police stations, he wasn't even at Portnall Road at the time of the clash. The same argument was put forward by Rothwell Kentish: he had swung by the demonstration on his way to a prayer meeting to give a speech for another cause and was at that other meeting at the time he was supposedly inciting a riot.[74]

Frank Crichlow used his time on the stand to explain the wider purpose of the protest and get the attention of local leaders. He had complained to the Home Office, Sir Learie Constantine (the former high commissioner of Trinidad and

Tobago who was involved in the Bristol Bus Boycott) and the National Council for Civil Liberties to no avail. Character witnesses were called in to counter the slander against Crichlow, including the MP for North Kensington, who had frequented the Mangrove. MP Bruce Douglas-Mann called Crichlow 'extremely intelligent with a social conscience about the problems of black people'.[75]

Near the end of November, Jones-LeCointe was on the stand. She recalled that she was helping a bleeding protester when a police officer told them, 'if you don't go, we will help you,' and he grabbed both of them but the bleeding woman escaped. Jones-LeCointe remembered, 'they did not tell me they were arresting me. They just took me away. There were about five of them. They lifted me up bodily to a van. I was struggling and saying: "what have I done?" I was thrown into the van.'[76] Witnesses confirmed Jones-LeCointe's version of events. While in the van, Jones-LeCointe says she was called 'a savage' by a police officer and elbowed in the waist.[77]

The prosecution's case rested on the evidence of the police that they witnessed the defendants calling for attacks on the force. And it rested particularly on the testimony of the police in nearby vehicles surveilling the situation. The police had taken photos, but so had the protestors, and the problem with bending the truth when there is photographic evidence is that there is photographic evidence.

Darcus Howe and the team used the testimonies and photos to take down the prosecution in the cross-examination. Some of the lies were easy to question, the placard slogans such as 'kill the pigs' the police claim were used weren't even in the photos presented by the police.[78] The claim that Howe jumped over a six-foot wall was also quickly taken down. Howe requested to take the jury to Portnall Road to see the wall or reconstruct a six-foot wall in the courtroom but was denied both times.[79] Despite that, it was still obvious that there was no way he could have done it; six foot is really, really high. And the claim that Howe stood on a wall shouting 'kill the white pigs'? A photo showed that there was a police bus between the observation van and the wall so there was no way anyone in the observation van would have seen the wall Howe supposedly stood on.[80]

The biggest takedown required a little more creativity. Much of the police testimony was based on the story that four officers saw the proceedings from an observation van. All of the officers gave the same testimony. But observation vans were meant to be clandestine and had just a thin slit to allow for outward observation, so the four officers couldn't possibly have all looked out of it at once. Howe replicated the size of the slit in a piece of paper and showed the jury how small it was: how could four people have possibly looked through it at once? Howe put this to Pulley, who claimed that they all had one eye on the slit at the same time, 'and where was your face?' Howe asked Pulley.[81] The courtroom howled.

The prosecution's case crumbled but it wasn't a slam-dunk as there wasn't much precedent for police testimony to be questioned. The jury, however, seemed to have warmed to the defence, their use of humour and Howe's use of Shakespeare quotes.[82]

The trial ended with as much tension as it had unfolded with, both inside and outside the courtroom. Shortly before the end of the trial, a Black protestor was arrested and charged with assault after he refused to stop protesting.[83] The tensions outside reflected the atmosphere in the courtroom. In his final statement, prosecutor Michael Hill said, 'this trial has been disfigured and at times almost totally disrupted by expressions of passion, of emotion, of prejudice . . . by betraying a childish petulance and sometimes by sheer stupidity'.[84] Ian Macdonald's final statement for the defence focused the jury's attention on the 'naked judicial tyranny' of Judge Clarke, and the impact of the intimidating set-up of the courtroom.[85] The defendants used their closing statements to discuss the prejudice faced by Black people in the UK and persecution at the hands of the police. 'The judge says he has thirty-five years of legal experience,' Howe said, 'well, I have had four hundred years of colonial experience.'[86]

Judge Clarke warned the jury to disregard everything they had heard about racial discrimination in general (like Howe's closing statement) and advised them to 'keep your cool and concentrate on the evidence you have heard'.[87] And with that it was time for the jury to deliberate. It was now 15 December 1971, ten weeks after the trial had started, four weeks longer than it was expected to take, and sixteen months after the protest.

The jury deliberated for eight hours and fifteen minutes.[88] On the incitement to riot charges, all were found not guilty. Five of the nine – Barbara Beese, Frank Crichlow, Darcus Howe, Rothwell Kentish and Godfrey Millett – were acquitted of all charges brought against them. On charges of affray and possession of a weapon, some were found guilty. Of the original thirty-two charges only seven stood at the end.

The four found guilty received suspended sentences for the charges, which meant they would be on probation for two years and if they complied with the requirements their sentence would be dropped. This wasn't met with all-round jubilation, though, as suspended sentences were seen as a ticking time bomb, a tactic used by the legal system as a form of social control.[89] 'Whatever sentence you have in mind I do not really care,' Gordon told Judge Clarke, 'whether you send me to jail or not does not interest me but I would ask that you do not pass a suspended sentence.'[90]

Judge Clarke thought he was being generous; being so close to Christmas he thought the sentence demonstrated the spirit of goodwill of the season. The gallery laughed when he said this to the court.

A bittersweet victory, then, for some of the Mangrove Nine. But they celebrated nonetheless: no one had gone to jail and the remaining charges were minor.[91] Members of the jury celebrated with the Mangrove Nine outside the Old Bailey and in the pub.[92] Some of them later went to the Mangrove for a celebratory meal.

For some of the Mangrove Nine, their ordeal wasn't over with the end of the trial. Rhodan Gordon was arrested two days later after an altercation with a police officer.[93] Rothwell Kentish was soon put on trial again, this time for the attempted murder of a police officer. He was eventually charged with assault and possession of an offensive weapon, and was sentenced to thirty-six months in prison. The

Mangrove was raided at various points after 1971 – the most serious incident was in 1988 when forty-eight officers raided the premises. Defended again by Michael Mansfield, Frank Crichlow eventually received a settlement of £50,000 from the Home Office as compensation for false imprisonment, battery and malicious prosecution.[94]

Frank Crichlow kept the Mangrove restaurant open until 1992. He also set up the Mangrove Steel Band and Mangrove Community Association, as the blue plaque affixed to 8 All Saints Road reads. Number 8 is now a private residence, sold in 2020 for a cool £2.7 million.[95] Crichlow died in 2010.

The trial lived strong in the minds of the Notting Hill community, and Howe would be greeted with cries of 'where's ya face!' And it lived strong for the entire Black community in the UK for another reason, as not only had the mostly white jury voted against the actions of the British police and state, but for the first ever time in a British court of law, it was stated that there was evidence of racism from the police force. Judge Clarke said, 'what this case has shown apart from anything else, and shown regrettably, is that there is evidence of racial hatred on both sides'.[96] 'Evidence of racial hatred' had finally been admitted in a courtroom by none other than a judge, and it was a phrase that etched itself onto the minds of Black people in Britain. The Metropolitan Police assistant commissioner tried to get Judge Clarke's statement retracted, and the home secretary even got involved, but it was not withdrawn. What is that I can taste . . . is that the sweet taste of . . . justice?

# Chapter Five

## The Fasimbas, the Oval Four and the Black Liberation Front

'We are our own liberators.'[1]

Black Liberation Front Working Platform

The Mangrove Nine trial had been won, a collective sigh of relief could be breathed and victory laps performed, right? Wrong. Some police officers were none too pleased with the outcome, and there were still no repercussions for the officers themselves. Sorry to start on a downer, but as we know all too well, the struggle is *still* not over.

So what came next? Special Branch were thought to still be monitoring Black Power groups and the leadership in particular, and there were many to monitor. Though probably the most well-known group today, thanks in part to the US namesake, the British Black Panthers weren't the only Black Power group in the UK. Groups sprang up independently of the Panthers, and broke off from the Panthers themselves after disputes and impasses. The Fasimbas were another example of a Black Power group. The Fasimbas, meaning 'young lions' in Swahili, were originally the youth branch of the South East London Parents Organisation, which was formed in 1969 to combat the miseducation of Black children (more on education in the next chapter).

The Fasimbas were a pan-Africanist organisation who provided a safe space for young Black people to get together outside of the gaze of both their parents and the state, through dances with consciousness-raising songs, discussions of ideas such as Marxism and Fanonism, and martial arts classes.[2] They tried to avoid attracting too much public or police attention by staying away from marches and they advised their members to escape from the police in case of a run-in.

It was the job of the Publicity and Propaganda Committee consisting of Winston Trew, Constantine Boucher, Sterling Christie, George Griffiths and Andrea Dixon, to design materials and recruit new members. More than half of the Fasimbas' 500-strong membership was female, but in a tale as old as time, the leadership was overwhelmingly male. Altheia Jones-LeCointe was the only female head of a Black Power organisation in the UK, though 'leader' was a title she didn't apply to herself. The disparity in representation was one of the reasons for the creation of female groups and spaces (more to come in Chapter Seven).

The north-London-based Black Liberation Front (BLF) shared a similar approach to the Fasimbas in that its members didn't take part in the big demonstrations that usually brought the coalition of groups together 'on the grounds that the police may use such an occasion to attack black militants', explained a 'plain man's guide to the New Left' in the

*Guardian*.[3] The overlap between the Fasimbas and the BLF led to an alliance at the end of 1971.

One of the reasons you've probably heard little to nothing about groups such as the Fasimbas and BLF is the media at the time only covered Black Power groups when there were clashes with the police or supposedly violent acts; popular portrayals of Black activism in the UK (when portrayed at all) often focus on the exploits of Michael X and supposed criminality of Black Power groups. What gets ignored is one of their main activities of education and community development.

Let's take a minute to correct that imbalance and discuss education as activism in Black Power.* As touched upon in the previous chapter, one of Black Power's main activities was education. Or rather, re-education. Adherents educated themselves and each other about the history of Black and all oppressed peoples worldwide; books focusing on key events such as the Haitian Revolution discussed in C. L. R. James's *The Black Jacobins* from 1938 were staple reading. And in the age before the internet, books needed bookshops.

The problem was, where could Black (and Brown) people even find books for them, and by them? If publishing is still so homogeneous today (shout-out to my publisher, one of a few working to change this) then what must it have been like then?[4] Yes, it was dire. The answer, therefore, was to do it themselves. Jessica and Eric Huntley were two such people who took this task upon themselves. They didn't grow up in Guyana surrounded by books, nor did they know anything

---

* We get to correct the imbalance and discuss books, double win!

about publishing.[5] But they did grow up with progressive politics and a passion for social justice, and they even named one of their sons Karl, after Karl Marx.

After they moved to the UK in the late 1950s, they became friends with historian and activist Walter Rodney, whose Black Power and anti-capitalist work unnerved many people. His politics was particularly unsettling to the Jamaican government. He held a post at the University of the West Indies, and after a trip abroad Rodney was prevented from re-entering Jamaica. This prompted the 'Rodney Riots', an uprising started by the university students that spread to the working class, and ultimately laid bare the underlying tensions in Jamaica. Some people see the 1968 uprising in Jamaica as the true start of the post-colonial era rather than independence in 1962.[6]

When this happened, as well as organising protests in the UK, Jessica Huntley decided to type up, print and distribute some of Rodney's lectures. The Huntleys put the lectures together in a book, and Bogle-L'Ouverture Publications was born with the publication of *The Groundings with My Brothers* in 1969, and soon after they bought a printing press from Fleet Street for £25.[7]

Bogle-L'Ouverture Publications wasn't the first Black publisher in the UK; New Beacon Books had been created in 1966 out of the Caribbean Artists' Movement, and publisher Allison & Busby started in 1967.

Bookshops by and for Black people sprang up across London and the country; from the Unity Bookshop, Shakti, and Centerprise in London to the Raddle Bookshop in Leicester and the Harriet Tubman Bookshop in Birmingham.

New Beacon Books and Bogle-L'Ouverture also opened shops to sell their publications and those of other publishers. The BLF opened one named after their newsletter, Grassroots Storefront, then a second shop, and then a third. The second shop was in Golborne Road, just a ten-minute walk from the Mangrove restaurant. Like the Mangrove, which was more than a restaurant, bookshops weren't just bookshops. They were community centres, impromptu citizens' advice bureaus, and safe spaces for events.

Like many symbols of Black excellence and success, a backlash soon followed. Eric Huntley recalls one woman who used to come to the store, buy greetings cards and then proceed to cut them up in front of him.[8] Stores were covered with graffiti with unimaginative slogans like 'Niggers Out' and 'KKK', windows were regularly smashed and shit was smeared on the walls.

The Black Panthers' Unity Books was firebombed, and Panther Farrukh Dhondy had to jump out of the first-floor window to survive.[9] They suspected the National Front was behind it, but it was hard to know as the police didn't pay much attention to what was happening to the bookshops. Eric Huntley recalls that the police said the Bogle-L'Ouverture bookshop isn't Buckingham Palace; they couldn't expect twenty-four-hour service.[10] In other cases, the police implied the bookshop owners themselves were to blame with lines of questioning like 'do you short-change?' and 'have you any enemies?'[11]

Bookshops and the Black community supported themselves and one another with the Bookshop Joint Action Committee, run from the Huntleys' place in Ealing, west London. When Soma Books in south London received a phone call threatening that the shop would be burned down, the committee consisting of seven bookshops at the time immediately sent a telegram to the home secretary which said: 'Urgently demand immediate meeting reference fascist attacks on black bookshops. Soma Books threatened with fire today.'[12]

It received no response. When it held a press conference a few weeks later in the burned-out wreckage of Unity Books, John La Rose of New Beacon Books reminded attendees that the Nazis had burned books and destroyed bookshops and libraries in their thirst for power.[13] There was then a burst of activity from the Crime Prevention Squad, but with an emphasis on the bookshops protecting themselves rather than what the police could do. The committee was ready: 'we won't be terrorised out of existence,' it responded.*

For Black Power groups, newsletters were also important. Weekly or monthly periodicals were published out of people's living rooms, community centres and book stores and sold for a few pennies at markets and outside Black-owned establishments such as barber shops and grocery stores.

So there you have it, some details on other activities of Black Power groups and activists that rarely get mentioned. And it just so happened that it was these publishing activities (and racism) that set off a chain of events in 1972 that lasted until 2020.

It was a Thursday in early spring in 1972, 16 March to be precise. Fasimbas member Winston Trew was going to his

---

* The importance of books only continued; from 1982 the publishers organised twelve fairs, the International Book Fair of Radical Black and Third World Books.

weekly appointment at the Peckham Labour Exchange (a job centre) to sign on, that is, register as having been unemployed that week. Trew had a standing appointment on Thursdays at 10.30 a.m., and that Thursday was no different. He was diligent about going to those appointments; he had a wife and two young sons to support.

Except, there was something in the air that Thursday. Just the week before Tony Soares, leader of the BLF, had been arrested while he attended his own standing appointment at a job centre. Soares was arrested by Special Branch for an article reprinted in the newsletter *Grass Roots* that detailed how to make a Molotov cocktail, a bottle petrol bomb. His arrest caused an uproar among the Black Power groups as Soares wasn't even editor at the time the article came out, and the original article was in print and legally available in bookshops and some libraries with no repercussions. As I said, the police were not done with the Black Power movement yet.

But Trew left the job centre unscathed and went about his day. As well as the underlying anxiety of police action, there was a lot to organise internally within the Fasimbas as the South East London Parents Organisation had faded away at the end of 1971 so they no longer had a premises, and there was the regular fundraising to do.[14]

That evening, Trew and the other members of the Publicity and Propaganda Committee joined the BLF at their HQ to discuss a campaign to free Soares and collect books for the Saturday school they ran. On their way home, Trew, George Griffiths, Constantine Boucher and Sterling Christie got off at Oval tube station around 11.30 p.m.[15] On the platform they noticed a plain-clothes policeman, recognisable from the blue anorak he wore, trying to look nonchalant as he stood on the platform eyeing them up.

The four passed him and started up the escalator, three of them choosing to walk up while Boucher stayed put to stand and read the paper (presumably standing on the right). The three walking up the escalator didn't get very far. Their path was blocked by two white men, so they just stood behind them and rode the rest of the way up. At the top of the escalator, all three were suddenly accosted by the fellow escalator riders, pushed and shoved to the wall with screams of 'get over there! Get the fuck over there!'[16]

'What the hell do you think you're doing? Who the hell do you think you are, pushing us like that?'

'We're police.'

They certainly didn't look like it: none of them was in uniform and they didn't present ID when asked to. They had the trappings of undercover police officers.

Boucher was also accosted as he reached the top. The supposed police officers wanted to search the men, whom they accused of theft. But the Fasimbas were trained, they knew their rights and weren't afraid to exercise them. The four shouted, 'Show us your ID!' while the suspected police shouted 'Turn out your pockets' and neither side was going to back down.[17]

It was a stand-off.

As stand-offs are wont to do, it soon erupted into a fight. The supposed police certainly didn't shy away from an altercation, and the Fasimbas had trained in Wado-ryu martial arts precisely for situations such as this. Punches and kicks were dealt and a lot of salty and racist language was thrown about. The brawl ended with the arrest of three of the four men and a white female onlooker. The suspected police were indeed police.

Sterling Christie managed to escape and would go for help. This would surely be over soon. As the others sat in the police van, an officer said to Trew, 'just you fucking wait till we get to the station.'[18]

It wasn't going to be over soon.

One of the officers from the altercation, and the officer in charge, was Detective Sergeant Derek Ridgewell. Ridgewell was 'the Transport Police equivalent of PC Pulley', in charge of the 'anti-mugging' squad on London's transport.[19] Trained with the British South African Police in what was then Rhodesia, now Zimbabwe, he said he left after three weeks as he wasn't happy with the way he was instructed to treat Black people.[20] But it was more likely that he left after independence was unilaterally declared, for fear of repercussions against the colonial power.[21]

It was a long night at Kennington Road police station. The arrested three were separated, and it soon transpired that Christie had been chased down, bitten in the face by a police dog and scratched by barbed wire, 'his face transfigured into rakes of blood', according to the Fasimbas, and arrested.[22] He wasn't treated by the police doctor for his injuries.[23] One of the charges was that he supposedly ran off with a police officer's handbag. So much for him being able to get help. All four were being accused of pickpocketing and assaulting police officers.

What followed was classic divide and conquer – Ridgewell and the other officers took each arrestee in turn, presented them with a statement of guilt, and tried to intimidate and beat them into signing.[24]

When Trew refused to sign the statement, he was presented with the statement signed by Boucher, implicating only Trew in the alleged offence, to encourage him to give himself up.[25] When he refused again, he was slapped twice by Ridgewell and his head was smashed into the wall by another officer.[26]

And Trew should not only give himself up for that offence, but also for other unsolved crimes in the area. As it turned out, the police didn't know that the four men were part of the Fasimbas so they weren't attacked for their political activities. Instead, the police read off crimes from their 'Big Book of Unsolved Crimes' (there was an actual book but that's not the actual name) and tried to get Trew to admit to them.[27] Trew didn't back down, and neither did the police.

Trew played it out in his head, what happens when the police say they saw you stealing and you say you didn't steal? It's one story against another, and most of the time this hasn't gone well for the defendants. Trew quickly weighed up his options and took another tactic instead: he admitted to crimes he didn't commit. But not any and all crimes. He admitted to crimes for which he knew he had an alibi, such as crimes committed on Thursday mornings when he had his appointment at the job centre.[28]

That way, when the charges came up in court he could prove he didn't commit them and undermine the police's entire case against the four men. A risky move, to be sure, and not one he'd seen in action before.[29] The pattern didn't go unnoticed by the police officers: why did Trew always choose Thursday mornings for his criminal activities? That's when women were out shopping, Trew lied.[30] So he signed the statement, as did the other three. Christie also used a similar false confession tactic when he saw Trew's statement.

The long night ended with an appearance in Camberwell Magistrates' Court the following day. As the seventeen charges were read out against them, Trew's heart sank. He hadn't even remembered some of the things he'd made up and was starting to think it may have been a bad idea.[31] The 'Oval Four' pleaded not guilty and were released on bail, but only just. It was lucky they were, as some of them had received some real beatings during the fight and overnight, and none had been treated. Between them they had swollen eyes, split lips, broken teeth and a dog bite to the face.

They didn't have to wait as long as the Mangrove Nine to be summoned to court, but their trial was also to be held at the Old Bailey. In the meantime, they checked in at the police station every Friday as per the conditions of bail, continued to volunteer with the Fasimbas and prepared legally. The Four decided they would not admit to suspecting the undercover police officers were in fact police officers. If they admitted to this, then they would be accused of resisting 'legitimate' police actions like stop and search, and that would not end well for them.[32]

They each had a trusted lawyer. Trew was the only one with a white barrister as he had a prior conviction and had used the false confession tactic, and they thought a white lawyer might help his case.[33] During preparation, Trew swung between complete confidence in their case given the obvious false confession, and a complete lack of confidence.[34] Taking on the police was never easy, and an emerging narrative was taking hold in the UK which would make it even harder.

This emerging narrative centred on a new word that was

seeping its way into vocabulary in the UK and USA. This word was more insidious than 'floppy disk', 'telecommute' and 'user-friendly', which were also new words in 1972.[35] This word was 'mugging', originally used in the USA and brought to the UK by the *Daily Mirror* in August of 1972. What made this word so insidious? On the face of it, the word is slang for 'robbery', but it was used almost exclusively for crimes supposedly committed by Black people. Once it took hold, it was hard to shake. It was used by the media, and even judges, to cause a 'moral panic' in the community.[36]

In September 1972, Ridgewell was involved in another case, against defendants who became known as the 'Stockwell Six'. The Six, all Black males, were charged with assault and intent to rob Ridgewell himself. All but one of the group was sentenced to prison, a detention centre or borstal (a type of youth detention centre no longer used).[37] The supposed leader of the group received a three-year prison sentence. Judge Alexander Karmel said, 'Mugging is becoming more and more prevalent, certainly in London. As a result, decent citizens are afraid to use the Underground late at night and indeed are afraid to use the underpasses for fear of mugging.'[38]

The spectre of mugging and Ridgewell's credibility were not going to make the trial any easier for the Oval Four.

Almost a year to the day after the Mangrove Nine trial, on 9 October 1972, the Oval Four appeared in court. The same towering Lady Justice stared down at them as they entered the Central Criminal Court and walked into the ominous-sounding courtroom 13. Members of the Fasimbas supported the Oval Four every step of the way, watching the trial unfold from the public gallery.[39]

As expected, the case rested on whose testimony the jury would believe: the Oval Four or the police. Arguably this is exactly how every case works, the jury has to decide whether they believe the prosecution or the defence. Though usually the prosecution's case is accompanied with, oh what is it called again, ah yes, *evidence*. Evidence is usually produced to support their case. To prove what the prosecution said happened at Oval station that day, for example, they could have called in witnesses to the altercation, who also would have seen Christie running off with the police officer's handbag.

They didn't do any of that. The case was based on police officer testimony after officer testimony, but they couldn't get their story straight. Did Christie have the bag over his shoulder, or under his arm? One officer who had initially said he saw the robbery took it back and said he in fact didn't see it.[40] And conveniently for the other charges, since the police claimed the pickpocketing was only attempted and did not result in anything being taken, there were no victims to call as witnesses.

The Oval Four didn't have much more evidence to support their case: how do you prove you didn't try and rob someone? They had Mrs O'Connor, the white woman who had seen the way the police treated the Four and been arrested along with them. The prosecution tried to discredit her by stereotyping her as a drunk Irish person.[41] But the ace up the sleeve was the false confessions that Trew and Christie had made.

Surely, once the confessions for all the other crimes were proven to be false, victory would be a slam-dunk, case closed. The manager of Peckham's job centre was called in to testify, and he could indeed confirm that Trew attended his weekly standing appointments at the job centre without fail,

10.30 a.m. on Thursdays. The manager even had signed papers. The lawyer for the prosecution almost fell out of his seat.[42]

Not to be shown up, the prosecution went to great lengths to try and prove the confessions were real, including timing the bus routes to and from Peckham to see if there was any way that Trew could have done the crimes he admitted to and still make his appointment at the job centre.[43] There was no way. The statements and associated charges would surely be thrown out? Throughout the trial, the feelings of hot and cold that Trew had experienced while on bail followed him round: they would surely be found not guilty, nope, they were sure to be found guilty. There was no way to tell which way it was going to go.[44]

The charges from the Big Book of Unsolved Crimes weren't thrown out. On the contrary, the judge let the confession statements stand, and the prosecution used them to paint the defendants themselves as liars![45] If they lied in their statements, then surely they were lying about what happened that night in March at Oval station? To admit that the confessions were indeed false would invite too many questions about how they were obtained and what that meant for the police. The false-confession strategy had backfired. And an attempt to question Ridgewell's credibility based on what had transpired recently in the case of the Stockwell Six and another case, against the Waterloo Four, was deemed irrelevant. The judge swerved any attempt to explicitly bring the issue of race into the courtroom.[46]

There was still hope, however. It was ultimately up to the jury to decide whom they believed. The jury – ten white, two Black – deliberated for four hours. They had two separate groups of charges to discuss: the ones from the confessions, and the ones arising from the events at Oval station. To the former, they returned a unanimous verdict of not guilty. Hurrah! It was clear that the confessions were suspicious. But the jury hadn't reached a unanimous verdict on the charges of attempted robbery and assault at Oval station. Judge Cussens sent them away – a majority decision would do (as is allowed in certain circumstances when a unanimous decision is not possible). This wouldn't do for the Oval Four, however; after another hour and a half, the jury returned a ten-to-two verdict of guilty. It's not known whether the two jury members who decided 'not guilty' were the Black members, but it's quite a coincidence.[47]

Judge Cussens handed down the sentence the next day, Wednesday 8 November 1972, to a packed courtroom and public gallery. He started:

> You must know, as all must know, that interference with citizens using the Underground railway will not be tolerated by the court. Fortunately, in the public interest, there were on the platform and escalator officers of the British Transport police who were there for the purpose of protecting the ordinary citizens of London who were using the Underground on the Northern Line. Their vigilance detected you and when they sought to arrest you there was a tremendous struggle in which you sought to escape.[48]

Winston Trew, Sterling Christie and Constantine Boucher were sentenced to two years in jail for each guilty charge, and not a suspended sentence either, but the 'Go to jail, do not pass Go, do not collect £200' kind of sentence. George Griffiths was sentenced to two years in borstal. Thank goodness the 'ordinary citizens' of London would now be protected.

Two years. A crushing blow, as it would be to anyone innocent of a crime, but for Black men in their early twenties in 1970s Britain, some with young children, this was even more devastating. Trew thought he would be in jail for eight years as he was found guilty on four charges from that night. 'Luckily' it would be concurrent, rather than consecutive, so two years in total. The defence was surprised by the harshness of the sentencing. By giving two years for each charge it would make appealing the case even harder: if one charge was somehow dropped, they would still be in prison for the other charges.

Winston Trew fell ill with a bad cold, and by the next day, 9 November 1972, was in the hospital unit of Wormwood Scrubs Prison. It was the birthday of his son, Mark.[49]

That wasn't to be the end of it. The Fasimbas created an Oval Four Defence Committee, supported by the Black Liberation Front, Black Unity and Freedom Party and British Black Panthers and others. Even with the majority of their Publicity and Propaganda Committee behind bars, they managed to pull together to design materials to spread the details of the wrongful conviction and they leafleted Lewisham, Camberwell and Peckham.[50]

By January 1973 they had raised enough awareness to host a meeting at Lambeth Assembly Hall, which more than 300 people attended, including Black Power comrades, press and, of course, plain-clothes police officers posing as press.[51] The walls were plastered with pictures of the Oval Four with the line 'indiscriminately imprison our warriors but the spirit of resistance lives'.[52] One Black Panther attendee summed up what the Oval Four case symbolised to the Black community: 'The case of the Oval Four is one of a chain of a whole plot by the State against black people. We are not going to be used as cheap labour and we are not going to live in slums.'[53] Fists were raised in solidarity with the victims of 'police muggers'.[54]

Through the Defence Committee funds were raised – they needed at least £2,000 to pay for a QC for the appeal and support the families of the Four. Stories of Ridgewell and his gang circulated quicker than trains on the Underground. Black parents warned their sons not to use public transport late at night. The Defence Committee called for an inquiry into the handling of the case and the actions of the Transport Police, and created a petition for this.[55]

In a rare break from their general heads-down policy, the Fasimbas organised a march from Oval Underground Station to Lambeth Town Hall to draw attention to the case. The national media had been relatively uninterested in the Oval Four compared to cases like the Mangrove Nine, and an eight-page press release the Fasimbas circulated was picked up only by *Race Today*.[56] It drew attention not only to the plight of the Oval Four but to the general situation for young Black people vis-à-vis the police. One of its most shocking statements is that 'during the months of September and October [1972] at the Central Criminal Court, sentences of approximately thirty-five years in total, ranging from six

months to three years, have been passed on Black youths'.
[57] The Fasimbas collaborated with the BBC, which was collecting information on cases in which Ridgewell had been
involved. They were determined that the truth about the
Oval Four be known.[58]

People were encouraged to send messages of solidarity to
the Oval Four in prison. They got so much mail it annoyed the
wardens.[59] Publishers such as the Huntleys were enlisted to
support the campaign. Jessica Huntley sent books to prison,
including *Things Fall Apart* by Chinua Achebe, *How Europe
Underdeveloped Africa* by Walter Rodney and *To Sir, With
Love* by E. R. Braithwaite, and wrote letters to the Four. In
a response from Constantine Boucher to Huntley, he writes:
'The letter was really beautiful. It gave me a lot of strength,
to tell you the truth sis, it was an inspiration, it make one
feel that there are a lot of our people outside of maximum
who are aware – care – so we are not for a moment forgotten.'[60] The public support and tireless campaigning from the
Fasimbas lifted the spirits of the prisoners, even temporarily,
which was much needed.[61]

In the meantime, Ridgewell's chickens were coming home
to roost. In August 1972, he had accosted two Black men,
failed to identify himself, and arrested them on charges of
assault and attempted robbery at Tottenham Court Road
station. The Tottenham Court Road Two were two Jesuits
studying at Plater College in Oxford, and coincidentally
from Rhodesia. The parallels to the Oval Four were striking, but their case had more success than that of the Oval
Four in court.

Judge Gwyn Morris stopped the trial partway in April

1973 and acquitted the defendants when it became clear that 'six different accounts were given by police officers in relation to the movements of these two men ... how is one to decide which is the accurate account?' and declared that 'I find it terrible that here in London people using public transport should be pounced upon by police officers without a word that they are police officers.'[62] Boom! The three in prison read about the good news in *News of the World*; Ridgewell's conduct was finally being questioned in court.

The case of the Oval Four went to the Court of Appeal on 30 July 1973. John Platts-Mills QC, for the defence, argued that Ridgewell's credibility was of paramount importance and allegations against him in other cases should be allowed, especially given what had happened with the Tottenham Court Road Two. The judge disagreed.

Platts-Mills also argued that the jury's verdict was inconsistent: how can they agree the confessions were unbelievable and yet believe the police's account of what happened that night in March? The judge disagreed.

Platts-Mills brought in two new witnesses, women who had been with fellow arrestee Mrs O'Connor and testified that not only did they see Christie running away empty-handed, sans police handbag, but that the female police officer in question had asked if they had seen a handbag on the platform as it seems she had misplaced it. The judge wasn't moved. The convictions were upheld.[63]

The judge did, however, end their sentences. Trew, Christie and Boucher were released from prison the very next day, and Griffiths was released from borstal. But the convictions still stood, and with all four under the age of twenty-five, those convictions would follow them around for a long time. Not to mention the psychological and social impact; one literature review concluded that people who are wrongfully convicted may experience a unique form of PTSD, and trauma comparable to that of prisoners of war and refugees.[64]

At a press conference held at the Black Liberation Front's Grassroots Storefront bookstore, Trew said: 'I am out of prison but the conviction is still on my record. We wanted to clear our names. The wounds are too painful to leave it at that. Prison was horrible. At first we were full of hope that we would be released but everything seemed to drag on . . . I shall try to get some redress for my bitter experience.'[65]

The Fasimbas faded away soon after the release of the Oval Four in 1973. The efforts of the campaign had worn down the energies of the group.[66] Some members reportedly joined the Black Liberation Front instead.[67]

George Griffiths and Constantine Boucher left the UK, and Winston Trew was a youth worker for a while before becoming a sociology lecturer for thirteen years at what is now London South Bank University. It may have seemed to have all turned out OK, all things considered, but Trew's marriage broke up shortly after he got out of prison, and when he met his current wife, Hyacinth, she said he was 'an angry young man' obsessed with clearing his name.[68]

Trew was indeed determined to have the convictions overturned. He collected all the material he could on the case, and wrote a letter of complaint to the director of public prosecutions, who responded, 'having carefully considered all the evidence, I have reached the conclusion that it is not such as to justify the institution of criminal proceedings against the Officers concerned'.[69] Those convictions followed them round for a long time – the story of the Oval Four didn't end in 1973, it actually ended in 2020.

Trew would have to wait considerably longer to clear his name, but thanks in part to the publicity actions of the Oval Four Defence Committee, the wheels soon came off Ridgewell's steamroller. He was the subject of the BBC programme *Cause for Concern* (to which the Fasimbas had contributed) that aired on the same night as the appeal on 30 July 1973. The documentary investigated Ridgewell and the cases of the Oval Four, Waterloo Four, Stockwell Six and Tottenham Court Road Two, and showed the heavy-handed tactics Ridgewell was accused of.

In response, he was quietly moved out of the Transport Police to a team looking at mailbag theft. He soon got involved with a criminal operation, stealing from mail and splitting the spoils totalling £300,000.[70] He was imprisoned for conspiracy to steal in 1980 and died from a heart attack in prison at age thirty-seven in 1982. When questioned by the governor at Ford Prison about what had happened to him, Ridgewell responded, 'I just went bent.'[71]

Winston Trew picked up the fight against the convictions with renewed enthusiasm again decades later. In a beautiful full circle, he meticulously researched and wrote a book on his experience and on Ridgewell to educate the next generations, which he self-published in 2010 as he was unable to find a publisher and was concerned he would be censored if he went the traditional route.[72] Called *Black for a Cause . . . Not Just Because*, it uses files obtained through Freedom of Information, newspapers and his own recollections to outline what happened. It doesn't hold back on the details and makes it clear that the confessions were made under duress.

But after the book's publication, nothing happened: the convictions weren't revisited in light of what Trew had said and found. Then in 2017 the darndest thing happened. Stephen Simmons (a white man) called into the LBC radio station during its legal advice show. He said he was wrongfully convicted of mailbag theft in London in the 1970s and had served time. How could he go about overturning his conviction at this stage? He was advised to Google his arresting officer, who was, you guessed it, Detective Sergeant Ridgewell.

He learned about Ridgewell's arrest and imprisonment, found Trew's book and realised he wasn't the only one Ridgewell had wrongfully imprisoned. He brought the case to the attention of the Criminal Cases Review Commission (CCRC), the body in charge of reviewing criminal cases and applying for appeal, as the name suggests. The CCRC only refers about 3 per cent of cases that come through its doors, and Simmons's case was one of them.[73] Trew's book was invaluable in its investigations into Ridgewell, and he was present at Simmons's appeal. When Simmons's conviction was overturned, Trew formally submitted his case to the CCRC. After all, the case of the Oval Four helped get Simmons's conviction overturned, yet their convictions still stood.

In December 2019, Winston Trew, Sterling Christie and George Griffiths finally had their convictions from 1972 overturned by the Court of Appeal. They were officially innocent. Christie died soon after.

The astute among you may be wondering, it was the Oval

Four, not the Oval Three, what about the fourth? Constantine Boucher eventually saw the news of the appeal and contacted the CCRC too.[74] His conviction was overturned in 2020.

After forty-eight years, the Oval Four finally got the justice they deserved. After nearly fifty years of Trew having Ridgewell living rent-free in his head, he could evict him.[75] Though it provided the closure he had sought for so long, Trew's celebration was muted; nearly five decades of injustice had left him exhausted.[76]

The bittersweet outcome was not lost on those involved. Lord Justice Fulford, who overturned the final conviction, said, 'it is highly unfortunate that it has taken nearly fifty years to rectify this injustice', and Boucher's lawyer said 'the British Transport Police and the Home Office have known about this officer's corruption for decades. Yet they have done little to right his wrongs.'[77] Meanwhile, the CCRC was just 'very pleased that all of the Oval Four have now had their convictions quashed thanks to our work'.[78] Cheeky. It was also thanks in large part to the work of Winston Trew and, as Sterling Christie said, thanks to 'everyone who supported us over the years in trying to right this miscarriage of justice, those who attended meetings, raised funds and distributed leaflets'.[79]

It was a victory not only for the Oval Four, but for those who continue to feel the scales of justice weighed against them. As Trew said when the conviction was overturned, 'if you are innocent, don't give up.'[80] At the time of writing the CCRC are working on the cases of the Stockwell Six and have had convictions overturned for four of them.[81] As Trew told me, 'the case of the Oval Four has started a conversation about the miscarriage of justice that cannot be stopped.'[82]

# Chapter Six

# Black Education Movement

'Education for liberation.'[1]

Black Parents Movement

Imagine you're a child, born and raised in the 1960s in the UK, who enjoys doing the things children do. You like to play with your friends, eat chocolate and try to watch TV past your bedtime when you think your parents won't notice, assuming you are lucky enough to own a set. But there is one thing you don't enjoy so much, and that is going to school. Not because you'd rather stay home and play (though part of you would), but because something is just ... off.

You seem to always be getting into trouble, even though you don't know what you did wrong, and your classmate didn't get in trouble for doing the same thing last week, did they? You are rarely picked to answer questions in class, even though you know the answer and not only raise your hand, but you wave to get the teacher's attention and emphasise you are bursting to answer the question. One day you are given a test to do by the school doctor and someone you don't know who said they are a 'sicolojist'. The test was OK, it asked peculiar questions like 'how does Big Ben tell the time?' and the distance between London and Edinburgh, but you think it must be fine because who would really know the answers to questions like that? And who would take that test seriously?[2]

Your mum is called in for the test results. That seems odd – your mum doesn't get called in after other tests you do in school. You sit with her in the headteacher's office, along with the mums of other children who did the test, and you are all told that you have been given places in a special school. Your mum is over the moon! She knew you were smart, and now it's been proven with a test and you're going to a special school. You know she's just dying to tell the whole family and she'll call every auntie later today to tell them the good news. You feel less excited, though. Something just feels . . . off. You don't know how to express this to your mum, though, so you guess you're going to the special school.

As it turns out, your hunch was right. You are at 'The Special School' because you have been labelled as 'educationally subnormal' and the special school is actually a remedial school, the treatment for your condition. And it seems to be a condition disproportionately experienced by Black children, since there are more Black children here than in your regular school.

This happened up and down the country, and parents and activists and those working with children had their suspicions, but no one had the hard, cold data to back it up. Until they did.

*

Bernard Coard arrived in the UK from Grenada with big ambitions. He was an economist in training and in 1966 started his master's degree at the University of Sussex. Little did he know, five years later he would publish something completely unrelated to his degrees that would shake up the UK's education system.

To earn money as he studied, Coard got a job running youth clubs for children from seven educationally sub-normal (ESN) schools in the area, and later taught at two ESN schools. As he got to know the children better he was surprised; they didn't *seem* subnormal, most were perfectly average, or above average. Just regular children. So why were they at ESN schools? To understand this, we have to go back another twenty years or so.

'Educationally subnormal' was a term first used in 1945, to replace the uncouth term of 'mentally deficient'. It was one of eleven categories of condition that warranted special educational attention, according to the 'Handicapped Pupils and School Health Service Regulations'. An estimated 10 per cent of all pupils were thought potentially to be ESN, while an estimated 2 per cent or less of all pupils had other special needs.[3]

But the process that led to a child being classified as ESN was inconsistent at best and malicious at worst. The main indicator was meant to be school performance. A pupil who performed at a lower level than someone 20 per cent younger in age was ESN.[4] So, a ten-year-old with the work level of an eight-year-old or younger would be ESN. But ESN was essentially a catch-all term that could be applied to those with medical needs or learning difficulties too. For example, dyslexia wasn't one of the eleven categories for special needs in the 1945 Regulations and yet dyslexic children could find themselves categorised as ESN. School performance wasn't usually the preferred tool; instead an IQ test overseen by a doctor or educational psychologist was frequently the indicator of choice.

If your hair stood on end reading the phrase 'IQ test', your spidey senses are working well. IQ tests in the UK have a murky history of their own. They were based on the idea of 'innate intelligence', that people are genetically predisposed to a certain level of intelligence. You see where this is going: since intelligence is *genetic*, entire groups of people could therefore be seen as intellectually inferior. Psychologist Cyril Burt's ideas on intelligence heavily influenced the development of education policy in the UK.

Burt did research with separated twins that had been raised apart yet supposedly showed similar or identical 'intelligence', informing the conclusion that intelligence was genetic and had nothing to do with the environment. This is the rationale that led to the formation of grammar schools and the eleven-plus exam via the 1944 Education Act.[5] There was no point in giving all children the same education if some could never be intelligent. It was these ideas that led to the belief that intelligence was something objective that could therefore be tested, regardless of how culturally specific the questions were. That's right, education policy was heavily influenced by a eugenicist.

Some people did champion the nurture side of the nature versus nurture argument. It was recognised that the circumstances in which a child finds themselves, that is, poor teaching, irregular attendance or frequently changing school, could impact performance. Some studies showed that teachers could influence the test results of Black children in their interactions with them.[6]

One piece of research showed that the place of birth must be accounted for, as children born in the West Indies had lower scores than UK-born children of West Indian parents. It was suggested that this could be because some children born in the Caribbean suffered malnutrition, which would have stunted their growth and development.[7] Many people also realised the inherent cultural bias in so-called IQ tests meant that anyone not from a certain social standing would inevitably do worse.

In practice, though, the assigned cause of subnormality didn't really matter. The method of measuring whether a child was ESN was inconsistent and not always targeted at children underperforming at school. Along with the category of 'maladjusted' pupils, it was a convenient mechanism to channel students whom the teachers did not want to deal with. Ask too many questions? Special school. Too loud? Special school. Seem emotionally unbalanced? Special school. Black? Special school.

Black children were more likely to be placed in ESN schools than Brown children. It was recognised that most Asians spoke English as a second language and therefore they were (sometimes) offered additional language help. Whereas Black children, especially those whose languages such as Patois or Creole were recognised as dialects and not languages, were labelled as stupid, as it was expected that they knew 'proper' English. A couple of studies found that among immigrant groups, Turkish Cypriots actually had the largest proportion of low reading scores, but that was beside the point.[8]

You may be thinking that special schools to help address the particular needs of pupils sound like a good idea – they exist today – and surely they would provide the best possible education for pupils? Unfortunately it is not that straightforward. Deaf or blind students in special schools might be in luck as teachers were at least required to have an additional qualification on top of their regular teaching one to cater to students' special needs, but no additional qualification was required for teachers of educationally subnormal children.[9]

And it was supposed to be government policy to integrate children with mild conditions into mainstream schooling. Under the 1944 Education Act, special schools were only to be for pupils with the most severe disabilities, including those who were severely 'educationally subnormal'. Despite the official policy being mainstream assimilation of ESN children, new special schools for them were opened at a speedy rate. Between 1945 and 1955, 64 per cent of new special schools opened were specifically for children deemed to be ESN. By the end of 1954 there were 22,895 children in ESN schools.[10]

ESN schools may not have been created for Black children, but they provided a handy way to keep them out of mainstream education. This was what Coard suspected from his work with ESN pupils, that ESN schools were nothing but a 'convenient dumping ground' for Black children.[11] But, like all the others who suspected this, he had no proof beyond his personal experiences.

That is, until Coard was given something by a cousin of his, a report entitled 'The Education of Immigrant Pupils in Special Schools for Educationally Subnormal Children', an Inner London Education Authority (ILEA) document. It doesn't sound like the most exciting gift, I'll give you that, but it was pure gold at the time. This report was meant for internal use only and contained hard statistics to prove the suspicions that Coard and others had. The following are some horrifying findings:

1) In ESN day schools (i.e. not boarding schools) in 1970, 34 per cent of the children were immigrants, compared to just 17 per cent of students in ordinary schools in the area.

2) There were comments from nineteen headteachers of ESN schools. Of those nineteen, thirteen headteachers thought that immigrant children had been wrongly placed in their schools and nine heads thought 20 per cent or more of their pupils had been wrongly assigned to the school.

3) Despite the widespread acknowledgement of wrong placement, only 7 per cent of immigrant children ever returned to ordinary schools.

4) West Indian children constituted *75 per cent of immigrant students* in ESN schools, compared to only 50 per cent of immigrant children in ordinary schools.[12]*

So what do all these statistics tell us? It means that immigrant children were wildly overrepresented in ESN schools covered by the ILEA, and West Indian children were disproportionately represented among those students. And these weren't just remedial schools – treatment for a condition – they were end-of-life hospices.

*

---

* Emphasis added.

Now that Coard had the report, what was he going to do with it? He didn't have many contacts in the media in the UK. It was spring 1970 and he had spent most of his time since he arrived in 1966 studying, or working to fund his study. At a friend's party one Saturday night in Tulse Hill, London, word got round that he was a teacher at an ESN school and soon the party turned into a discussion as the guests wanted Coard's insider insights as he was one of the rarest of findings: a Black teacher at an ESN school.

They persuaded him to present a paper at an upcoming conference, organised by the Caribbean Education and Community Workers Association (CECWA), part of the umbrella, wide-ranging Black Education Movement that was already in full swing.* At the conference Coard was 'virtually ordered by all present to turn that paper into a book'.[13] So he did. He spent the summer of 1970 furiously writing and researching a book aimed at Black parents to expose what was happening in the school system. The book was called *How the West Indian Child Is Made Educationally Sub-normal in the British School System*. The title was no accident: Coard emphasised that the West Indian child was *made* educationally subnormal, that there was intention behind children being categorised as ESN. It wasn't titled 'why West Indian children are educationally subnormal'. And although it used the ILEA data as a starting point, the book was relevant to

---

* CECWA had formed because Black parents and teachers suspected that there was foul play in the education system in the 1960s. Bussing was already happening in pockets around the country and children were being sent to special schools. CECWA brought together a powerful group of parents, educationalists and concerned community members.

parents of Black children across the UK as the ESN issue was not just confined to London.

As well as uncovering the statistics from the ILEA report, Coard argued that ESN schools weren't about education but rather socialisation, trying to ensure that people could contribute a basic minimum to society. They didn't learn science or history but cookery, woodwork and needlework.[14] He explained that teachers' low expectations of students had a real effect on their performance, and highlighted experiments that showed that Black children tested by white people performed less well than when tested by Black people, and if Black pupils knew that the test would be compared to white children, that was enough to bring down their scores.[15] Coard exposed the deep-seated self-hate held by some Black children and made concrete recommendations for self-help and what to demand of the authorities.

The experiences Coard relates of the children he encountered and their self-hatred is the hardest part of the book to read. Children hated their Blackness on top of hating themselves for their perceived lack of academic ability. The impact of being labelled as stupid, dumb and backward sticks. A 2021 BBC documentary, *Subnormal*, revealed it was hard to recruit people to talk about their experiences in ESN schools, such was the continued shame all these decades later.[16]

After the book was turned down by major publishers (surprise surprise), Black-run New Beacon Books decided to publish it. Owner John La Rose was one of the members of CECWA and he was supported by Bogle-L'Ouverture Publications (Jessica Huntley was also a member of CECWA) and more than twenty-five Black organisations who worked to raise the £750 required for publication.[17] Distribution of the 10,000 printed copies was largely done door-to-door, in Manchester and Birmingham as well as London. And behind the scenes, Coard learned publicity tricks from a media consultant who advised him pro bono how to garner media attention. And it worked!

The *Guardian* printed almost an entire chapter of the book two days before publication, and the headline of *The Times* the day before publication in May 1971 read 'Injustice to children in subnormal schools'.[18] There was a huge outcry from parents, educationalists and concerned community members across the country. Parents organised, young Black people formed groups, and Coard was kept busy with speaking engagements, sometimes up to five a day.[19]

The reception wasn't wholly positive, though. A reader's letter to the *Guardian* in response to the extract said that 'this is a community problem, not a racial problem', and was echoed by another letter which said the criticisms levelled against the schools 'apply equally to the English child at those same schools . . . it is too much to ask of a group of people that they provide a better education for immigrant populations when they neither see enough need nor make enough effort to provide it for their own children'.[20] School funding was a hot-button topic and regarded by some as the main issue of the day rather than the treatment of Black children in schools.

Coard's book wasn't a revelation for some Black parent-activists as the leaked ILEA report had already made its way into *The Times* in 1969, and this wasn't the first time they had fought against racist education policies.[21] Black parents and teachers formed the North London West Indian Association (NLWIA) in 1965 to take action on the issues they saw before them as well as 'to promote and encourage social, cultural and economic activities'.[22]

The NLWIA raised the issue of ESN schools with Haringey in 1967, after careful investigation including undercover work in schools, and two years later the chairperson of the Haringey Education Committee admitted that errors had been made.[23] The numbers of Black children in the area classified as ESN reduced, from around 68 per cent in 1966, to 54 per cent the next year and then 47 per cent by 1968, but as Jeff Crawford, chairperson of the NLWIA, said, 'we contended in 1967 and still contend that this figure is unrealistic by any law of averages; that is, if it is accepted that there is no inherent difference in intelligence quotients between black and white races.'[24]

Due to the persistently high figure, the NLWIA made an official complaint to the Race Relations Board (RRB) in 1970, calling the classification of West Indian children as ESN 'unlawful discrimination'.[25] In February 1971, three months before the publication of Coard's book, the RRB released a report on six local authorities, including Haringey. The RRB did not find that Haringey had acted unlawfully, though it confirmed the number of Black children in special schools was disproportionate.[26] Haringey's defence was that parents had agreed to the placement of children in special schools.[27] The NLWIA's response to the RRB decision said that this was 'an implicit admission of the existence of discrimination' and called ESN schools 'permanent educational dustbins'.[28] It called on the RRB to investigate further.

Another issue taken on by the NLWIA was against the banding of students in Haringey, that is, grouping them according to ability. This may not seem controversial on the face of it as grouping students by ability has been practised for years in different forms. In 1970 an estimated 70 per cent of secondary schools were using some form of banding, or the related concepts of streaming and setting.* But this is a controversial topic, then and now.

Streaming and setting, where pupils are grouped together for some or all classes based on ability, are supposed to enable teachers to better tailor material to the ability of the children, but studies point to worse outcomes for children who are set into lower-ability classes than those in mixed-ability classes.[29] In the early 2000s I was in set classes for maths, English and science in secondary school and I remember thinking even as a teenager it was unfair that the highest grade those in the lower set could attain was a C at GCSE. Grouping based on perceived ability and intelligence takes place as early as primary school these days.[30]

Banding came in from 1965 when there was a push away from grammar schools and towards mixed-ability 'comprehensive' secondary schools instead. Many areas saw their grammar schools turned into secondary comprehensive schools, though some areas retained a hybrid system and others never changed at all. Banding was promoted to ensure a spread of abilities within each school in an area by placing pupils in a broad 'band' of ability as they left primary school

---

* Streaming and setting are slightly different but related ideas, see: M. Baker, 'Setting, streaming – how schools teach', BBC News, 14 February 2001, http://news.bbc.co.uk/2/hi/uk_news/education/1170241.stm.

and distributing them equally around the school system to ensure each school had a mixture of abilities.

For some this was desirable as the comprehensive school project was fairer than the grammar/secondary division, but for others banding was unwanted. Black parents knew that their children would be disproportionately put in the lower bands. And as with the decision of who was ESN, there was no consistent way of banding pupils.

Depending on the school, each child would either be assessed, or the headteacher and teachers would provide their recommendation on which band a child would be in according to their academic achievement, and then assigned to a secondary school.[31] Haringey's proposal also included allocated secondary-school places based on the reputation of the primary school of the child.[32] Banding would lead to children having to go to schools further away from home, and disregarded parental choice in schools.

Haringey proposed banding in March 1969, and a leaked report from January explained where the proposal came from. Andrew Doulton, a Haringey headteacher of a private school, wrote, 'On a rough calculation about half the immigrants will be West Indian at 7 of the 11 schools, the significance of this being the general recognition that their IQs work out below their English contemporaries. Thus academic standards will be lower in schools where they form a large group.'[33]

This confirmed the suspicions of Black parents: the policy was not based on what was educationally best for all children, but based on a fear that high numbers of Black children would affect the education of white children. The figure of 50 per cent of the student body being immigrant children suggested by Doulton was higher than the state recommended 30 per cent stated in the government's circular of 1965, which led to bussing (as discussed in Chapter Two on the Indian Workers' Association).

White parents feared that 'ghetto schools' would develop, which some thought would disadvantage the white children in the schools. Banding was just another means of dispersing Black students, like bussing. Banding would also conveniently mean that white children would have greater access to the five former grammar schools that were in areas with a lot of immigrants.

The NLWIA went to work. Its members lobbied Haringey Council and its Education Committee through demonstrations outside meetings and written statements and petitions. They spread the word among Black parents about the banding proposal and its consequences with multiple meetings in April and May 1969 to reach as many people as possible. They held a conference in June. They aired their views in the local and national press. They relentlessly campaigned for months. A flyer for a meeting in September read:

**ALL WEST INDIAN and other BLACK PARENTS ... BEWARE**

**YOUR CHILDREN'S EDUCATION IS STILL THREATENED**

**By the RACIALIST DECISIONS OF HARINGEY BOROUGH COUNCIL**

**Earlier this year they said among other things that:**

- **Black children have a lower I.Q. than white children**

- **We are creating 'ghetto' schools**

- **We are too ambitious for our children**

- **They are going to 'band, 'stream' and 'disperse'[34]**

Instead of banding, the NLWIA argued, the focus should be on proper resourcing of schools. Teacher turnover in primary schools in Haringey was found to be up to 31 per cent per year.[35] An organisation called the Haringey Parents Group also campaigned on the issue. They wrote to all the Haringey councillors to ask them to think carefully about the proposal, questioning point by point the arguments put forward by Doulton. In response to the idea that banding would make sure no school has 'too many immigrants', they asked 'if – as the scientists show – there is no difference in intelligence between the races, how can banding have any effect at all? Or is the assessment not on intelligence? If not, what is being assessed? Good manners and clean hands?'[36]

It wasn't just Black parents who were against this idea. Teachers were against the idea of banding. Dispersal through banding wouldn't improve the quality of education in the borough, they argued, but more teachers and resources would.[37]

Haringey Council didn't appreciate the onslaught from the NLWIA. Its schools had been praised in 1968 for their ability to help all children with their different needs, including special language provision, though the news report which praised them did say this had been helped by 'a pattern of housing that spreads the immigrants reasonably evenly over the schools'. The Haringey Education Authority was even called progressive.[38] The council reacted by crying racism at the NLWIA itself, complaining that a leaflet it distributed in Haringey discriminated against white people. The leaflet in question invited Black people to a meeting to discuss a demonstration, which Haringey Council said excluded white people. The leaflet also called Haringey councillors 'mini Enoch Powells', which I imagine would have riled them up somewhat.[39] Crawford from the NLWIA said the criticism from the council was simply part of the feud that had started after the Doulton Report.[40]

The NLWIA's efforts eventually paid off. Haringey Council put the banding proposals on the backburner, though it didn't throw them out entirely. The Conservative council was then defeated in the 1970 election and banding was put to rest. The NLWIA had won.

So it was within these campaigns that Coard's book was published. The NLWIA, and Coard, believed that schools could be improved. Among other measures, they recommended hiring Caribbean teachers, improving nursery provision for better early childhood development, and having more community and parental involvement in schools. Black leadership in schools was still a rarity. One of the first Black female headteachers, Yvonne Conolly, was appointed in 1969 and she had to endure racist abuse and threats to burn the school down.[41]* Changes could not be achieved by the Black community alone, they required the authorities to recognise the problem too.

But despite the cold, hard evidence of misuse and racism at play, it wasn't the end of Black children being labelled ESN.

The first reaction of the establishment was to deny it.[42] Then, as media coverage grew and its own report was quoted at them, the response softened. A few months after Coard's book was published, a National Foundation for Educational Research (NFER) report backed up the statistics he presented, showing that there were three times as many West Indian children in ESN schools than non-immigrant children.[43]

However, the report did not support the argument that this was due to racial bias; it attributed the allocation to 'difficulties in dealing with a new situation [of immigration]'.[44] The government, too, was keen to stress that racism wasn't taking place. Though they now admitted that the statistics were indeed accurate, and even added Coard's book as recommended reading in teacher training, the government was keen to look for alternative explanations to racism.[45]

It wasn't enough that West Indian children were being labelled as ESN at greater rates than other children, that their teachers thought they had been wrongly placed, and that educators came out and said that they thought Black children had a lower IQ with absolutely no evidence. It wasn't

---

* Beryl Gilroy also became a head teacher in 1969.

enough to convince the government that racism might have had a teeny part to play.

The question of why ethnic minorities, West Indians especially, boys in particular, were underachieving became one of the million-pound questions of the day. Research proliferated. While genetic predisposition still had its proponents, especially with Arthur Jensen and Hans Eysenck, the new eugenicists on the block, not everyone agreed with the government. There was also a shift to focus on the role of school itself as continuing the race and class divisions of society, which was in no small part due to the campaigns of groups such as the NLWIA and CECWA.[46]

Some studies now focused mostly on what was happening in school rather than an individual's intelligence or the family and social environment. One study looked at teachers' perceptions of children at the beginning and end of the first year of primary school and found that, in ordinary schools, ethnic minorities were rated lower than their classmates in categories like 'character, sociability, brightness' and this ranking didn't change over the year, while in ESN schools ethnic minorities were actually ranked higher than their peers in the same categories.[47] The study concluded 'that intake to these [ESN] schools may be biased' as there didn't seem to be any obvious indication as to why the students would be in those schools.[48]

Research and debate on the topic raged on. Studies would be published saying that teachers were biased, and then would be criticised for their research methods. Criticisms of the criticisms would be published. Then criticisms of the criticisms of the criticisms would be published.[49] I imagine that in the days before Twitter this was how academics argued.

Those in the academic Ivory Towers were trying to quantify the unquantifiable: they were trying to pin down the long, looping, elusive tendrils of racism that grew around school structures and influenced the behaviour of teachers and the lives of students. The debate that raged unmasked the fundamental problem: how can we define racism in education? Was it only the explicit behaviour of the teachers, or was it in the curriculum, the policies and regulations that replicated the white supremacy of the day?

Depending on how you defined racism, the results of your research would show something different to someone else's, and thus the debate continued. Although much of the research would seem to support the argument of the campaigners, for many in the Black community, there was no debate to be had. White people could argue among themselves all they liked about the best methodology to prove racism, Black communities were going to keep fighting against the racism they knew was there. And if the cold, hard data of the ILEA report wasn't enough to convince people that there was an issue, no research would.

Substantial change would have to wait. (We are still waiting.) The recommendations Coard made for the authorities were certainly not adopted wholesale. In the meantime, what about the children? The children taught by teachers who had low expectations of them? The rate of West Indian children admitted to ESN schools did actually reduce, some returned to mainstream schooling, and others were even able to achieve academic qualifications.

And what about the curriculum? It was so, so, *what's the*

*word?* Oh yes, white. The curriculum lived and breathed whiteness, and changing that would take longer than hiring more Black teachers. What was needed was some sort of education to go alongside mainstream schooling, to supplement it, to help Black children excel in the regular subjects like maths, but also to fill the large, Black holes (if you will) in the curriculum. That's where the aptly named supplementary schools came in.

Two of the first supplementary schools were set up in 1969 in north London. They were run out of the homes of John La Rose, the co-founder of New Beacon Books, and Albertina Sylvester, homemaker and childcare provider at 57 Victoria Road, N4. La Rose held classes on weeknights, and Sylvester on Saturdays. Free to parents and voluntarily run, the classes started off small, and through word of mouth and after Coard's exposé in 1971 supplementary school enrolment across the country increased. By 1972, the George Padmore School run by John La Rose had gone from five students and one teacher to nearly forty students and three teachers.[50] By 1975 it had outgrown its location, and combined with two other schools in the area to try and buy a new premises.

Supplementary schools differed in their approach but were all united along one factor: the importance of Black environments and leadership for the education of Black children. One parent said, 'it wasn't just about reading and writing. They taught the kids about Black history and showed them that they had nothing to be ashamed of because Black people are as good as anyone else'.[51] This idea was widely shared, including by organisations such as the Black Parents Movement, which believed in 'education for liberation'; that is, the power of people to learn whatever they need and want for their own social liberation.

As well as ensuring children could do the three Rs (reading, writing, [a]rithmetic), it was also important to learn about Black history, culture and traditions that did not appear in the mainstream curriculum. Many supplementary schools were boldly African and Black in their approach and weren't afraid to tackle the big subjects. Reading comprehension could be improved using texts entitled *How the Slave Trade Started* and extracts from *Soledad Brother.*[52] English language would be tested with questions like: 'When the Europeans first came to the West Indies they were under the illusion it was India. This was a big mistake. Illusion means 1) Good idea 2) Wrong idea 3) Sky 4) Idiotic idea'.[53]

The proliferation of supplementary schools was met with a range of reactions from Local Education Authorities. On the one hand, support was given in kind (provision of school premises to hold classes), or in cash, and on the other hand, some authorities feared the schools were fertile ground for Black radicalism, spurred by the fact that Black Power groups ran supplementary schools too.

Government support was welcomed by many who ran supplementary schools, who saw this as their due since the state was failing their children in mainstream schools, and funding was needed as demand for schools grew.[54] Others saw state funding as selling out.

Accessing state funds meant satisfying certain terms and conditions, one of which was usually to show the impact supplementary schooling was having. The government was particularly keen for supplementary schools to show their success in hard, academic terms. The success of supplementary schools had occasionally been measured using results of students who attended the schools compared to children in the wider education authority. They often showed that supplementary school students did better than the average.

Some schools focused more on supporting children in their mainstream subjects and less on the Black studies aspect to satisfy the government's academic requirements. Thus, two strands of school emerged in the supplementary school movement: one emphasised their independence, often with a focus on cultural education (these have also been called 'self-help' schools); and the other had to jump through hoops to access and maintain state funding – these became the 'official' schools, which often sacrificed some of the Black cultural education along the way.[55]

It is hard to know exactly how many supplementary schools there were, or how many students attended them. Schools were formed on a local community basis, as grass-roots initiatives, and many were not linked to other schools or the wider supplementary school network, which was formed in the 1980s.[56] It is even harder to know the holistic ways in which schools helped children. As Akala mentions in his excellent book *Natives*, thanks to his time in a supplementary school he was able to challenge his teacher's claim that William Wilberforce was the person who single-handedly freed enslaved people.[57] Liberation from white supremacist narratives is a hard thing to measure.

It would take ten years after the publication of Bernard Coard's book for a state report to admit that racism was the reason for West Indian children being disproportionately labelled 'educationally subnormal'.

The Select Committee on Race Relations and Immigration spent its 1976–7 session looking at the West Indian community. The members interviewed people from prominent organisations such as the Runnymede Trust as well as community groups such as the Caribbean Teachers' Association, set up by headteacher Yvonne Conolly, to help promote the role of Caribbean teachers in British schools and to contribute to the wider development of the community. The committee heard about all the hardships faced by West Indians, and other Black people in the UK, from housing to education to employment.

It concluded that discrimination against West Indians was indeed widespread and had led to their alienation, especially young people. For education, it recommended that an independent inquiry should look into the causes of West Indian underachievement, alongside remedial classes and increasing the number of teachers with a Caribbean background.[58] And they said that the alienation of young Black people was an urgent issue, which proved prescient given what happened in 1981, which will be covered in Chapter Eleven.[59]

The Committee of Inquiry into the Education of Children from Ethnic Minority Groups was convened by the government in 1979. It was tasked with publishing a report specifically on West Indian children. An interim report published in 1981, *West Indian Children in Our Schools*, known as the Rampton Report after the committee chairperson, Anthony Rampton, said: 'The Committee concludes that, whilst racism, whether intentional or unintentional, cannot be said alone to account for the underachievement of West Indian children, it can and does have an important bearing on their performance at school.'[60]

As well as finally acknowledging the 'R' word, it acknowledged the role of inadequate pre-school provision and the poor community links between schools and parents. It was a game changer. Now that it was out in the open, the discourse would have to change, surely? The report was not well received by everyone. One reader response said, 'this [racism] is a very unhelpful term . . . in my twenty-one years in the [teaching] profession, spread across five schools and four authorities, I have not met a single teacher who can be described as prejudiced'.[61] Thatcher's government fired Rampton from his position as chairperson due to the conclusions he had drawn, and the committee worked towards its final report with Michael Swann in charge instead. Meanwhile, the Education Act of 1981 ended the use of the term 'educationally subnormal' and discussed 'special education needs' instead.

The committee's final report in 1985, entitled *Education for All*, or the Swann Report after Rampton's successor, did not change the conclusion from Rampton's report. It stated:

> Our own investigations leave us in no doubt that IQ is *not* a significant factor in underachievement . . . A substantial part of ethnic minority underachievement, where it occurs, is thus the result of racial prejudice and discrimination on the part of society at large, bearing on ethnic minority homes and families, and hence, *indirectly*, on children . . . Not all of underachievement, where it occurs, is to be

accounted for in these terms, and the rest, we believe, is due in large measure to prejudice and discrimination bearing *directly* on children, within the educational system, as well as outside it.[62]

Though Swann had been brought in to dampen down the accusations of racism, his report concluded, in no uncertain terms, that racism in society at large was a major reason for the underachievement of West Indians, and other ethnic minorities.[63] The Swann Report quoted the Select Committee's 1977 report to recommend making the curriculum more diverse:

> The black child goes to a white school, he is taught by white teachers, he sees pictures of white persons, he uses books written by white craftsmen, he hears and sings songs about white people, he learns poems written by white people about white people. All this necessarily accustoms him to appreciation of white values only ... The primary purpose of Black Studies is the adjustment of this imbalance, and to help black people in this country, particularly the children who try desperately, as one writer puts it, to escape from the 'prisons of their skins'.[64]

Black Studies had been introduced into the curriculum at some schools, most notably in south London's Tulse Hill Comprehensive and William Penn Comprehensive, but never fully took off. There were fears that it would lead to politicisation as it was not just a discussion of 'things Black people did' but 'things done to Black people', which would open a can of worms that the government would prefer to put at the back of the shelf and never touch, not even in case of the apocalypse.

Additional recommendations from the Swann Report included school policies to combat racism, improved teacher training and hiring advisors at the education authority level to enact change. Surely change was gonna come now, right? Like the Rampton Report, the recommendations weren't exactly welcomed. And with Thatcher's chokehold on Local Education Authorities, and deep budget cuts, anti-racism in schools was about to become even harder to institute.[65]

While strides have been made, many of the Swann recommendations remain chillingly relevant today; Black Caribbean and Pakistani students are still more likely to be deemed to have moderate learning difficulties than their white counterparts.[66] And as ESN schools for Black children fell out of fashion, 'disruptive units' aka 'sin bins' were formed instead, and now we have Pupil Referral Units and Alternative Provision. So it continues.

The wider Black Education Movement continues in a form to this day. Supplementary schools reached a peak of membership in the mid-1980s and then reduced in number by the early 1990s, as far as one can tell without a definitive list. Today, supplementary schools still exist, and a new National Association of Black Supplementary Schools was set up by parent Nia Imara in 2007 to connect parents to schools, and schools to each other. State control over supplementary schools continues to be an issue, with ever more boxes to tick for reduced funding. Supplementary schools are prominent among other ethnic minorities, too, and one estimate puts the total number at between 3,000 and 5,000.[67]

After his death in 1971, Cyril Burt's theory of innate intelligence soon unravelled; evidence emerged to suggest that he made up some of his research on twins, and he was even accused by fellow eugenicist Jensen.[68] The fraud was later reconfirmed by Burt's biographer, but the debate rages to this day, with defences of Burt's work still being published as recently as 2015.[69] It is said that the debate matters because of the integrity of science and psychology. But I smell a lab rat. This was fifty-odd years ago now and I think science is doing just fine. Could the defence of Burt's work have anything to do with the persistent idea that intelligence is related to race? A 2017 study of racial prejudice in Britain showed that 18 per cent of people still believe that 'some races or ethnic groups are born less intelligent'.[70]

It is easy to be disheartened at the snail's pace of change. But the very fact that the conversation was even happening, that committees were formed, independent inquiries commissioned, was a victory. Without the Black community speaking up on the issues, how many more West Indian children would have been declared 'dull', 'stupid', 'educationally subnormal' and funnelled into a special school with impacts on the rest of their lives? How many more people would believe that intelligence is based on genetics?

If this were fiction, it would end with a rousing victory speech from John La Rose, Jeff Crawford or Yvonne Conolly, heralding the dawn of a new era in British education, an 'education for all' where the history of Black and Brown people was just called 'history'. Unfortunately I can't give you that; change isn't linear but continuity is.

However, organising and campaigning against racism in education continues to challenge the status quo. Grassroots movements such as No More Exclusions aim to abolish the use of exclusion in schools, including Pupil Referral Units and Alternative Provision. Coalition projects such as No Police in Schools want to decriminalise classrooms. And there are also multiple organisations developing Black education materials for use in schools, and thanks to the work of Black activists and historians, Black British activism in Notting Hill even features in a GCSE textbook, which includes discussion of the Mangrove Nine.[71]

Bernard Coard returned to Grenada as planned. He formed a Marxist political party and after the party staged a coup he became deputy prime minister in 1979. With Prime Minister Maurice Bishop he formed a People's Revolutionary Government to reform society, known as the Grenadian Revolution. Another coup led to PM Bishop's death, and Coard was in charge for a few days before enemy of the state US President Ronald Reagan invaded and took over the country, sentencing Coard and others to death. A death penalty turned into life in prison instead, from which he was released in 2009. While in prison, Coard continued teaching; this time his inmates were his students. Weren't expecting that ending, were you?

# Chapter Seven

## Brixton Black Women's Group and OWAAD

> 'Until the lions have their own historians,
> the history of the hunt will always glorify
> the hunter.'[1]

African proverb

Of the varied medical and technological breakthroughs that have happened since the Second World War, which do you think has done the most to transform the lives of women in many societies? Is it the washing machine and other white goods, which reduced the time required for domestic work? Is it the rise of the ready meal in the 1970s? Or is it the small, innocuous-looking pill? No, not the pill you took at warehouse raves in the 1990s, but the other one, the one that can be used to prevent pregnancy. Nowadays, the right to choose is one of the biggest campaigns for feminists, and the introduction of contraception that was controlled by women was a game changer. But ready access to contraception hasn't always categorically been a good thing, especially for Black and Brown people. In the 1970s, Black women were integral to the campaign against a particular type of contraception.

Before we launch into it, you may have noticed by now that the discussions have been quite man-heavy and women have been conspicuously absent from many of the movements. Even in 2017, the TV show *Guerrilla*, a fictional retelling of the British Black Panthers created by a Black man, largely ignored the role of Black women in the movement and (Brown) Frieda Pinto was used as a proxy for all the non-white women who were part of the group.[2] Women, as usual, were integral to many of the movements but so much of that history is only now being uncovered or focused on, and there are certainly still issues with representation.

I have consciously attempted to promote and centre the role of women, and now we go into two chapters focusing almost exclusively on women. Hurrah! The women in these pages embodied Girl Power before Girl Power was a thing. I usually avoid the word 'badass' to describe women as it is only used to describe women, but it is so well suited to the women that follow; they were, and are, badasses to the highest degree. To start with, what led Black women to organise as Black women? Why wasn't participation in the Black Power or feminist groups enough?

After the Second World War, some white women were forced out of the workplace, their role in the labour force being important during wartime but deemed uncouth during peacetime. And of course, the men needed 'their' jobs back. In the 1950s, working women could be fired if they got married, and married women could be fired if they got pregnant.[3] Where women could get work, they were funnelled into gender-specific roles; that is, repetitive, low-paid jobs.

Meanwhile, with the labour shortage in the UK, Black women came over from the Caribbean and countries in Africa where the British had had colonial interests, including Nigeria, Sudan and Sierra Leone.[4] Many worked in the NHS, often tricked into signing up as State Enrolled Nurses rather than the better paid State Registered Nurse position for which many were eligible. If working white women were at least a rung below working white men on the wage scale, Black and Brown working women were a rung or two (or three) below them.

With a lack of representation at the political level (there were just 24 female MPs out of 640 in 1945 and 26 by 1966, and they were all white), the role of advocating for women fell to the women's movement. Second-wave feminism, also known as the Women's Liberation Movement, rolled in from the late 1960s. The movement's demands were formulated at its first conference in 1970, attended by 600 women from the UK and other countries.

While the first wave of feminism had secured suffrage in the interwar period, the second wave now wanted equal pay, equal education and employment opportunities, free contraception, abortion on demand (it was legalised under certain circumstances in Great Britain in 1967 but there was pushback), and free, twenty-four-hour nurseries.[5] 'The personal is political' was a rallying cry for second-wave feminism. What was happening at home wasn't a private matter between spouses, but was directly related to wider political structures.

They were partially successful in their campaigning; the first Equal Pay Act was signed in 1970.

Meanwhile, Black women faced a double whammy of discrimination, not just based on their gender but based on race too: what we today call 'misogynoir'. Black female activists in the sixties and seventies in the UK found that it was constant work to justify and legitimise their concerns and existence. Many Black men couldn't understand the implications of gender discrimination. Within Black organisations, like Black Power groups, women faced accusations of undermining the movement if they brought up concerns about sexism in the Black community or 'women's issues', as the bigger issue at hand was the state repression of Black people, especially Black men. And the women may have been regarded as easy sexual targets for the men. In their landmark 1985 book, *The Heart of the Race*, Beverley Bryan, Stella Dadzie and Suzanne Scafe said, 'We could not realise our full organisational potential in a situation where we were constantly regarded as sexual prey. Although we worked tirelessly, the significance of our contribution to the mass mobilisation of the Black Power era was undermined and overshadowed by the men. They both set the agenda and stole the show.'[6]

Social movements led by Black and Brown people were not universally progressive by virtue of being anti-racist: there was patriarchy, sometimes misogyny and very often homophobia.

Black women did not find the solidarity they were looking for within the women's movement either. Most Women's Liberation Movement groups were predominantly white, and you were expected to get on board with demands such as free contraception and abortion on demand while ignoring that Black women had a different relationship with the medical establishment. Many medical professionals and so-called healthcare specialists bought into the idea of the 'promiscuous Black woman', an overly fertile woman who needed protection from her own uterus.

So Black women had no problems getting an abortion, but what about the right to *not* have an abortion? Equal pay was certainly needed – there was no legislation for it in the 1960s – but what about equal pay between Black working women and white working women? Twenty-four-hour nurseries as a demand was fine, especially as there was a shortage of childcare in areas with a large Black population, but Black women didn't necessarily want to be out working at all hours of the day any more; some also wanted to be at home once in a while.

Black women were tired of the racism in the white women's movement and the sexism in the Black movement. They needed spaces that were just for them. They were inspired more by Angela Davis than by Gloria Steinem. To provide a space to discuss and organise around issues important to them, many Black women started women's caucuses within the Black Power groups.

But the Black Power movement crumbled in the early 1970s amidst a steady scratching away from the government and infighting, largely among the male members. Many of the women involved in the groups wanted to keep fighting the good fight. As we know, a woman's work is never done, and the work of these women was certainly not done. They included Olive Morris, who had joined the Black Panther Youth League after being arrested and beaten by the police for coming to the defence of a Nigerian diplomat who was being accosted. And through Morris, Beverley Bryan also joined the Youth League. Bryan became a teacher and hung a poster of Angela Davis on the wall of her primary-school classroom. She also taught at the supplementary school run by the Black Panthers on Saturdays. During the Mangrove Nine trial, Bryan organised volunteers to go to the public gallery and distributed the *Freedom News* newsletter, which covered the case.[7]

At the same time, Black women disillusioned with the Women's Liberation Movement were also looking for alternatives. Gerlin Bean, a nurse and former member of the Black Liberation Front, had been one of only two Black women at the first Women's Liberation Movement conference in 1970, out of the six hundred attendees. She didn't find it to be a place for Black women.

Black women of the former Black Power caucuses and others dissatisfied with the state of organising around Black women's issues in the white women's movement soon came together and solidified as the Brixton Black Women's Group (BWG) in 1973. Around the same time Black women's groups were also formed in other cities, such as the Manchester Black Women's Co-operative and Liverpool Black Women's Group, which later became Liverpool Black Sisters.[8]

The BWG started off as a study group. It would meet in people's houses on Sunday afternoons for three to four hours, an act which felt radical in itself as that was usually a time when women would be at home in the service of their families.[9] Self-actualisation through studying was not the end goal, however; the BWG was a political group. Its members did not campaign solely on 'Black women's issues', but they campaigned on issues as Black women. They campaigned as Black women, Black mothers, Black workers and Black community members.

Nationally, there wasn't an issue affecting the Black and other marginalised communities in which the group wasn't involved in some way: from police brutality and abuse of the 'sus' laws (the 'Scrap Sus' campaign was started by Black women), to children being categorised as educationally subnormal, to substandard housing, to restrictive immigration laws such as the rule of 'sole responsibility' to prevent children from joining their parents in the UK.[10]* They protested to pull troops out of Ireland. They opened a Black Women's Centre, which provided information and advice on legal and welfare rights, and healthcare. There was a craft workshop, a library and resource centre, regular seminars and films and discussion and study groups, and a crèche for women as they used the centre.[11] It was as if the Citizens Advice Bureau, the local playgroup and your favourite radical bookshop-cum-community space had a lovechild.

Their scope wasn't just limited to national issues: they protested the war in Vietnam, and supported the anti-apartheid campaign events in Zimbabwe. As a socialist, anti-imperialist group, they campaigned against all manifestations of imperialism, including when white actor and model Bo Derek wore braids in 1979 and started a style craze with no attribution

---

* In simple terms, this rule said that a child could only come to the UK if there was no one else to look after the child or make important decisions about their life, even if this person was not a parent of the child. 'Sole responsibility' still exists in UK immigration law.

of the style to Black women. Beverley Bryan stated that, 'we resent this attempt to trivialise our heritage and regard it as the worst form of cultural imperialism'.[12] Whatever the issue, BWG was involved.

BWG co-founder Olive Morris was particularly passionate about housing issues. Houses in Brixton were crumbling and within a few years would be uninhabitable. Lambeth Council had to build or refurbish at least 4,000 houses a year, and even then it still wouldn't be able to accommodate the 13,000 people waiting for council housing.[13] Houses and buildings earmarked for demolition were emptied even though there were no funds to do anything with them, and by 1971 there were 5,225 houses sitting empty.[14]

Squatting became not only a way to deal with the housing crisis but a political statement against the plans for the area to make it more middle class, increase property prices (which had almost doubled over three years) and encourage a nuclear style of living.[15] Lambeth soon became the squat capital of the capital. Councils all over London were formalising squatting, handing out licences to squatters' associations.[16]

Olive Morris was a keen squatter, having left home in her teens and joined squatters' movements. Morris and fellow Black Panther and soon to be fellow BWG co-founder Liz Obi squatted in a flat at 121 Railton Road in Brixton, above an abandoned launderette. On at least three occasions they had eviction attempts; Obi was arrested for possession of an offensive weapon in one raid, and when police followed Morris into the flat she climbed on to the roof of the building and waited for three hours until the police left.[17] The BWG later opened Sabarr bookshop on the site.

Reaction from most Black men towards the BWG remained lukewarm, though the issues they were fighting for largely over-lapped, like an end to the 'sus' laws. The women were seen as dividing the Black movement. BWG member Gail Lewis was asked, 'do you think that Black feminism is becoming so strong now that all Black women are going to become lesbians?'[18] When the BWG helped form the Brixton Defence Campaign in 1981 (more on that in Chapter Eleven), the members had to be clear that their role wasn't just to take meeting notes and provide meeting space via the Black Women's Centre. The men who did support the women's groups provided much needed logistical and operational support such as driving, set-ting up sound systems for events and caring for children while women attended meetings and, later, conferences.

Relationships with white women's organisations depended on the aims of the group; if they were socialist and anti-imperialist, and concerned with racism, then connections were formed, but a distance was still maintained. The BWG could be 'in solidarity with' white women's groups but not 'in sisterhood with' them.[19]

At the same time, Black women in other male-dominated groups were also looking to carve out a space for themselves. Female members of the African Students' Union, such as Stella Dadzie, wanted to set up a women's caucus in the group, but were advised by women in the African women's movements that this wouldn't lead to the autonomy they wanted. Taking this advice, they decided to separate them-selves from the men and created the Organisation of Women of Africa and African Descent (OWAAD) in February 1978 in conjunction with Black women from other groups.[20]

OWAAD was an umbrella organisation connecting the various Black women's groups in London and around the UK. They also had a strong focus on liberation and anti-imperialism in Africa, and made links with groups such as the ZANU Women's League in Zimbabwe. The constitution opened with 'all oppressed suffer, whether they live in the Third World or the industrialised West. But women suffer the most.'[21] As a large, well-known and London-based women's group, the BWG was one of the key groups holding up the umbrella.

Brown women were organising and campaigning in parallel to the Women's Liberation Movement and Black women's groups. Groups such as Awaz, meaning 'voice', were formed to fight many of the same issues as Black women's groups, such as stringent immigration laws. They read a lot of the same books, such as Walter Rodney's *How Europe Underdeveloped Africa*. They also wrote books about the issues, with activist Amrit Wilson highlighting the life of Asian women in their own words in her award-winning 1978 book, *Finding a Voice: Asian women in Britain*.

And, similar to Black women, Brown women did not feel welcome in the male-dominated Asian Youth Movements, or what Birmingham Black Sisters called the 'Asian Young Men's Association'.[22] A former member of the Southall Youth Movement, Harwant Bains, said that 'any girl who tries to take an active part in the running of SYM is popularly regarded as "loose"'.[23]

A few months after OWAAD was formed, they changed the name to the Organisation of Women of *Asian* and African Descent. The shared struggle between Brown and Black women was now recognised in the name of the organisation. A statement accompanying the original constitution states that: 'Although the specific circumstances may differ, the causes and effects of our arrival in this country are strikingly similar ... if OWAAD was to be an effective fighting organisation, which takes up the issues effecting [*sic*] black women in a meaningful way, then unity between ALL black women is of the utmost importance.'[24]

OWAAD was the first national organisation of its kind. Its internal structure was also different to the usual group organisation. After a brief flirtation with a formal hierarchical structure consisting of an elected executive, this was ditched in favour of a collective committee approach. OWAAD's approach was fluid so groups could bring forward issues that were important to them, and this information was then disseminated and other groups encouraged to support where they could.

There was no dictating which issues OWAAD members would take on.[25] And there was flexibility in how involved women were expected to be, as they recognised other pressures like childcare. For example, groups did not have to send the same representative to OWAAD's monthly meetings.[26]

The fluid approach was successful, OWAAD soon propelled forward like a jet ski. By March 1979, it had organised the first ever national Black women's conference at the Abeng Centre in Brixton. Nearly 300 women attended, far more than expected. Some of them were just in the area and convinced to attend by enthusiastic members such as Mia Morris, who said, 'I remembered being so excited that I was stopping grandmothers going to church, we kind of, grabbed them from the bus stop and tell them to, you know, forget about their rice and peas and God for the day.'[27]

With 'Black Woman' by Judy Mowatt playing on repeat, it was a day to discuss all the issues that affected Black and Brown women, from education, to law, to employment, imperialism and health. The conference was a rousing success. The organisers did not expect the turnout they had and in attendance were established activists as well as those just learning about the issues, old and young women, African, Caribbean and Asian women.[28]

With a renewed sense of empowerment, groups took on issues in their local areas with vigour. One of OWAAD's founders, Stella Dadzie, was part of the United Black Women's Action Group in Tottenham who, following the conference and discussions around education, took the lead to form the Haringey Black Pressure Group on Education, another group under the Black Education Movement umbrella.[29] More women's groups were formed out of the waves of the conference, such as Southall Black Sisters, created a month later after Blair Peach was killed (more on that in Chapter Ten), and the East London Black Women's Organisation, both of which still exist today. Groups were not confined to London either; by the early 1980s there were groups around the country, including Cambridge and Wolverhampton.[30] The impact from the conference rippled outwards to prompt even more grassroots action.

Groups within OWAAD instigated and joined protests together. In June 1979, the BWG, Awaz and Indian Workers' Association marched together from Hyde Park Corner to Downing Street to protest immigration laws and the 'sus' laws.[31] Awaz organised a sit-in against the virginity tests at Heathrow Airport, which many OWAAD members joined, and Awaz and BWG organised a demonstration against the practice in London.[32]

And that is why and how the Black women's groups came to be. I mentioned at the beginning of the chapter that Black women were involved in campaigning against a particular type of contraception. So far, we haven't really discussed health as an arena for anti-racist activism, what with the bin fires of racism in every other aspect of life that Black and Brown people were trying to douse. That's about to change, but keep a safe distance, because this bin fire is scorching.

It is hopefully clear by now that the demands of the Black women's movement were not exactly the same as the broader Women's Liberation Movement. While white women wanted easy access to contraceptives and abortion, Black women wanted to defend their fertility and right to actually have children. Black women were hypersexualised as much as men were – they were supposed jezebels who couldn't be trusted to make good decisions about their own bodies. Enter: an unappetising smorgasbord of unwanted sterilisation, freely available abortion and easy access to contraception.

One of these contraceptives was Depo-Provera.

Depo-Provera first came on the scene in the UK in 1976. A contraceptive injection, one shot of which would provide three months of protection against pregnancy. It was originally approved for one-off use in just two circumstances. Firstly, if a woman had been given a rubella vaccine in order to give time for the vaccine to kick in, as rubella is dangerous in pregnancy. The second scenario was if their male partner had just had a vasectomy and they were waiting for the sperm count to reduce.[33]

It wasn't approved for longer-term use as it hadn't gone through enough testing to ensure its safety. Produced in the USA by Upjohn (which sounds like it would be making Viagra rather than contraception), it wasn't even approved for use there. Trials on beagle dogs showed that the drug could cause breast cancer, and it caused endometrial cancer in some rhesus monkeys.[34] This was enough for it not to be approved by the Food and Drug Administration in the USA.

Apart from the two approved uses in the UK, a doctor could also administer the drug if they thought it was in the patient's 'best interest'. That is to say, it could be used a lot more widely than originally intended. This raised two issues: was consent sought from the woman? And was this consent informed? That is, were they properly informed of the potential side effects and risks? In many cases, unfortunately not.

One study found that as few as 25 per cent of women were actually told what the side effects were and what the shot was.[35] And it soon emerged that Depo-Provera was being administered disproportionately to Black and Brown women.

It wasn't that Black and Brown women were asking for the injection and the enlightened medical institutions were fulfilling their right to choose. In some cases, women were administered Depo-Provera without them even knowing it. A fourteen-year-old girl of Caribbean descent was in hospital for tonsil removal surgery and while under general anaesthetic was given the shot without her knowledge or consent.[36] Some concerned doctors started doing their own investigations and in one case found that in some hospitals Brown women were on the receiving end of 30–60 per cent of the Depo-Provera shots, while only making up 20 per cent of the women who gave birth there.[37] Though statistics were hard to come by, another estimate says that around half of all prescriptions of Depo-Provera were given to Black women.[38] Black and Brown women were being disproportionately targeted with the drug.

Some doctors thought they were providing a public service beyond helping people's health. The doctor who administered the shot to the unconscious teenager said it was his 'moral duty' to do so.[39] In supposedly protecting Black and Brown women from themselves, the rest of unwitting society would be protected too. Statements like 'what's the use of putting an end to immigration when you can't put an end to immigration through the uterus?' were apparently common, according to a 1981 report on family planning in ethnic minorities.[40]

Immigration controls could stop Black and Brown people from coming into the country, but could not stop them from procreating. A report by Brent Community Health Council recognised that this was why hospitals and councils were endorsing Depo-Provera, saying that 'the use of Depo-Provera comes out of a very different approach to health care … the desirability of reducing the black birth rate and the assumed ignorance and unreliability of black women – and seeks to change people's behaviour accordingly, whatever the suffering this may cause'.[41] A senior gynaecologist defended their actions, saying that Brown women didn't know where their vaginas were, so informing them about alternative, barrier methods of contraception was unnecessary.[42]

It was no secret that so-called 'family planning' was really

Control of Black and Brown Families. The chairperson of the British Family Planning Association, Margaret Pyke, had said in 1963 that 'differences of intelligence are inherited – and it is a fact that children who belong to small families do better in intelligence tests than children of larger families. A possible explanation is that the less intelligent parents find it more difficult to practice birth control.'[43] We've been here before, haven't we? The secretary of state for social services, Keith Joseph, echoed this sentiment, saying that 'our human stock, is threatened ... a high and rising proportion of children are being born to mothers least fitted to bring children into the world ... they are producing problem children, the future citizens of our borstals, subnormal establishments, prisons, hotels for drifters.'[44]

It wasn't just Black and Brown women who were disproportionately administered Depo-Provera. White working-class women were seen as untrustworthy and undesirable enough to have the shot. (Female) Doctor Wilson in Glasgow had a points-based system for administering Depo-Provera. Lived in substandard housing? Have some points. Supposedly of low intelligence? Have some more points. Those with enough points would have their reproduction controlled, which she did to 162 women, including white working-class women. In 1977, an estimated 33,000 women in the UK received Depo-Provera.[45]

The widespread use of a drug meant for restricted use was bad enough, the disproportionate use on Black and Brown women, often without their consent, was even worse, but to really rub salt in the injection site, Depo-Provera's side effects were plentiful, and real, real bad.

Reported side effects of Depo-Provera included: heavy bleeding, absence of menstruation altogether (amenorrhea), depression, weight gain, breast cancer and endometrial cancer, as shown in the trials.[46] Through breastfeeding, the hormones could pass to the baby and impact its immunity.[47] After just one injection there could be a long delay to return to normal fertility, and it could even cause sterility.[48] Black women in an Upjohn-funded experiment in Atlanta in the USA (yes, where the drug was banned, it's complicated) were told that they shouldn't use it if they wanted more children.[49]

Reproduction was an issue that the Black women's groups already approached as they had heard that some hospitals, like King's College hospital in London, gave Black people abortions without any questions, and the group had free pregnancy testing sessions for women.[50] On top of this, the use of Depo-Provera was an issue many Black women understandably felt passionate about. As Stella Dadzie says, 'it made absolutely no sense whatsoever not to begin to raise those issues, because this is where we were and this is where our daughters were being born'.[51]

They convinced white women to tackle the issue jointly with them.[52] The national Campaign Against Depo-Provera, colloquially known as the 'Ban the Jab' campaign, was born. It's a rare example of a campaign in which Black, Brown and white women fought together. Dadzie was part of the small central committee for a time, contributing to strategy meetings and literature, and she even designed a badge and logo for the campaign.[53]

The campaign produced a detailed leaflet clearly outlining what Depo-Provera was and how it was being used. It soberly stated, 'if you're mentally retarded, a "promiscuous girl", working class or black, you may be offered Depo-Provera'.[54] Ban the Jab was unequivocal in its objectives: it called for the withdrawal of Depo-Provera, for a 'contraception that does *not* endanger people's health' (original emphasis), and it aimed to expose how Depo-Provera was being used.[55]

Black women's groups used all avenues they had to spread the word. Their publications like *FOWAAD!* and *Speak Out* drew attention to Depo-Provera. The very first edition of *FOWAAD!* reviewed ITV's *London Programme* show on the contraceptive, stating that 'no real attempt was made by the *London Programme* journalists to investigate more thoroughly the allegation that DP is being given to large numbers of Black women, particularly to Asian sisters in the East End of London'.[56]

Black women's groups helped to distribute the Ban the Jab campaign leaflet and encouraged people with information on the use of Depo-Provera to come forward with their stories. Many members of the women's groups worked for the NHS, so they were crucial in ensuring that accurate information was reaching marginalised women.[57] OWAAD also supported other campaigns and groups that had formed around the issue, such as 'Fight against DP on Black Women', which produced literature specifically on the racialised use of Depo-Provera, highlighting that, in Haringey, West Indian single women made up 66 per cent of those administered the contraception.[58]

Thanks to the campaign, the use of Depo-Provera wasn't ignored by the mainstream media, though little attention was paid to the race and class implications, and even less to its use in the Global South. The Black women's groups made sure that the impact on Black and Brown women globally was central to the campaign against the jab. At the first OWAAD conference, a video on the exports of Depo-Provera to the Global South was played.[59] It was clear that the use of Depo-Provera was an imperial one, not a million miles from the eugenics arguments put forward by the likes of Cyril Burt, as seen in the education debate.[60]

Depo-Provera wasn't just being used in the UK to control the population in the way the establishment wanted. It was first tested on women in Jamaica in the early 1960s.[61] By the mid-1960s it was being administered in over sixty countries, and in eighty countries and by an estimated ten million women by the mid-1980s.[62] New Zealand authorities were using it on Polynesian women, and largely in psychiatric institutions, maternity homes and clinics.[63] It was used in South Africa, where a Black doctor said it was being used on Black girls without their consent.[64] In Zimbabwe it was used freely on women, in the name of overpopulation, at the same time that white people were being encouraged to emigrate there.[65]

Foreign aid, including World Bank money, was used to purchase and administer Depo-Provera in the Global South.[66] At a refugee camp in Thailand, women were given a chicken in exchange for taking the shot.[67] Buses kitted out with loudspeakers were said to travel round telling women that their figures would look better with Depo-Provera.[68] In India, women feared it would be administered alongside vitamins, without women knowing what it was.[69]

Even though it wasn't approved for use in the USA and so technically couldn't be used by US-funded programmes, the development agency USAID funded non-US organisations, which could then buy it. It was used by the UN Population Fund and the World Health Organisation. Only the Swedish government banned its use in its aid programmes in 1980.[70] Outside of the foreign aid sector, Upjohn was also actively marketing it to countries of the Global South where formal approval processes for pharmaceuticals were shaky or non-existent, spending $4 million between 1971 and 1976 to persuade government officials or intermediaries to purchase Depo-Provera.[71]

The Ban the Jab campaign shifted the public discourse around the drug. Upjohn submitted an application for a full licence in the UK in September 1979. A few months later, the Committee on Safety of Medicines rejected this application because it needed to look into the research more thoroughly.[72] By the time the committee granted the licence two years later for women who could not use other contraceptives long-term, the health minister Ken Clarke, instead of rubber stamping the committee's view as was usual procedure, actually rejected its recommendation. (Yes, *that* Ken Clarke, who was an MP until 2019 and is now in the House of Lords. We have the term 'career politician' for a reason.)

It was the first time that one of the committee's recommendations had been rejected since it was created in 1968.[73] Clarke's concern was that Depo-Provera would be given to women without their informed consent, with him singling out women with mental illnesses in particular rather than acknowledging the racialised aspect.[74] Though he was quick to point out that 'we have not allowed ourselves to be influenced by any "political" campaigning about this product', it is widely believed that it was the campaigning efforts of women's groups that swayed his decision.[75] Upjohn appealed against the rejection, worried that a ban in the UK could affect its use elsewhere in the world and would almost certainly hurt its chances of approval in the USA.

A five-day hearing followed. Upjohn, UK doctors and other 'experts' defended the merits of the drug and the professionalism of health professionals, arguing that to prevent its use by women who were able to provide consent was unacceptable, and that it had 'saved millions of Third World women from misery, illness, and death as a result of unwanted pregnancies'.[76] A doctor of family planning in London said that looking at a sample of 73 of the people administered Depo-Provera, they'd had 114 abortions between them, and there would have been more if it wasn't for the contraceptive.[77] The accusation that doctors were administering Depo-Provera without informed consent was seen as insulting to the profession.

Clarke eventually relented in 1984 and approved Depo-Provera for long-term use in the UK, with many provisos, such as: it would be used exceptionally, it was not to be used on breastfeeding women until the baby was six weeks old, and the importance of informed consent was recognised, especially for those who did not speak English.[78] It was approved for use in the USA in 1992.[79]

Though the war was ultimately lost, many battles were won. The Committee on Safety of Medicines had actually asked to look at further research, and then Depo-Provera wasn't allowed to be used willy-nilly and the importance of informed consent from everyone was recognised. And that's not counting the women who decided not to accept Depo-Provera, or were encouraged to ask questions of their doctors because of the campaign. Depo-Provera also wasn't the only health issue OWAAD worked on: it raised awareness of sickle cell anaemia, supporting the work of people such as Elizabeth Anionwu.

After the success of the first OWAAD conference in 1979, it held one annually, growing in the number of days and number of attendees. The second one, in 1980, was called 'Black Women Fighting Back' and more than 600 women attended.[80] Through the Depo-Provera campaign and others, the Black women's groups powered forward, until they came to a grinding halt.

Both OWAAD and the BWG had political objectives from the beginning, but they didn't want these objectives to be determined by a certain class or background of Black woman either because then they would be no better than the Women's Liberation Movement, which was overwhelmingly middle class. OWAAD was successful in bringing together Black and Brown women in sisterhood and mutual support in an unprecedented way.[81] But the problem with a wide tent is that it's hard to see and hear everyone.

Lesbian members hid their sexuality, and members in interracial relationships kept them secret. Gail Lewis, a lesbian in an interracial relationship when she joined the BWG, 'felt this enormous split in my life, in terms of living as a lesbian and with a white woman then, yet being involved in anti-racist and Black women's liberation politics'.[82] When a group of Black lesbians wanted to use the Black Women's Centre, there was a lot of internal debate. What would the community think?[83]

Sexuality was just one issue that drove a wedge into the movement. How to work together as diverse Black and Brown women was a sticking point, as was whether or not to call themselves 'feminist', the term being so strongly associated with white women.[84] It wasn't easy breaking new ground in collective organising with no one to tell you how to use the spade, or whether a spade is even the right tool to use. (For any fellow movement-heads out there, the BWG and OWAAD provide excellent case studies for the danger of ignoring multiple intersectionalities in a collective.)

By 1982 and the fourth OWAAD conference, OWAAD had the momentum of a pedalo rather than a jet ski, and it ceased to exist by 1983. But many of the organisations and groups that were formed because of it continued. And a few members, Stella Dadzie, Beverley Bryan and Suzanne Scafe, went on to publish the aforementioned *Heart of the Race: Black Women's Lives in Britain* in 1985, a book about the Black British female experience based on interviews with Black women. It remains one of the only books that does just that.

The BWG continued until 1986. Things changed somewhat in the 1980s (as we'll see in a later chapter). Some campaigns had been won, and acceptance of state funding meant a jungle of administration and management. And more than that, as former member Melba Wilson said, 'we were just tired. I mean it is hard to get across the level of intensity during that period. It required a lot from all of us, in addition to the rest of our lives.'[85]

Brown women's groups largely turned their focus to domestic violence and the development of refuges. Though there was also the Sari Squad, which campaigned against deportation and would beat up racists outside clubs in east London and then 'burst into song', according to Benjamin Zephaniah.[86]

Depo-Provera, now made by Pfizer, is one of two main inject-able contraceptives used in the UK today.[87] About 10 per cent of women who use hormonal contraception use an injection.[88]

It should be said that I am not a doctor (sorry, Indian community) and I am discussing what is reported to have happened with Depo-Provera forty-odd years ago, but I cannot comment on the safety of the drug today – please talk to your doctor if you have any concerns. What I can tell you is what the current information says; that among other things there's a risk of bone thinning and weight gain, and a small increased risk of breast cancer.[89] After an injection, it can take up to a year for normal menstruation to resume and fertility to return.[90]

Depo-Provera is still used widely in the Global South. Injectable contraceptives are the most popular method of contraception in sub-Saharan Africa and Depo-Provera is the most common.[91] Zimbabwe is the only country to have banned it, in 1981, by which point up to 9.5 per cent of women of reproductive age were using the contraceptive.[92] The minister of health banned it on the basis of both the health effects and racism involved in its administration. Research into the effects of Depo-Provera continues, and recently indicated that Depo-Provera users are at a higher risk of contracting HIV, double the risk of transmission and contraction in fact.[93] Unsurprisingly, this is hotly debated.[94]

Some things have stayed the same, some things have

changed. The population debate has changed now. Where population control was once discussed as a complement to immigration control, population control is now discussed in the context of climate change. The argument is that climate change is primarily driven by 'overpopulation', not overconsumption and the actions of big industries and all of us that fund them, and therefore population numbers must be controlled. Overpopulation is an imperialist straw man often used to justify family-planning initiatives in the Global South while falling birth rates in Europe and Japan are met with alarm.[95] The UN Department of Economic and Social Affairs says that 'higher incomes contribute more to environmental degradation than population growth', yet overpopulation as the driver of climate change is a stubborn myth.[96]

As recently as 2012, the UK was found to have funded forced sterilisation in India under the guise of fighting climate change, with many dying on the operating table.[97] In 2021, sixty NGOs called for the use of the UK's £11 billion climate-change fund to be used for family planning in the Global South.[98] One of those NGOs was the Margaret Pyke Trust, the same Margaret Pyke who said that smaller families are better for children's IQ. You can't make this stuff up.

As you read this, you may be reminded of the unrolling of the COVID-19 vaccine in the UK and the high rate of hesitancy among ethnic minority groups in taking the vaccine. In early 2021, 44 per cent of Black/Black Brits were said to be vaccine hesitant, and 16 per cent of Asians/British Asians.[99] Is it any wonder that given the history of control of Black and Brown women's reproductive systems and bodies more generally there was such hesitancy? Trust needs to be earned; this can't be fixed with a few trust falls.

Women who had been involved with BWG and OWAAD took what they had learned into their future workplaces, trade unions, relationships with the state and their homes. They looked at the world through an intersectional lens before the term was coined, able to see how issues affected people differently depending on the multiple identities they held.[100]

Olive Morris died in 1979 at just twenty-seven years old, of lymphoma. She is remembered by her friends and fellow activists for the silver bangles on her arm, her inseparable relationship with her bike and the unwavering dedication she had to radical liberation.[101] Number 121 Railton Road was a squat until 1999, twenty-seven years after Morris and Obi first squatted there, and one of the longest-running in the country.[102] In 2020, on what would have been Morris's sixty-eighth birthday, Google created a Doodle in her honour, with a street sign for 'Railton Road SE24' a prominent feature.[103]

Many of the other former members of the BWG and OWAAD continue their activism today. Stella Dadzie is an author, historian and educationalist. Gail Lewis, who only learned to read at ten years old due to discrimination in the school system, has an illustrious academic career in psychotherapy. Liz Obi has helped keep the legacy of Olive Morris alive through exhibitions and creating an archive about her. Gerlin Bean, who had been a nurse in the UK, went to Zimbabwe in the 1980s to work on health and education, and then to Jamaica to train parents of children with disabilities. Beverley Bryan became a professor of education at the University of the West Indies.

Well, that's part one of the 'women's section' wrapped up, and if you thought this was jaw-dropping just wait till you see what's in store in part two.

# Chapter Eight

# Grunwick Strike

'We are the lions, Mr Manager.'[1]

JAYABEN DESAI

Grunwick strikers at the TUC Congress in Blackpool, 1977. Jayaben
Desai is on the right.

© TUC Library Collections at London Metropolitan University

If you were asked to name the most important strike in the
UK since 1945, what would you answer? If you are anything

like me you might go for one of the miners' strikes, or maybe the strike at Ford Dagenham. Essentially, if there's a film about it, that's what I'll think of. But there is one seminal strike that rarely gets mentioned, even though the Trades Union Congress (TUC) calls it the strike that 'changed the face of British trade unionism', and the trade union GMB refers to it as 'one of the most defining events for unions of the twentieth century'.[2] This was the Grunwick strike. Race, gender and class all intersected in this epic struggle that began in a sleepy London suburb and captured the nation's interest. It was an unprecedented show of working-class solidarity.

The Grunwick Film Processing Laboratories opened its doors in 1965. Amateur photography was on the rise, and Grunwick capitalised on this by printing photos through a mail-order model; individuals and businesses mailed in used camera film and Grunwick posted printed photos back to the customer. If you came of age in the eighties or nineties, the chances are you would have used Bonusprint, Tripleprint or Doubleprint for your holiday snaps – those brands were all processed at Grunwick.

Grunwick was founded by three male business associates: Tony Grundy, George Ward and John Hickey. 'Grunwick' was a portmanteau of their names, the original 'Brangelina', if you like. Grunwick was hugely successful as it processed photos up to seven times faster than its competitors, in just three to four days.[3] The company rapidly expanded as demand grew, and in 1975 Grunwick opened new premises in Willesden, a quiet suburb in north-west London.

The company's success was due in large part to the tactics

used by management to keep costs down and production high. It is a formula for success as old as capitalism itself. They automated what they could, but productivity in the mail-order department relied on employees, and lots of them, since opening customer envelopes and handling payments couldn't be done by a machine.

Grunwick squeezed its employees to maximise profit; workers were paid less than half of the average national wage, earning £28 for a forty-hour week instead of £69.[4] This was also lower than wages typical for the industry: its competitor Kodak paid £49 a week.[5] Director and co-owner George Ward, meanwhile, earned £163 a week.[6]

The pay was low, and yet this wasn't the employees' main grievance. Working conditions were oppressive and stripped workers of their dignity. Overtime was compulsory and often demanded at the last minute. While some workers were glad to bolster their income, it could result in sixty-hour weeks.[7] Management sat in a glass-walled office to keep a close, intimidating eye on the factory floor. Laurie Pavitt, the MP for the area, described Grunwick as 'a sweatshop with a management which could have been lifted straight out of the Dickens era'.[8] Other reports say that the conditions inside the factory were acceptable and that the only problem was the draconian management style of supervisor Malcolm Alden.

Companies such as Grunwick could get away with sub-standard treatment as there weren't many alternatives for workers at the time because the economy was suffering and jobs were scarce. The economy shrank in both 1974 and 1975, unemployment was high and rising, and inflation reached an eye-watering 23 per cent in 1975.[9]* A former Grunwick employee, Chandrikaben Patel, said, 'there was no question of whether you wanted to or not – you had to work, so you did. And wherever you found work, you had to take it'.[10]

Companies such as Grunwick took advantage of the double whammy of the country's economic situation and the tough circumstances for recently arrived migrants, and actively sought out migrant workers. George Ward, who himself was Brown, was in charge of the day-to-day management at Grunwick, and recruiting Brown women was a key part of his strategy for cheap labour. The company distributed leaflets door-to-door telling people, 'Come and we will give you a job. We give jobs to everyone.'[11]

Not only did Grunwick actively recruit Brown women, it actively turned away white women. A former employee overheard management say to a white woman looking for work, 'You don't want to come and work here, love. We won't be able to pay the sort of wages that'll keep you here!'[12] Let's repeat this for those at the back: Ward himself was Brown.†He knew all too well the stereotype and expectation of Asian women as docile and submissive, and he aimed to exploit that to Grunwick's advantage. Ward's targeted recruitment strategy was successful and around 90 per cent of the mail-order department employees were Brown.[13]

Ward reportedly called his employees 'my Asians' (yeah, eugh), which succinctly highlights the low status he gave his fellow Brown workers. However, he grossly overestimated

---

* As measured by the Consumer Price Index. The Retail Price Index in 1975 was 24%.

† Ward was Anglo-Indian and Brown, but cagey about his family background.

the docility of 'his Asians'. Most of the women at Grunwick were part of the East African Asian diaspora and had lived comfortably in Kenya, Uganda and Tanzania. Life in the UK was quite different to the one they left behind. The women and their families went from being distinctly middle class to working class in the space of one flight.

Many of the women had not had paid jobs before, and those that had been employed had usually had white-collar jobs or worked from home. They had servants in East Africa; they certainly did not work in factories. Now, in the UK, their decent English skills and good education did not afford them the same status as they were used to in East Africa, and they had to get any job they could. The conditions at Grunwick and management's bullying tactics were quite an affront to these women.

Jayaben Desai was one such member of the East African Asian diaspora employed at Grunwick. She was also soon to be the leader of one of the biggest strikes of the century. Born in the Indian state of Gujarat, Desai moved to Tanzania after marriage, where she lived a comfortable life and didn't do paid work outside of the home. The Desais moved to the UK after Africanisation policies made life harder in Tanzania, arriving in London in the late 1960s in the era of tension caused by Enoch Powell's 'Rivers of Blood' speech. There was an immediate shift in status for the Desais. Jayaben's husband, Suryakant, went from being a white-collar manager in Tanzania to a manual labourer. Jayaben raised their children and did some part-time tailoring before joining Grunwick in 1974.

Desai watched the management closely from day one. She

watched as management made employees ask to use the bathroom. She watched as pregnant women were denied time off for visits to the doctor. She watched as management publicly ranked employees in order of performance and threatened to sack those ranked lowest. She watched as supervisor Malcolm Alden threw wage packets at the employees 'as though we were dogs' and told them 'how lucky we were to earn such a lot of money'.[14] Desai had some run-ins with management, but the tipping point came in 1976.

It was Friday 20 August 1976, near the end of summer, after a relentless few months at the factory. That summer was one of the hottest in 300 years, temperatures reaching over 30°C for days on end, leading to melted roads, wildfires and even the appointment of the first minister for drought. The end of summer didn't mean an end to the workload at Grunwick. Quite the contrary, as people came back from their summer holidays they were keen to have their photos processed as soon as possible to relive the sun, sea and sangria. The mail-order department had to work at full capacity to process orders.

As usual, the mail-order department hired student workers over the summer to help, who were not exempt from the sour attitude of Grunwick's management, especially that of Malcolm Alden. One of the student workers was Jayaben Desai's son, Sunil. Sunil had already clashed with Alden earlier in the summer – both Sunil and a female student worker had taken a driving test on the same day, and the female colleague passed but Sunil failed. When Alden found out he scoffed, 'Well, women are better than men,' to which Sunil replied, 'I know, that's why your wife is better than you.'[15] Jayaben warned her son to keep his mouth shut and head down, which he mostly did. But on that fateful Friday, Sunil and a colleague were messing around, and he let out a yelp, provoking Alden's wrath: 'Sunil, this is not a zoo!'[16]

Tensions were high across the department. That same day, employee Devshi Bhudia and a few student workers were given a day's worth of work and expected to complete it within an hour. It was far too much – but Alden wouldn't listen.[17] Undeterred, Bhudia and the student workers went on a go-slow. When Alden realised what was happening, he was furious. He fired Bhudia on the spot, and the student workers left with him in solidarity.* They waited outside the factory as they planned their next move.

This dampened the mood more than the summer humidity. After a long day fraught with tension, Jayaben Desai was packing up to leave at the end of her shift when a foreman requested she do overtime. She refused. Alden called her into his glass-walled office. He jabbed his finger at Jayaben and questioned her lack of compliance, saying, 'It's not good business to leave work behind.'[18] She had endured enough of Alden's bullying and didn't want to be on the receiving end of his indiscriminate sackings. Jayaben squared up to him and jabbed her finger right back, 'You never told me this before, why are you telling me today? If you are not happy with me, give me my cards!' And with that she quit and stormed out of his office. Sunil threw down his tray and joined her as

---

* It was later noted that Bhudia had already lined up a new, better-paid job and so was on the verge of quitting anyway.

she walked out. As they left the factory, Jayaben told Alden: 'What you are running is not a factory, it is a zoo. But in a zoo there are many types of animals. Some are monkeys who dance on your fingertips. Others are lions who can bite your head off. We are the lions, Mr Manager.'

I like to imagine there were cheers and whooping as the Desais left.

The Desais ran into the now ex-employee Devshi Bhudia and the student workers outside the factory, who were waiting for Alden to leave to rough him up. Jayaben talked them down from the beating and persuaded them to go the route of collective action rather than criminal action.

Grunwick did not recognise the right for its workers to join a union. There was a Works Committee, but some workers didn't even know it existed. It also included one of the bosses, which defeated the purpose of it representing workers' interests.[19] On two occasions in the previous ten years there had been attempts at unionisation; in 1973 a group of drivers had attempted to unionise and were all sacked. The message was clear: unions were not welcome at Grunwick.

The lack of union rights was a Big Deal in 1970s UK. Trade unions were powerful organisations, which is hard to imagine for those of us that grew up after Thatcher dismantled them, but they were one of the key political players of the time. Historically, there have always been workers' groups, going as far back as medieval guilds. During the Industrial Revolution trade unions emerged to bargain collectively for workers' rights.

Union actions ranged from negotiating pay to organising and supporting strike action, and they fought for the rights we take for granted today, such as the eight-hour workday and the two-day weekend. They were also central to the creation of the Labour Party. After the Second World War, around 6 million workers were trade union members, which increased to over 9 million by 1970. By the end of the decade, membership peaked at 13 million, or over half of the total workforce.[20] The majority of union members were blue-collar, and membership was a way to prevent exploitation at the hands of employers. Grunwick workers did not have the privilege of such protection as they were part of the non-unionised half of the workforce.

Even if the workers had been part of a trade union, it would not have guaranteed better working conditions. For all the good they did, the trade unions did not have a glowing record protecting the rights of marginalised members in their ranks, including women and Black and Brown people, as we saw in the Bristol Bus Boycott and with the Indian Workers' Association. Unions were the domain of white men.

The main body representing unions in the UK, the Trades Union Congress, opposed the arrival of Black and Brown Commonwealth migrants after the Second World War, and supported restrictive immigration legislation enacted by the government.[21] The TUC argued that Black and Brown workers didn't integrate well with white ones. Unions had simply refused to participate in some industrial disputes led by Black and Brown workers, such as at Imperial Typewriters, and in others took some convincing to support, such as at Mansfield Hosiery.[22]

The unions were also influenced by a deal with the Labour government known as the 'Social Contract'. This delicate agreement aimed to rein in the wayward inflation by preventing large wage hikes. To do this, trade unions would see that workers would only negotiate wage increases at specific times and for 'reasonable' amounts, and in return workers would have subsidies for food and transport, rent control and full employment.[23]

With this as a backdrop in the UK, the small group of aggrieved Grunwick workers hatched a plan over the weekend. As the employees arrived at work the following Monday, 23 August 1976, they were met by Jayaben Desai and the others wielding placards, a petition for union recognition, and a plan for a mass walkout later that day. Despite the bad reputation of the unions, there was still hope that their support would make a difference. Most of the workers signed the petition, but the walkout was less successful: about half walked out at the planned time.[24]

Meanwhile, Jayaben's son Sunil visited the nearest Citizens Advice Bureau to ask about contacting a union, and with their advice the strikers contacted the Brent Trades Council and the trade union APEX: the Association of Professional, Executive, Clerical and Computer Staff.* Within days, the strikers joined the union as official members and formed a Strike Committee, with Jayaben Desai as treasurer.

APEX was not a progressive trade union. It was actually quite right-wing, which was not uncommon at the time. The secretary of the Brent Trades Council at the time, Jack Dromey, has noted that APEX was an 'unusual home' for the

---

* Trades Councils are the local representation of trade unions that work across all types of unions to provide support to their communities.

strikers.[25] And as said before, trade unions were not exactly champing at the bit to welcome Black and Brown people into their ranks, which begs the question – why did APEX support the Grunwick strike?

The cynical, and likely the most accurate, answer is that it saw the increasingly militant industrial action being taken by Brown and Black workers around the UK and was concerned about putting the Social Contract in jeopardy.[26] With Black and Brown workers kept out of the ranks of the trade unions, their tactics were unpredictable. If they were brought into the union they could be controlled, and as long as the Grunwick strike was first and foremost about the right to unionise rather than racism in the workplace, then it was something APEX could get behind. It was also desperate for members as its competitor union was growing at a much faster rate.

The less cynical answer would be that APEX was progressive compared to other unions and that unions were, and are, about 'decency that sees the value in every human being, regardless of their background or the colour of their skin', as the general secretary of the union GMB (who absorbed APEX) said in 2016 in a book about Grunwick.[27] However, given what we know about how many unions acted at this time, this would be a stretch.

The first demand of the strikers above all else was union recognition. The workers couldn't begin to tackle the discrimination motivated by racism and misogyny until Grunwick accepted the right to unionise. With APEX and the support of the Brent Trades Council, the Strike Committee planned to persuade George Ward to allow workers to unionise.

Ward would not be persuaded. He argued that he was

not anti-union but rather that the workers that remained at Grunwick did not want a union. According to him he was merely serving his workers and he offered to allow the strikers back without any issues if they dropped their demands for unionisation. The strikers refused, and in early September, less than two weeks after the first walkout, Grunwick fired all 137 workers that were now on strike, around 28 per cent of its total workforce.

The Strike Committee decided to use another tactic and formed a picket line, while APEX continued to look at other pathways for persuasion. The small band of Brown and Black strikers picketed daily, often taking shifts of one to two hours at a time, especially as the colder weather set in.[28] The female strikers dressed in long winter coats, with saris and salwar kameezes sticking out of the bottom, earning them the moniker 'Strikers in Saris'. Though they were few in number to start with, the strikers were dedicated to the cause. A reporter's interview with Desai captures the commitment:

REPORTER: How long will you stay here?
DESAI: Until we finish this dispute.
REPORTER: A year?
DESAI: Any time.
REPORTER: Five years?
DESAI: Ten years.
REPORTER: You'll stay?
DESAI: We'll stay.[29]

Striking was a new experience for most of the women. One striker, Sananda, said, 'I had never heard of a strike before, never been on a strike.'[30] Some of the strikers faced pressure from their families or the wider community as it wasn't appropriate for women to be so publicly exposed, and there was an element of shame in admitting the fall in social status they'd experienced over the past few years. Men were also on the picket line, and disproportionately represented on the Strike Committee. This was not without its tensions.

Jayaben's own son suggested early on that men should be on the picket line while women make the tea.[31] This was soon quashed, thankfully, and it was established that men and women were to play an equal role in the strike.

Unfortunately, this didn't change the view of many men that a woman's primary role was in the home. A husbands' meeting was organised where for three hours the men asked questions of Dromey, an APEX official and members of the Strike Committee. The hoped-for outcome was that they would support their wives' actions.[32] Some women stopped picketing due to the community pressure, while others picketed day after day despite the fear of repercussions. They had simply had enough.

Ward used his knowledge of norms in the Asian community to reduce the numbers on the picket line by spreading rumours that a young female striker only came to the picket line to meet her boyfriend; Ward knew that her family would stop her from participating.

Ward taunted the pickets. Desai said: 'He would come to the picket line and try to mock us and insult us. One day he said "Mrs Desai, you can't win in a sari, I want to see you in a mini [skirt]." I said "Mrs Gandhi wears a sari and she is ruling a vast country."'[33] Verbal taunts were not the only risk to the strikers. In September alone, Jayaben was hospitalised when a manager drove his car over her foot, and in another case a manager drove his car into a female striker.[34] The police did nothing.

As the strikers held up the picket line, APEX tried to negotiate with Grunwick. APEX asked Grunwick to engage in arbitration through the new government body ACAS, the Advisory, Conciliation and Arbitration Service. In practice, the union was asking for Ward to cooperate with an ACAS investigation into the dispute. However, there was no legal obligation to cooperate, and George Ward simply refused to participate.

The picket line did not persuade Ward to change his stance and many Grunwick workers didn't join the strike, even if they wanted a union, because they couldn't afford to be out of work. With Grunwick's management refusing to budge and the number of strikers fairly static, they needed reinforcements in the form of other workers. Solidarity action was common at the time, whereby workers from one union would strike to support workers from another union. It was less common, however, to see solidarity across the racial divide, but Grunwick's persistent refusal to allow its employees to join a union really riled up a lot of workers for whom unions were essential.

APEX and especially the Brent Trades Council worked behind the scenes to try and cut Grunwick off. Grunwick operated not only nationally but internationally too, so APEX encouraged workers to block Grunwick's shipments in and out of the country.[35] It issued and circulated lists of the different names that Grunwick operated under to ensure its business was cut off from all sources, tried to block sales of nitrogen gas cylinders necessary for processing and investigated who printed the envelopes used by the company to get them to stop supplies.[36] It turned out that company was also part owned by George Ward.[37]

The situation ramped up in November with a remarkable show of worker solidarity. Desai wanted to call on the Union of Postal Workers (UPW) to cut Grunwick off from its customers. She urged APEX to enlist the support of the UPW, but it refused.[38] Desai took it upon herself and requested support from the UPW's branch in Cricklewood, where Grunwick's mail was processed. The postal workers threw their support behind the cause and 'blacked' Grunwick. This unfortunate turn of phrase meant they would not process nor deliver its mail. Without the postal service, the mail-order model that Grunwick used would be ruined. Ward likened the blacking to cutting Grunwick's jugular.[39]

The strikers had Grunwick by the throat. But legal action put a stop to the blacking. Even though solidarity action was legal, it was against the law to interfere with the mail. In a show of good(ish) faith, Grunwick began arbitration proceedings with ACAS. If the blacking had continued, Ward would have been brought to his knees and forced to concede, and the strike would have been over in less than three months. Instead, the strike turned into one of the longest since the Second World War.

As the strike attracted more attention from the wider union movement, it also caught the attention of the political parties. The incumbent Labour government had a lot riding on the Social Contract with just a three-seat majority in Parliament, and it couldn't afford for it to fail. The Conservatives were also keenly watching what happened at Grunwick as a general election was due by 1979 and they wanted to tip Labour off its shaky pedestal. To help assure this election victory, the strikers had to be defeated.

Enter the National Association for Freedom (NAFF).

The NAFF was founded in 1975 as a right-wing pressure group to 'support individual freedom and resist ever bigger government'.[40] It was the perfect way for the Conservatives to influence events without getting their hands dirty. The NAFF technically wasn't affiliated to any political party but its membership included Conservative MPs and aristocrats, and it was in cahoots with the new leader of the Conservatives, Margaret Thatcher.[41] The NAFF became Ward's special advisor.

The strikers were not deterred by the setback of the failed blacking. The picket continued, and now also targeted pharmacies, where customers would often go to send their camera films to Grunwick. Solidarity action became a regular routine for nearby workers. One labourer recalls that every day at 6.30 a.m. his whole household joined the picket line for a couple of hours before going to work.[42] Spurred on by the outpouring of local support and with the help of Brent Trades Council, members of the Strike Committee toured the country to spread the word.

Two men and two women at a time would visit mills, dockyards, mines and factories to win support for their cause.[43] In total, over forty-two weeks the committee members visited 2,000 workplaces and were met with rousing enthusiasm and support wherever they went.[44] The picket line swelled beyond the initial 137 workers as others joined in solidarity. Ward meanwhile bought the loyalty of his remaining employees by increasing their wages by 15 per cent, and hired a bus to transport employees in and out so pickets couldn't recruit them.

ACAS published findings from its investigation four months after the arbitration started, in March 1977. It was good news for the strikers; ACAS urged Grunwick to recognise the union. But the victory was short-lived. The report was not legally binding, so Ward still refused to recognise APEX, and even appealed against the ACAS decision. Buoyed by the ACAS report and angered by Ward's reaction, 1,400 people took to the streets in solidarity to march against Grunwick. In April, as a throwback to an earlier tactic, Ward increased wages for Grunwick workers by a further 10 per cent.[45]

The strike was back to square one. George Ward would not compromise as long as he had the support of the NAFF and no legal consequences for his actions, and the strikers would not back down now that they had the support of workers countrywide. Workers from all trades had been spotted on the picket line, from renowned lawyers to Labour MPs. The government was scared by the escalation of events and intended to end the strike in its own way.

It sent the Special Patrol Group (SPG) unit of the police to the picket line. This 'special' unit was modelled after the Northern Irish paramilitary branch of the same name and deployed in exceptional circumstances of 'public disorder'. It had never been used in an industrial dispute before, despite the hundreds of strikes that had occurred since the SPG's creation in 1961. A member of the SPG later killed teacher Blair Peach at an anti-racism demonstration in 1979 while attending to a display of 'disorder', but that's for Chapter Ten. The SPG, and police more generally, demonstrated their broad mandate and ferocious tactics in the 'week of action' organised for June 1977.

The week of mass pickets aimed to harness the national enthusiasm and support for the strike. The first day of the 'week of action' was a women's only day, and resulted in 84 arrests out of around 200 pickets.[46] Arrest was not the only risk on the picket line. Ten (male) police officers encircled Mary Davis, then secretary of Haringey Trades Union Council, and stomped on her feet until they crushed her bones and she couldn't walk.[47]

On a more positive note, solidarity didn't just come from white workers and activists: Black people from the women's movement, such as Gail Lewis, were on the picket line every day, and members of the Asian Youth Movements and activists such as Farrukh Dhondy showed up.[48] Striker turnout was in the thousands by the end of the week, and with it the acts of police brutality and arrests increased.[49] In total there were more arrests during Grunwick than any strike since the national General Strike of 1926; around 550 in total.[50]

The week of action morphed into a 'fortnight of action'. The violence did nothing to deter people showing up on the picket line. Against explicit orders from their party leader, Labour MPs continued to visit the picket line. MP Audrey Wise was arrested. The strongest union in the country, the National Union of Miners, and its leader Arthur Scargill joined the picket line. Scargill was arrested. Throughout all of this, the newspapers were dominated by stories of injured police officers with headlines like 'Shouts of kill as PC is hurt' with photos of injured PC Trevor Wilson in his hospital bed.[51] They rarely showed the police choke-holding strikers. The pickets were likened to a mob.

If the government was afraid before, after a tumultuous two weeks it was petrified of the consequences on its tenuous hold on power. Notes from a meeting on 26 June 1977 between key officials including the prime minister, chancellor, home secretary and attorney general state: 'The Prime Minister said that people have to realise there was indeed a crisis. If things continued on the present basis there could well be fatalities and in circumstances which might be in danger of bringing the government down.'[52]

The government was well aware of the violence used by the police against the protestors, and feared a murder on the picket line at the hands of the police would be bad press for the shaky administration. All the tactics discussed at the meeting, such as cordoning off or closing access to the area, were dismissed as unworkable or risked antagonising the strikers further.

Instead, the government's first response was to send the home secretary, Merlyn Rees, to the picket line to see for himself what was happening. He was met with shouts of 'police out!'[53] The second action of the government was the launch of an inquiry, with Lord Justice Scarman in charge. Remember the name Scarman; he will come back in Chapter Eleven when we discuss the events of 1981.

It wasn't just the government that had concerns; some of the unions were growing increasingly cautious. APEX watched the violence on the picket line and suggested a limit of 500 pickets at a time, and tried to use the ongoing Scarman inquiry to urge the strikers to hold off on any major action. The strikers rejected this proposal. Meanwhile the UPW refused to support a second blacking of Grunwick's mail, so the Cricklewood postal workers took unilateral action to cut Grunwick off.[54]

A hundred postal workers were suspended and threatened with dismissal, and as the action was unofficial, they received no strike pay from the UPW. Without business coming in, Grunwick was haemorrhaging money fast, and for a while it looked as though the postal strike would achieve what it hadn't in 1976, but then Ward's buddies at the NAFF came to the rescue.

With the cooperation of the police, the NAFF organised a pick-up of 80,000 processed films from Grunwick, affixed £7,000 worth of stamps to the packages and then posted them from post boxes across the country so Grunwick's customers received their orders.[55] They called it 'Operation Pony Express' in reference to covert transportation missions in the Vietnam War. According to The Freedom Association, NAFF's successor, 'the actions taken by members of the Association were privately described by Margaret Thatcher as the "best thing since Entebbe"'.* They directly helped to save the now nearly bankrupted firm.'[56]

Following government procedure clearly wasn't working, and neither was relying on union-backed action. Cutting off essential services such as the post was the quickest and most effective way of bringing Grunwick to its knees, assuming

---

* 'Entebbe' is a reference to Operation Thunderbolt, a hostage rescue mission in Uganda, 1976.

that the NAFF didn't find ways around it. Without calls from the union movement for the withdrawal of more services, the strikers had to take matters into their own hands.

One of the strikers commented at the time, 'if this is to work we need ten thousand people every day'.[57] By this point, the strike was about more than just Grunwick. A member of the strike committee commented that 'we are getting a lot of Asians from this area and other parts of the country who say that they are waiting for us to win and they will unionise their factories too'.[58] A victory at Grunwick would change labour rights for all Asian workers in the UK.

This led to the 'Day of Action' on 11 July 1977, which saw one of the largest labour solidarity marches the UK has ever seen. Twenty thousand people travelled to Willesden from all over the UK to support the Grunwick strikers. I'll put that in digits to help it sink in: 20,000 people. This included 3,000 miners from Yorkshire. There weren't enough buses to transport everyone from Yorkshire that wanted to go to the march. The strikers' country tour had clearly worked. Even the dockers from east London showed up. Striker Gita Sahgal reflects:

> There were dockers and post office workers and miners . . . it was an amazing moment and I remember it particularly because what we'd known about the dockers was that they were racist. They were famous for their marches when Enoch Powell had made his inflammatory speeches . . . my abiding memory is that these white men had come in solidarity with Asian women and in order to protect the idea of solidarity itself.[59]

The sea of people pumped their fists and chanted in unison, 'Workers, united, will never be defeated!' and 'APEX, in! APEX, in! APEX, in in in! Ward, out! Ward, out! Ward, out out out!' Desai addressed the cheering crowd, 'Brothers and sisters . . . there's no doubt in my mind that victory is near. With your support, we will win . . . with unity we will win.'[60] With a show of support like that it was easy to believe that Grunwick had to budge, but the management, government and their mercenaries, the police, had other ideas.

The excitement and energy of the pickets were countered with fear and anger from the state and the police. They were afraid of what they saw as the potential 'that this could develop into one of the largest and potentially violent demonstrations ever seen in this country'.[61] In response they sent one police officer for every five protestors. Four thousand police officers, 15 per cent of the entire Metropolitan Police force, were in Willesden that day to police the picket line and protect the Grunwick factory.[62] The day was indeed violent, though not the most violent by Grunwick strike standards, and with a lot of the violence instigated by the police themselves.

The first objective of the strikers was to prevent the Grunwick worker bus from arriving at the factory. This would show Ward, the NAFF, the union and the government that the workers were powerful enough to take down Grunwick themselves with or without full union support. This in turn meant that the first objective of the many, many police officers was to clear a path for the Grunwick worker bus to reach the factory. The very narrow residential roads were full to the brim with pickets.

Police vehicles certainly couldn't enter the crowds to clear a path, so horse-mounted police arrived with hopes of dispersing the pickets. They failed too. More than two hours behind schedule, the bus still hadn't arrived. So, the police went the old-fashioned way and marched in to open an entrance. They linked arms to form human chains and pushed pickets into shopfronts and against houses to make space for the Grunwick bus. The sheer force of the throng of people demolished the garden walls along the road to the factory. The bus reached the factory. While the police helped the Grunwick bus, they were less welcoming to buses carrying pickets and prevented the arrival of buses of solidarity strikers, and diverted people away from Dollis Hill tube station.[63]

The second objective of the police seemed to be arrest, attack, or both. *The Times* reported that there were seventy arrests and thirty people injured, including eighteen police officers.[64] This is probably a conservative estimate as the papers liked to focus on the police injuries and not the protestors. A doctor from the area reported that the most common injuries were a result of testicle squeezing and breast grabbing.[65]

It was on the streets of Willesden that day that the police practised and perfected their kettling technique.[66] Some police officers seemed convinced that white workers were their secret allies and sought to help them. A local (white) attendee, Derek McGuinness, remarked: 'I went down on the floor, there were people in heaps on the floor, there was punching and kicking and gouging, a cop pulled me up, did my arms up the back ... he got me on the police bus ... he said to me "thank fuck we're out of that".'[67]

\*

The Day of Action has a mythical status in British labour history. For all the horrors of the day, it is remembered fondly by many strikers and the labour movement in general for the show of solidarity. The strikers seemed to be close to victory.

Ultimately, the Day of Action didn't help the strikers' cause. Grunwick, with a lot of help from the police, had shown that it could take on the workers of the whole country and win. The strikers didn't give up. The very next day the momentum continued when the High Court rejected George Ward's appeal against the ACAS recommendations. The *Scarman Report* was published in August and also sided with the strikers. Scarman called for Grunwick to recognise union membership and reinstate the strikers.

The celebrations could not continue for long. Soon after, the unofficial postal strike ended, forty-four days after it began. On the same day, the High Court decision was overturned and Ward's appeal against ACAS was upheld. Ward also, predictably, rejected the *Scarman Report* and its findings. Like the ACAS recommendations, Grunwick was under no legal obligation to accept the results of the inquiry, and though it was an unprecedented move – he was the first employer to ever reject a result – he had the backing of the powerful NAFF. He was untouchable.

The situation was now a stalemate.

By October 1977, the strikers were losing hope and some started to drop out. After over a year they could not believe that the strike would now be successful.[68] As a final push to keep momentum going, calls for another mass picket led to a

'Day of Reckoning' in November 1977. The SPG was out in force again, using the 'flying wedge' formation to disrupt the crowds this time (it's where they form a triangle, or wedge, shape and essentially drill into the crowd). A crowd of 8,000 people turned up and it led to 113 arrests and 243 injured pickets.[69] The day was the most violent in what had been a very violent strike.

What was left of APEX's enthusiasm dwindled by this point, and this was the death knell. The TUC was conspicuously quiet. In a desperate last-ditch attempt to rally support for a blacking of essential services, Jayaben Desai, alongside strikers Vipin Magdani, Johnny Patel and Yasu Patel, took inspiration from Gandhi and went on a hunger strike outside the trade union headquarters, Congress House. APEX was furious with the unauthorised action and suspended their membership for four weeks without pay.[70]

The strike petered out and officially ended on 14 July 1978, just shy of two years after it started.

The strike failed. The workers did not get union recognition, nor were they reinstated.

There were two main reasons it failed. One was the conservative-with-a-small-c Labour government that implicitly supported George Ward, and the other was the wavering trade union support.

The government supported Grunwick rather than the strikers through its application of the law and use of the police. Desai reflected that 'all the laws were in our favour, but they [the government] didn't apply it, and didn't try it.'.[71] It condoned the violent actions of the police and Special

Patrol Group, and was scared to lose its precarious hold on power. Labour lost the 1979 election anyway. Ward knew there would be no repercussions for ignoring the recommendations of ACAS and even ignoring a Court of Inquiry, an unprecedented move.

For its part, the Trades Union Congress and its general secretary, Len Murray, paid lip service to the strike but failed to enact the idea of halting Grunwick's operation by shutting off its power and other suppliers. The TUC was afraid of the potential lengthy and expensive legal proceedings that would follow. APEX's tepid support dissolved over time as the dispute became protracted. Jayaben Desai described union support like 'honey on the elbow – you can smell it, you can feel it, but you cannot taste it'.[72]

Perversely, by withdrawing support for the strike, the trade unions undermined their own cause and centuries-long fight for union rights. They didn't have to wait long to see the ramifications. Desai reflected in 1987, 'I don't think the Labour Party learned anything from Grunwick but I think the Conservative Party learned a lot of things.'[73]

It did. The leader of the opposition, Margaret Thatcher, closely watched the strike and used its failure as added impetus to dismantle the trade unions when she became prime minister. One of the ways she did this was to outlaw solidarity striking (also known as secondary picketing), which would have limited the Grunwick action to 137 instead of 20,000 people, and would make the infamous Grunwick mass pickets illegal today. Trade union membership today is low; in 2019 only 24 per cent of the total workforce were trade union members, and most of them white-collar.[74]

The fired workers went on to find new jobs, some with financial support from APEX until February 1979 to tide them over.[75] Some of them used their training from Grunwick to become union leaders in their new workplaces, and involvement with the strike helped build the confidence of some women to advocate for their rights. Jayaben Desai went on to tailor and teach. She received an award from the union GMB in 2007 for her part in the strike.

Grunwick continued to operate until 2011, and in the 1990s was one of the largest photo-processing labs in the world. In 2008 George Ward and family were worth £40 million.[76] The National Association for Freedom still exists, as The Freedom Association. It supposedly organises an annual get-together on Thatcher's birthday weekend to celebrate her values, and arranges pub quizzes in Westminster with Jacob Rees-Mogg as quizmaster.[77] They also have some snazzy Rees-Mogg cufflinks for sale inscribed with the quote 'I'm all in favour of nannies, but not the nanny state.'[78]

The legacy of Grunwick has been hotly contested. For some, Grunwick was a resounding success despite its failure. Former Brent Trades Council secretary Jack Dromey said, 'ultimately we did not win but you never lose a struggle like Grunwick'.[79] Firstly, conditions improved for workers who stayed at Grunwick. Christmas bonuses were distributed more fairly, and bank holidays were paid. With the two pay rises Ward introduced during the strike, wages increased by £6 a week. Striker Chandrikaben Patel said: 'because of us, the people who stayed in Grunwick got a much better deal. When the factory moved, the van used to come to their home and pick them up. Can you imagine that? And they get pension today! And we get nothing. That was because of us, because of our struggle.'[80]

Secondly, and more importantly, after Grunwick the trade union movement now recognised the rights of Brown and Black workers – with caveats. At the last meeting of the strikers, Desai urged her fellow strikers to be proud of what they had achieved: 'we have shown that workers like us, new to these shores, will never accept being treated without dignity or respect'.[81] There had been many times that Black and Brown workers had gone on strike before without union support or at best tepid support, but Grunwick was the first time that class solidarity won out over the prolific racism of the day. Arthur Scargill reflected that 'there were thousands of workers out there ... who for the first time began to identify with Asian workers, something that had never happened before'.[82]

Some say that given the failure was largely due to the lack of union support, Grunwick has been unduly celebrated by the trade union movement.[83] And unions did not unconditionally welcome Brown and Black people, especially Brown and Black women, into the inner circle. In 2014, Black and Brown people were still under-represented in many union positions.[84]

The true legacy of Grunwick probably lies somewhere in the middle. It didn't stop racism within the union movement, and certainly didn't stop employers being racist. But it sent a message to the nation not to underestimate Brown women.

It turns out there are some important strikes that don't get portrayed in film (Steve McQueen if you're reading this, call me). The history of Grunwick has been kept alive through a play, a temporary exhibition for the forty-year anniversary, public murals, a permanent exhibit in the People's History Museum in Manchester, and even through song.[85] A block of flats stands in Chapter Road where Grunwick once stood. The factory may be long gone, but the events are not forgotten. The enclave has been renamed 'Grunwick Close', and a plaque honours the late lioness Jayaben Desai as 'Leader of the Grunwick Workers Strike'.

# Chapter Nine

## Altab Ali and the Battle of Brick Lane

'Black and white, unite and fight.'[1]

Movement slogan

Sit-down protest outside police station, Bethnal Green Road,
London E2, 17 July 1978.                    © Paul Trevor

The Borough of Tower Hamlets spans many different realities
within London. The Tower of London stands on one side,

housing its stolen jewels with aplomb, and Canary Wharf stands on the other side, housing the who's who of finance and skulduggery. In Tower Hamlets also lies Brick Lane, famed for its Bangladeshi restaurants, lovingly known as London's 'curry mile' by white people. Forty-one per cent of the population of the street and its surroundings were of Bangladeshi origin in 2011.[2]

The borough also kisses the City of London Corporation, the rich, tax-haven square mile outside even Parliament's remit.[3] In 2020, Tower Hamlets had the worst poverty rate in London, with 39 per cent of its population living in poverty.[4] And in 2015 the borough had the worst child poverty rates in the whole of the UK, with 31 per cent of children living beneath the poverty line.[5] Its other neighbours include the poor boroughs of Hackney and Newham and it is cupped by the River Thames, the distinct 'U' bit you see in the opening credits to *EastEnders*.

The proximity of Tower Hamlets to the river meant that it was historically an important area for trade, spurring the appearance of dockyards, warehouses and other industries required for shipping. This really took off with the East India Company in the 1600s. And with Great Empire comes Great Exploitation. Cheap labour was imported from the Indian subcontinent, especially from Kolkata in the Bengal region, an important port city for the East India Company, and from Sylhet, a landlocked region in what is now Bangladesh. With few opportunities, many Bengalis decided to become sailors as a potential economic opportunity, tempted by signs that read 'Join the Navy: See the world'.[6]

Lascars – sailors – were thus hired by the East India Company or the British Merchant Navy, and later the Peninsular and Oriental Steam Navigation Company (what is now P&O), and ended up in the UK in areas such as Tower Hamlets.[7] Some lascars then deserted, while others were stranded after the East India Company refused to assure passage back. Bengali immigration to the area had begun. Bengalis were the latest in a long history of immigration to the area, with Irish, Huguenot and then Jewish communities all settling in Tower Hamlets.

Two hundred years later and a few thousand ships led to quite a few lascars knocking about, an estimated 1,100 at any given time in London in the early 1800s.[8] And given the lack of opportunities and hand-washing of the East India Company, a few hundred lascars a year would die on the streets of London.[9] A hundred years later, by the outbreak of the First World War, lascars also lived in Glasgow, Cardiff and Liverpool.[10] Men weren't the only ones to be brought over. Women were brought over as ayahs, as nannies and domestic help, and the latest fashion accessory. Like lascars, many were then dismissed with nowhere to go.

Lascars were used in both world wars, and 'used' is the right word; they were paid less than their white counterparts. In 1939 white seamen earned £9. 12s. 6d. a month while lascars earned £1. 17s. 6d.[11] No, I don't understand the old currency system either, but I know that there is a big difference between a 9 and a 1. We don't even have accurate records of how many lascars died in service, as these numbers weren't seen as worth keeping.[12] This is despite lascars comprising a stonking 20 per cent of the entire British maritime labour force at the end of the First World War, and 26 per cent on the eve of the Second World War.[13]

Recognising how important their labour was to the British, the lascars unionised to demand better pay and conditions, and their biggest industrial action happened as the Second World War broke out. Lascars went on strike all over the UK, from Glasgow to Liverpool to Southampton, and even in South Africa, Australia and Myanmar (what was then Burma). Demands included a substantial pay rise, in some cases up to 200 per cent, and basic necessities like soap, warm clothing and bedding.[14] Some were successful, winning pay rises of 100 per cent or even 125 per cent, but many were imprisoned instead, an estimated 500 by November, just two months into the Second World War.[15]

During the wars and after, Brown and Black people helped destitute ex-lascars in the ports and docks. Guest houses ensured there was a place to stay and learn from the experiences of other men in a similar position, like the one owned by Sylheti sailor Ayub Ali on Sandy's Row in east London, known as 'Number Thirteen' within the community.[16] The self-help model led to the formation of the Pakistani Welfare Association in 1961, helping people learn how to read and write. The Bangladesh Youth Movement was created in the late 1960s. It was focused on providing cultural activities, drama and sports, especially football. Cafés and restaurants ensured there was always plenty of food to go round, and jobs for some. Many others in the East End worked in the area's textile industry, known as the 'rag trade'.

More Bengalis migrated to the UK after 1945 and a second wave followed after the independence of Bangladesh in 1971, with migration and family reunification aided by a new direct flight from Dhaka.[17]

As we've already seen, life in 1970s Britain was increasingly grim for Brown and Black people, and this was the same in the East End. In a tale as old as time, and as depressingly common for many today, the working hours were long and the wages were low. It wasn't unusual for workers to clock up seventy hours per week in the rag trade.[18] Of a suit that would retail for £30, a Bengali worker would see £1.[19] Workers were not unionised.[20] Women also worked in the trade, usually from their homes.

Racism was frequent in school, on the streets and in housing. Racism in school led to some students dropping out, like Mohammed Abdus Salam who left Montefiore Secondary School after just a few months due to the abuse, and he joined evening classes instead.[21] On the streets, though exact numbers will never be known due to under-reporting, in the first three months of 1970 alone there were at least 43 separate incidents of racially motivated acts including robbery and molestation.[22] From March to May of 1976 there were at least 30 attacks, and in the autumn of 1977 at least 110 attacks were recorded.[23] Julie Begum, chair and co-founder of the community group, Swadhinata Trust, recalls, 'you went to school, you went home, you didn't hang around, you did your shopping and you hoped that you were not going to be attacked on your way there or back'.[24]

Those looking to find solace in their homes were out of luck as there was none to be found.

Poor housing conditions were quite commonplace in a lot of cities nationwide, in part a hangover from the rapid expansion of housing in the 1800s. Most housing had been built and owned privately and didn't have much planning or thought involved beyond profit.[25] Home ownership wasn't affordable for many (unlike today, amirite?!) so renting privately was the main option. In 1918, 76 per cent of houses were privately rented, only 23 per cent of houses were occupied by the owners, and for the mathematically savvy among you, the remaining 1 per cent of housing was socially provided.[26]

After the First World War, 'homes for heroes' was a slogan on voters' and politicians' lips, and councils started to build more housing, this time with some planning involved. The new housing wouldn't be cramped, and there would be facilities such as churches, shops and schools (though no pubs at first).[27] The fanciest of developments had inside toilets and fitted baths. Slums were cleared and people rehoused, often not in the same area where they had lived. After the Second World War, housing shortages led to the construction of prefabricated houses, a temporary solution, which could be put together in about forty hours.[28] New, faster, easier construction methods were used for longer-term housing. By 1955, 1.5 million new homes had been built.

By 1961, 26 per cent of people were now renting from the council, often in high-rise flats on specially built estates. Social housing – council housing – comes with a lot of stigma and residents are often seen as 'scroungers' on the welfare state. There was a time, however, when it was commonplace and even seen as a duty of the local authorities to provide affordable housing. In Tower Hamlets by 1976, the Greater London Council and London Borough of Tower Hamlets owned 87 per cent of the housing.[29]

The reality of building so quickly after the Second World War was that there was a lot of low-quality housing, and the spacious ideas of the interwar period had given way to high-density settlements instead. More people, in less space. And despite the rapid building there was still more needed; many buildings were condemned and seen as unfit for habitation but there wasn't enough money to rebuild quickly enough to meet demand.

The housing situation was therefore dire for many people, characterised by long waiting lists and substandard conditions. But Brown and Black people would be lucky to get the dregs: they would usually get the dregs of the dregs. Discrimination against Bengalis in housing was fivefold. First, there were barriers to access council housing, with a residency requirement of at least a year in the borough. In one case, a family was asked to prove their residency status every month for two years.[30] Second, if they could get on the waiting list, they could be waiting for years. Chand Ali lived with his wife and five children in one bedroom just nine feet by nine feet, shared a toilet with two other flats, and a kitchen with one other flat. When he was interviewed by a journalist, he had been waiting on the council list for five years already.[31]

Third, if a Bengali family was lucky enough to be housed, it could be in the most run-down places, known as 'sink estates', often built decades earlier, riddled with damp and mould, with seven people or more sharing a one- or two-bedroom place, and they'd be lucky to have a bathroom. To put this into perspective, at the time a house would be identified for demolition if it didn't have a water supply, an indoor toilet and a bath, so these homes were not adequate for living.[32] This was called 'low-demand' housing, meaning it was available to Bengalis as the demand was low from white folks. No shit: these were condemned buildings.

Fourth, if housing wasn't on a sink estate, it was often out of the E1 area and in places that were no-go zones for Bengalis. Families that were rehoused to adequate council housing would often face such racism that they would go back to their old, worse housing.[33] And for anyone still counting, the fifth way that Bengalis faced disadvantage was through constant insecurity. Evictions came thick and fast, justified by a lack of payments or a need to house the unhoused, never mind that families themselves could then be made houseless. Discrimination meant that in 1971 in Tower Hamlets, Brown and Black people made up 8.8 per cent of the population but only 3.7 per cent of the council-house tenants.[34]

To rub salt in the wounds, there were hundreds of empty houses in Tower Hamlets, as was the case in Lambeth too, awaiting a redevelopment plan that didn't materialise. The two boroughs, along with Newham, Hackney and Southwark, were regarded as having 70 per cent of London's uninhabitable housing.[35] In 1975, Tower Hamlets had at least 1,320 empty properties.[36]

Bengalis organised to fight against the abominable housing. In 1975, a group of around forty Bengalis picketed the offices of the Greater London Council (GLC), technically Britain's biggest landlord as it owned so many properties, and made demands: an end to evictions; that any rehousing be done within the same postcode area, E1; and the ability to exercise their right to view a property before being rehoused.[37] They told the GLC: 'By sending Bengalis into places like the Canada Estate in Poplar, you have exposed us to racial attacks and our children to isolation in schools, where the local children have not yet been taught that people who do not speak English are not culturally backward.'[38]

The GLC washed its hands of the issue, saying that responsibility lay with Tower Hamlets Council. It did, however, float a plan for an all-Asian estate, to great uproar about the attempted ghettoisation of Bengalis.[39] It was a catch-22, because Bengalis felt safer among the community, but also didn't want to be forcibly segregated.

Twenty-five young Bengali men were lucky enough to find a home at Toc H, a youth hostel. Opened in 1973 at number 7 The Crescent, it became not only a home but importantly a safe space for Bengalis to gather, to exchange ideas, play badminton, cook together and to organise. A group visited the Lake District in 1975, where they camped for the first time and befriended some white locals. There were tears from both sides when the trip ended and they stayed in touch for years afterwards.[40] That story has nothing to do with the fight against housing conditions but it was heart-warming, I think you'd agree.

As in other parts of London and nationwide, people started squatting as a means to meet their need for housing. At least a couple of hundred Bengali families were squatting, helped by organisations such as the Tower Hamlets Squatters Union, even if it meant that they had to pay to sort out access to gas, electric and water as many of the houses had dodgy wiring and no services.[41] Women were central to the success of the squatting movement, as they would be defending the home while the men were out at work.[42]

\*

One evening in February 1976, seventy Bengali families and activists including former Black Panthers Mala Sen and Farrukh Dhondy, and local Terry Fitzpatrick, came together at the Montefiore Centre on Deal Street to discuss the housing situation. Out of the window they could see the Pelham Buildings on Woodseer Street lying empty, and decided to occupy them.[43] They also formed the Bengali Housing Action Group, the acronym BHAG meaning 'share' or 'tiger' in Bengali, to demand better housing policy.[44]

Within a couple of months, around fifty families had moved into the Pelham Buildings, much to the chagrin of the GLC and Tower Hamlets Council. The Labour-run GLC had won a case against Bengali squatters a few months earlier and was in no mood to concede, or even negotiate. The GLC then became Conservative-led, and it had a different policy; if BHAG could tell it which were safe estates for Bengalis, then the families could be rehoused there, which it did. Taking the issue all the way to the chairperson of the GLC's Housing Management Committee, BHAG also managed to get the GLC to agree to an amnesty, allowing squatters to become legal tenants of a squat if they registered within a given timeframe.[45] As one of the founders of BHAG, Terry Fitzpatrick, reflected, 'for the first time a community had forced the British state to house them where they were safe from racist attacks'.[46] 'BHAG is on the loose', stated a *Race Today* article.[47] Yes it was.

Other communities around the UK were also taking housing into their own hands. The Black Liberation Front set up the Ujima Housing Association, at first to provide accommodation for young, unhoused people, including the facilitation of squatting, and then expanded to become a more general-ised association serving the most at-risk in the community. It merged with another association in 2008, London and Quadrant, by which time its assets were worth £2 billion.[48]

Safe housing was imperative as the streets certainly weren't safe. Determined to draw on the previous strongholds of Oswald Mosley in the East End, the National Front started campaigning in the area. It made sense as a place to rally support as in 1968 the dockers had famously marched in sup-port of Enoch Powell after his 'Rivers of Blood' speech. The Battle of Cable Street between anti-fascists and the police, who defended Mosley's British Union of Fascists, had been in Whitechapel in 1936.

Members of the National Front turned up at the Brick Lane Market on Sundays to sign up new recruits and sell their publications *National Front News* and *Spearhead*. In the very heart of Banglatown. They marched in the surrounding areas of Hoxton and Bethnal Green. National Front members would also go to Bengali-owned restaurants and dine and dash, or worse: dine, trash and dash.[49] Feel free to borrow that phrase, by the way. In the elections for the GLC in 1977, the National Front received 19 per cent of the vote in Bethnal Green and Bow.[50]

Spitalfields Bengali Action Group, which had formed in 1974 to campaign for a community centre, documented attacks on Bengalis in the area. In March–May 1976 it doc-umented thirty attacks alone, or one every three days.[51] The Bangladesh Youth Front was set up in 1976 in response to the simmering violence in the area. It met every evening in a café to discuss the latest attacks, which included urination through letterboxes, dog attacks and arson.[52] Nowhere was safe.

The police were no help. Or, at least no help to the Bengali community. They helped the National Front but would not protect the Bengalis from attack. Bengali groups therefore took it upon themselves to be prepared; the Progressive Youth Organisation sought training in kung-fu.[53] Groups formed to campaign for better protection, like the Anti-Racist Committee of Asians in East London with the catchy acronym ARCAEL, which was set up in 1976 to call out the inadequate police protection. It led a march of 3,000 protestors from Brick Lane to the Leman Street police station, demanding that the police keep blood off the streets.[54] Darcus Howe and the *Race Today* Collective called for self-defence patrols in the area.[55]

This was life in and around Brick Lane as 1978 came about. Nasty, brutish and, unfortunately for some, cut short. Bengalis lived with one eye over their shoulder outside, and on high alert to potential attacks even at home. Members of the National Front basked in their racist glory, no doubt buoyed by the leader of the opposition Margaret Thatcher saying on ITV that 'people are really rather afraid that this country might be swamped by people with a different culture', after which the polls swung in clear favour of the Conservatives, who went from being two points behind Labour to eleven points ahead.[56]

By 1978 anti-racism action was also widespread in the area and beyond, due to the unfortunate high demand. Knowing full well that the police only had part of the story since so many crimes went unreported, the predominantly white local trades council in conjunction with members of the Bengali community started compiling a report in 1976 on the racism faced by the community, which would be aptly named *Blood on the Streets*. An epic battle took place in Lewisham in 1977 between the National Front and anti-racist demonstrators. And while April 1978 saw the murder of ten-year-old Kenneth Singh in the East End, stabbed eight times in the head, it also saw the Clash headline a festival for Rock Against Racism, which 100,000 (mostly white) people attended.[57]

Monday 1 May 1978 was the first ever 'Early May Bank Holiday', and Thursday 4 May was local election day. The National Front had forty-one candidates up for election in Tower Hamlets.[58]

Altab Ali was one of the people actually planning to vote in the local election (turnout was only 29 per cent).[59] Twenty-five-year-old Ali went to work as usual as a machinist in a leather factory on Hanbury Street, a few steps from Brick Lane. He had been in the UK for nine years at that point, arriving as a teenager in 1969. His parents were still in the Sylhet region of Bangladesh and he would send them money from his meagre earnings to support them and his siblings. His wife also lived with his family in Bangladesh; they hoped she would be able to join him in the UK eventually.

After work, Ali did some shopping. He ran into Shamsuddin Shams, who worked close to Ali. They saw each other a lot, working so close to each other, and on Saturdays after work would watch wrestling together at Jim's Café.[60] Shams had just voted for the first time at the polling station on Brick Lane and was excited to have exercised his democratic right.

Ali hadn't voted yet, he was planning on doing so later with his cousin's wife, with whom he lived. This was around 7 p.m. and the polls were open until 10 p.m., so there was still plenty of time.

Ali started making his way home to Wapping, walking down Adler Street, a small street next to St Mary's Gardens. He was soon confronted by three teenagers, no older than he had been when he came to the UK. They attacked him, stabbing him in the neck. Ali managed to stagger 180 metres to Whitechapel Road before collapsing against a bus stop.[61] He was taken to London Hospital and died on the operating table two hours later.

Ali still had his money on him, all £51 of it; it was not a robbery.[62]

Labour held on to Tower Hamlets Council, but its share of the vote decreased by 18 per cent, and the Conservatives increased theirs by 13 per cent.[63] The National Front got 9 per cent of the votes.[64]

Altab Ali didn't get to cast his vote.

For a community that had been consistently racially abused, attacked and discriminated against, this was the breaking point. Jamal Hasan, who worked at Tower Hamlets Law Centre, said, 'as soon as we heard about Altab Ali, everyone in the East End was terrified. Being beaten up was one thing, being stabbed to death, that was the first one. It shocked us so much, we became ten times more angry.'[65]

The racists had attacked their last Brown person. There would be no more Paki-bashing. All the organisations in the area got together – Brown, Black and white, from the Bangladesh Youth Front to the Anti-Nazi League to the

Tower Hamlets Law Centre – to make a stand. Enough of the National Front, enough racism in the streets. Groups and committees sprang up, including the Action Committee Against Racial Attacks (ACARA), an umbrella group whose first objective was to organise a national demonstration against the persistent racist attacks and killings, and the inaction of the police.[66] Ali's killers hadn't been caught yet.

Desire for action wasn't just coming from the activist groups, there were suddenly hundreds of people who had been stirred to do something. Harnessing the fervour within the community and nationwide, ACARA was able to mobilise a demonstration within just a few days, the news spread by word of mouth and leaflets entitled 'Racist Murder'.[67]

Ten days after Altab Ali was killed, Sunday 14 May 1978, was a rainy day. Torrential rain, in fact, such that hundreds of signs and placards that had been painstakingly made actually dissolved in the wet conditions.[68] It couldn't stop thousands of people from taking to the streets, though. The exact number is disputed: numbers range from 7,000 to 10,000.[69] Whatever the figure, it was one of the biggest demonstrations to date of Brown people in the UK. People came from all over the country to London in solidarity, including from Wolverhampton where some West Indians had recently been shot at.[70] And it wasn't just the young who showed up; one of Hasan's elder clients from the Tower Hamlets Law Centre turned up with his wife, and said, 'we're not doing it for you, we're doing it for the community, for us, for our future children'.[71] The Progressive Youth Organisation stayed back to protect Brick Lane from anyone who would look to take advantage of it being empty.[72]

The protestors followed a hearse carrying a symbolic empty

coffin as they marched from St Mary's Gardens to Hyde Park with cries of 'Law and order for whom?', 'Who killed Altab Ali? Racism, racism', 'Self-defence is no offence' and 'Black and white unite and fight'.[73] They gathered in Hyde Park to listen to speeches from all of the major organisations, and prayers from religious leaders. A member of the Anti-Nazi League said, 'We must mourn, but we must also mobilise.'[74]

In the pouring rain a small contingent then marched to Downing Street where Taibur Rahman, the chairperson of ACARA, handed over a petition for Prime Minister James Callaghan that demanded a full investigation into the police handling of racist deaths, including Ali's, and for greater protection of immigrants. The last person to see Ali alive, Shamsuddin Shams, said, 'One of our community leaders told us that, if we killed racism from the political ground, it would automatically die on the streets, so we took Altab Ali's coffin to 10 Downing Street.'[75]

Unfortunately, racism didn't die on the political ground or on the streets. More Brown men would die, and many more would fight back to defend their lives, homes and dignity. Rajonuddin Jalal, co-founder of the Bangladesh Youth Movement, said of the march, 'it was the day we realised we are no longer to be treated as immigrants'.[76]

The Battle of Brick Lane had begun.

The police didn't step up protection of the community following Altab Ali's murder. They downplayed the race component to the attack, especially since at least one of the attackers was Black. Police tended to arrest the Bengali men, the victims, rather than the perpetrators of racism. Young men who took to the streets to defend themselves and their area and community would be stopped and searched, and charged with possession of offensive weapons; the ones they carried to protect themselves in the very absence of police protection. Over five years, Bangladeshi Youth Front members were stopped 2,000 times by the police.[77] Some members were given curfews so they couldn't be on Brick Lane on Sundays to defend it from the National Front.

From the perspective of the police, the Bengali community wasn't doing enough to report crimes, because 'their community is isolated, inward looking and easily frightened'.[78] From the perspective of the Bengali community, there was little point in going to the police since reporting crimes hadn't resulted in any charges, and the police were always so slow to respond to calls; in some cases they could be waiting over three hours for police to arrive following a racially motivated attack.[79] For at least two years, since the formation of ARCAEL, calls for greater police protection had gone unheeded. What more did the police want?

The community was explicit in its requests. Bengali groups asked the police to stop the National Front presence at the Sunday market on Brick Lane, but they were told it was first come, first served. Challenge accepted! On Saturday nights, groups of men would sleep on the corner of Bethnal Green Road and Brick Lane, the intersection where the National Front would set up its market stall. They were there first. They would sleep with banners and posters, and people from the area brought them food and drink. Some people were pre-emptively arrested on the grounds that their presence would cause a breach of the peace in the morning. They were told it was first come, first served, but simultaneously that their presence was a danger.

Brick Lane was under siege. On 11 June 1978, 39 days after the murder of Altab Ali, around 150 young white people, some sporting badges that read 'National Front Rules O.K.', went on a rampage on Brick Lane, smashing up shops, restaurants, cars, hurling concrete, and confronting anyone they could find to shouts of 'kill the black bastards'.[80] One shopkeeper said, 'they really went berserk. It has never been as bad as this before.'[81] One Bengali man, Abdul Monaf, had to have two teeth removed after he was hit by rubble thrown through his shop window.[82]

Young Bengalis were there to confront the white attackers, managing to kettle twenty of the perpetrators who were then arrested, but only three of the hundred-plus crowd were charged immediately following the incident.[83] The day's events were alarming: suddenly the National Front groups were bigger and more organised.

In response, the Bangladeshi Youth Movement, Bengali Youth Association and the Anti-Nazi League organised a march. Forty-six days after Ali's murder, on 18 June, around 2,000 to 4,000 people and hundreds of police officers took to the streets, as National Front supporters did 'Heil Hitler' salutes and sang 'Rule Britannia' from behind the safety of police lines.[84] The day passed relatively calmly considering the events that had led to it, and even initiated hopes that it would go some way to dissipate the tension in the area. It certainly gave the media a chance to celebrate the successes of the police: headlines read, 'Police avert East End clashes' and 'It's peace – thanks to a little help from police'.[85]

The tension didn't dissipate. Now fifty-three days after the murder, on 25 June, there were more attacks. Fifty anti-racists were attacked, but fewer than ten arrests were made.[86] On the same day, Ishaque Ali was walking home with his nephew in Hackney when they were confronted by three young white men, who demanded money and then attacked them. They punched Ali, who died in Hackney Hospital from a heart attack.[87]

There had now been two deaths from racist attacks in less than two months and there were fears a race war would soon break out.[88] The Hackney and Tower Hamlets Defence Committee was formed by a coalition of over twenty-five organisations.[89]

Fifty-six days after he was murdered, Altab Ali's killers were caught. They were seventeen-year-olds Roy Arnold and Carl Ludlow, and a sixteen-year-old known only as Mr Burns. Respectively, a white boy, a Black boy, and one possibly mixed (this racism stuff is more complicated than you might first think).[90] It didn't stop the fight against fascism in the area: this was now bigger than seeking justice for Altab Ali, it was about seeking justice for everyone in the community.

Sixty-three days after Altab Ali's murder, on 5 July 1979, as Bengali workers were leaving the Bass Charrington brewery in Bow they were attacked by 'carloads of whites'.[91] There was no police presence at the plant the day after the attack.[92]

The chairperson for the Commission for Racial Equality finally visited the area to reassure Bengalis that local racism would be got rid of, with increased police patrols.[93]

By July, Brick Lane was the most heavily policed area of the

UK outside of Northern Ireland.[94] The Special Patrol Group was also called in, and it became a training ground for police from different areas. Each Sunday, protestors were met by unfamiliar police officers using varying tactics to dissipate tension; stop and search one week, cordoning off the area the next.[95] One police tactic remained consistent, which was to arrest anti-racists in the name of crowd control. They faced the possibility of imprisonment for public order offences, a harsh punishment, intended to deter protests, handed out by a senior magistrate at Old Street.[96] What little remained of trust in the police was quickly waning.

Sundays were no longer a day for rest and family, they were a day of protest. As members of the National Front tried to get to their market stall on Sunday 16 July, seventy-four days after Ali's murder, they were met with 2,000 people trying to stop them, wearing 'Stop the NF Nazis' badges and chanting, 'We shall come back, Sunday after Sunday' and 'We are taking over Brick Lane – we shall not give it up'.[97] OK, not the catchiest slogans to be fair, but descriptively accurate. By now, Bengalis and the wider anti-racist movement had an impressive organisation and network, and they could mobilise hundreds of people with very little notice.[98]

The impressive organisation led to a Black Solidarity Strike the next day, arranged by the Defence Committee. It was the first ever strike against racial violence. It aimed to bring more people to the anti-racism cause, for Black, Brown and white to unite and fight. Workers were urged to stay at home, or protest or picket instead of going to work. Parents were asked to keep their children home from school.

At Robert Montefiore School in Tower Hamlets, only 50

students showed up out of 450.[99] Some employers tried to stay open, but by midday nearly 80 per cent of all offices and shops were closed.[100] Around 8,000 people took part. A thousand people gathered in the Naz Cinema in Brick Lane to listen to speakers, and some watched the documentary *Blacks Britannica*, an exploration of systematic racism in the UK.

Others went to picket factories and talk to workers, and hundreds marched and picketed police stations. Three men were arrested after confrontations with the National Front, prompting a sit-down protest of 2,000 people outside Bethnal Green police station to demand their release. After eighty minutes the men were let go, crowdsurfing over the cheering protestors, and the protest continued with a march to St Mary's, near where Altab Ali had been attacked.[101]

Though the strike was seen as useless by some members of the community, who lost a day's wages and saw self-defence as more effective than a strike, the community had finally got the attention of the police.[102] At a meeting with community groups, the police agreed to put up a temporary police station on Brick Lane itself. But in true police fashion, they set it up at the wrong end of the street, the opposite end to where the National Front gathered. Or maybe it was the right end of the street according to the police. Insert shrug emoji.

Concern about what was happening in Brick Lane also reached Westminster, at least among some politicians. Recalling concerns from Bengalis such as being constantly asked to show resident papers, Labour MP for Paddington, Arthur Latham, called for an independent judicial inquiry and for the home secretary to visit the area. He was met with scepticism and anger by both his own party and the opposition. One Conservative MP said Latham was 'in danger of abusing Parliamentary privilege by making accusations without giving any evidence'.[103]

Even after all that, nothing really changed in the area. Every Sunday, there would be a stand-off between the hundreds of National Front supporters and the Bengali community, supported by anti-racist organisations. Every Sunday, hundreds of police and SPG officers would use dubious crowd-control methods and guard the National Front.[104] To build on the momentum from Black Monday and have a show of solidarity, Sunday 20 August, 109 days after the murder of Altab Ali, was declared a 'Day of Action' for Brick Lane.

Every Brown and Black community and trade union was called on because as the Hackney and Tower Hamlets Defence Committee said, 'the National Front must not be allowed to grow and achieve its aim of smashing all its opponents and kicking its way to power.'[105] This was particularly timely as racist attacks continued to surface around the country; 'KKK' was painted in white on the door of a mosque in the West Midlands and a severed pig's head was left on the doorstep.[106] About 5,000 people showed up to the march, though Asian participation was noticeably lower than usual. People were growing weary.[107]

The National Front was apparently still undeterred, protected as it was by the authorities. In September 1978, it relocated its headquarters from the sleepy, white suburb of Twickenham to its intended heartland, Hackney. It moved into 73 Great Eastern Street, just a ten-minute walk from Brick Lane. The move was accompanied by a 2,000-strong march and a plan for a rally near the top of Brick Lane, permission for which the Tower Hamlets Defence Committee called 'an act of criminal insanity by the Home Secretary'.[108]

No wonder the Bengali community thought the state wasn't on its side. Around 3,000 Bengalis and supporters gathered around key points on the suspected march route on Shoreditch High Street and Bethnal Green Road to make sure the march couldn't reach Brick Lane. In the end, the march was diverted and instead held its rally from a lorry on Curtain Road, around the corner from the new HQ, under police protection.[109] It was a successful day for the National Front, one of its biggest turnouts ever.

The long summer of 1978 had seen triumphs and heart-ache, and unprecedented community solidarity, but was it enough?

There is no agreement as to when the Battle of Brick Lane ended. Though racial violence reduced over the 1980s, many of the other issues remained, including a lack of access to housing, and police mistreatment.[110] The Federation of Bangladeshi Youth Organisations was formed in 1980 to bring together the disparate groups into a force capable of advocating for Bengalis at an institutional level, which it had done by the end of the decade, for example with an increase in Bengali workers in the council.[111]

The National Front slowly lost its grip on the area, first stopping its appearances at Brick Lane Market, and later get-ting into a property dispute with Hackney Council, which refused to allow the premises to be used as an HQ. The NF claimed it was for printing and bookselling. The National Front put up over 300 candidates in the 1979 general election, the most it had ever fielded, but still failed to get anyone into Parliament. By 1981, it had moved the headquarters to Streatham. But a new British National Party emerged in 1982 and the confrontations continued.

Some would argue the Battle of Brick Lane ended in 1986 when the government published *Bangladeshis in Britain*, a milestone report recognising, for the first time, the concerns of the community and the nuances within the Asian communities.[112] Bangladeshis are one of the most disadvantaged communities in the UK, with consistently high rates of child poverty and unemployment. Nineteen per cent of Bangladeshis were living in the most deprived areas of the UK in 2019 compared to 9 per cent of white people.[113]

Some may say that the Battle really didn't end until the early 1990s when the first British National Party councillor, Derek Beackon, was ousted from his Tower Hamlets seat after a concerted campaign from the community and groups such as Women Unite Against Racism.[114]

Some would say that the Battle of Brick Lane is still going on. The Battle is slightly different these days – there are no longer any no-go zones for Bengalis in Tower Hamlets – but it has similar roots to the 1970s.[115] Spitalfields ward was renamed Spitalfields and Banglatown in 2001 but the label becomes more historical by the day. Gentrification has been in full swing for a good decade-plus in London's East End, which is now home to brunch places, an indoor mini-golf venue and even a Veggie Pret. And we all remember when the Cereal Killer café opened on Brick Lane.

Housing prices increased by 63 per cent in Tower Hamlets from the London Olympics in 2012 to 2021, more than the

London average of 61 per cent, and way more than the UK average of 49 per cent.[116] In and around Brick Lane itself, property prices are 20 per cent higher than the surrounding areas.[117]

All these big numbers lead to one big conclusion: Bengalis are being pushed out of the area. The number of restaurants on Brick Lane owned by South Asians plummeted from around sixty in the 2000s to just twenty-three in 2020.[118] Fun fact: more than 80 per cent of 'Indian' restaurants in the UK are actually Bangladeshi owned.[119] Shamsuddin Shams, the last person to see Altab Ali alive, went on to own a restaurant.

In September 2021, the council decided to approve plans for the Truman Brewery site to become a shopping centre and office complex. The #SaveBrickLane campaign sees this as a death knell for Brick Lane. The campaign's website is even called battleforbricklane.com. Some people have seen this coming for years. In 2006, BYM co-founder Rajonuddin Jalal said the 'saddest thing that has happened is that we haven't been able to acquire the Truman Brewery site for the community . . . had it been acquired by us it would have given us the true establishment for Banglatown. Without the Truman Brewery site, it is Banglatown without our freehold ownership.'[120] The struggle continues.

Everyone agrees, though, that the murder of Altab Ali was a turning point. A founder of the Bangladesh Youth Approach, Suroth Ahmed, said 'the killing of Altab Ali gave the voice to the Bengali people that we are here to stay and to live. We can no longer tolerate racism and such kind of brutal activity. It was the beginning of the progression of the community.'[121] There is even a community history project called 'Brick Lane 1978: The Turning Point'. Bengalis would not take things lying down, they would not be quiet.

The legacy of the Battle of Brick Lane is evident in other ways today. Bengalis formed the Spitalfields Housing Association in 1979 to serve the community and it is still running today.[122] It owns and manages 850 properties, which it renovates to make liveable and rents at affordable rates to those most in need, and it aims to get that up to 1,000 properties. The Bangladesh Youth Movement still exists today as a community self-help organisation, providing legal advice, support to young people, and has a dedicated women's centre.[123]

Many members of the organisations went on to become local councillors. Though some young Bengalis had tried to become Labour Party members in 1978, and were rejected, this changed after 1981 and by 1982 the first Bengali councillors were elected.[124]

In June 1978, Altab Ali's body was returned to his family in Bangladesh, where he was then buried. In November his attackers were sentenced. The youngest was given seven years for stabbing Altab Ali, the other two were given three years for robbery, even though we know it wasn't a robbery.[125] So what was their motivation for the murder? According to one of them, there was 'no reason at all, if we saw a Paki we used to have a go at them. We would ask for money and beat them up. I've beaten up Pakis on at least five occasions.'[126]

Ali hasn't been forgotten by the Bengali elders and officials. 'Altab Ali Day' is officially marked every 4 May by Tower Hamlets and those who aim to keep the importance of Ali alive. In 2020, his tattered grave got a new headstone befitting someone who means so much to many in the Bengali and East End community.[127] Julie Begum wrote a play called *The Altab Ali Story* about his life and death. The younger generations know Ali's name but there is still a lack of knowledge as to what really went down at the time, which organisations like the Altab Ali Foundation are working hard to rectify.[128]

Next time you are in the area, as you walk down Whitechapel Road past Brick Lane, maybe on your way to Starbucks, take a look up at the name of the park on your right. Altab Ali Park. It was renamed from St Mary's Gardens in 1998, and since 1989 it has had an arch at the entrance in Altab Ali's honour. The bus stop has also been renamed from Adler Street to Altab Ali Park in his honour. He won't be forgotten.

# Chapter Ten

# Asian Youth Movements and the Bradford 12

'Self-defence is no offence.'[1]

Asian Youth Movement slogan

Commemorative plaques outside Southall Town Hall mounted by the group Southall Resists 40 in 2019.                    © Preeti Dhillon

It was a Friday night in June in the hot summer of 1976 and young, turban-wearing student Gurdip Singh Chaggar was out with a couple of friends in Southall. Normal eighteen-year-old teenager stuff. Only, this time, Chaggar wouldn't return home.

A pool of Chaggar's blood still lay on the ground close to the Dominion Cinema the following morning as twenty-two-year-old Suresh Grover walked by. A police officer stood next to the blood. Grover asked the police officer what had happened. 'It was just an Asian,' was the reply.[2] *Just an Asian.* Grover, alarmed by the carefree response, bought some red cloth at a fabric store and carefully covered up the pool of blood with the cloth and some bricks so no one could step on it.[3] By the afternoon, the community had found out who had died there, and people were pissed. Chaggar had not only died, but had been killed.

Later that day, a few hundred people had gathered around the spot where Chaggar was murdered and painted slogans on the floor – 'We'll get you you racist scum' – and attacked cars going towards Norwood Green, known to be a white area.[4]

The next day, Sunday 6 June, the Indian Workers' Association (IWA) held a public meeting where its members discussed what action they would take, including the possibility of organising a march. This was too much talk and not enough action for many of the younger generation, and that very day Brown and Black men and women made their way to Southall police station to protest what was strongly suspected to be a racist killing, and the dismissive handling of it by the police.

Two people were arrested, including one of Chaggar's friends who had been with him when he was attacked. By the afternoon the crowd was 5,000 strong and they staged a sit-in at the station to demand the release of those arrested. It seemed to have worked: the two came out and announced to the crowd that they hadn't been charged, and the group dispersed, satisfied with their efforts. But it was all a ruse. The elders had convinced the two to lie to the crowd to end the protest and disperse people, and they were actually charged afterwards.[5]

The community elders such as those of the IWA called for calm and a measured response; they didn't support what they saw as the more extreme actions of the younger generations. From the other side, the youngsters saw the elders in the IWA as ineffective and too friendly with the establishment. Young people were done with the politicking of the IWA and the mainstream political parties. By Monday 7 June, the Southall Youth Movement (SYM) was officially founded.

What made the young people different was that they had spent most of their lives in the UK. Many were born there. These were the teenagers and young men who had been bussed to schools far from where they lived, to schools where they were rarely wanted. These were the teenagers and young men who had been bullied on the playground and banded together to protect themselves.[6] These teenagers and young men didn't know South Asia in the way their parents did. They knew England, Britain, the UK. The UK was their home, they didn't entertain thoughts of returning to the 'motherland'. And nor did they feel the gratitude that some of their parents did for the new life in the UK. This was their home and they didn't like the way they were being treated. They knew they would be here for the long term and had to make it a place that included them; where they could feel welcome, or at least safe and able to go about their lives without fear of attack.

The diaspora from all around South Asia was involved in the SYM. It was a secular group, not based on culture or religion; instead, it was race and class and an anti-colonial stance that bound the members. This is in such contrast to what comes later, the divide-and-conquer approach the state took to drive wedges between groups and define people based on faith. This is not to say there wasn't a lot of enmity and distrust between Brown people of different religions, for example Islamophobia among Sikhs and Hindus is not new, but to the younger generation it mattered less. The ties that bound were stronger than that which divided them.

The first thing some members of the SYM wanted was revenge for Chaggar's death, using the slogan 'blood for blood' as they huddled around the spot where Chaggar was murdered.[7] The de facto leaders of the new SYM managed to talk the members out of this tactic, recognising that they could do without more violence right now.[8]

Meanwhile, the official line was that this wasn't a racist attack and police reports did not admit a racial motive. John Kingsley Read, the former National Front leader and by then council member for National Front splinter group the National Party, said: 'I have been told that I cannot refer to coloured immigrants. So you will forgive me if I refer to niggers, wogs and coons. As for the murder of one Asian youth in Southall last weekend. That was terribly unfortunate. One down, a million to go.'[9]

For this speech, he was found not guilty under the Race Relations Act of inciting racial hatred after just ten minutes of deliberation by the all-white jury, and was even supported by the judge who said, 'you have been rightly acquitted ... in this England of ours we are allowed to have our own views still, thank goodness'.[10]

The two white teenagers responsible for Chaggar's murder, Jody Hill and Robert Hackman, were found. However, they were only charged with manslaughter, they pleaded not guilty to murder, and got four years in prison.[11] The judge took the same line as the police and repeated that this was not a racially motivated attack.[12] But the SYM didn't stop there.

The Southall Youth Movement formed because of racist violence and police apathy, and it continued to fight that cause in the following years. It wanted to scare off the National Front from Southall to make it a safe area to live in. The main method to achieve this was for the members to literally defend themselves and the streets from the National Front. Large groups would go to where National Front supporters would meet or roam, and push them back. They had insider information from a white supporter who became a mole in the National Front, telling the SYM where the NF was planning to meet so groups of SYM members could go to confront them at the pub or meeting place.[13] The SYM also organised social activities and sports.

For the SYM to be effective, it had to operate with certain rules. Firstly, no one outside the SYM should know who was in it. Balraj Purewal, one of the co-founders, was the only external face of the SYM.[14] To facilitate this, no photos should be taken during SYM operations. Secondly, you should only ask people to do something you were prepared to do yourself. If you didn't want to be fined, arrested, roughed up, then you couldn't ask other members to put themselves in situations where that was a possibility. Lastly, SYM members had to take care of other members' families if they got in trouble.[15]

This finely tuned organisation had a reach in every sports team, college and workplace in which young Brown Southall residents had a presence. With just an hour's notice it could have 600 people at its disposal. Purewal describes it like pressing a button and people would show up.[16]

The young people of Southall gained quite a reputation; in a parliamentary debate about the 1976 Race Relations Act and hate speech provisions, Conservative MP Ronald Bell said, 'I have no doubt that the Southall young would demonstrate against anything'.[17] He also went on to say, 'The kind of people who demonstrate are not usually very academically minded. People of any intellectual achievement do not have to demonstrate. They can express themselves with words, which is a rather more sophisticated form of expression.' He sounds like he would have been a lot of fun at parties.

Regardless of Bell's opinion on their members' intellectual abilities, Asian Youth Movements (AYM) sprang up all over the country: in Manchester, Bradford, Luton, Leicester, Nottingham, Sheffield and Birmingham. Each AYM differed slightly in approach and sometimes in its direct aims, though many AYMs had similar activities such as martial arts classes and self-defence patrols.[18] All the AYMs connected with each other and supported each other's campaigns. They featured each other's struggles in their newsletters, such as *Kala Tara* of AYM Bradford and *Liberation* of AYM Manchester. It wasn't unusual to jump on a bus to go to another city at the weekend to march in a demonstration.

Members of the Asian Youth Movements were courageous by necessity, the kind of courage that comes from being constantly oppressed, ignored and threatened with murder. When a planned National Front march was stopped by the authorities in Hyde, near Manchester, in October 1977, the leader of the NF led a one-person protest, protected by 2,000 police officers. This didn't stop Ramila Patel from the Bolton Asian Youth Movement from walking in front of him with a sign that read 'This man is a Nazi'. At least, it didn't stop her walking for about 70 metres before the police grabbed her placard and broke it.[19] My hero.

Like other anti-racist groups, the AYMs had a strong sense of international solidarity. There was an affinity with Ireland, and AYM members from Birmingham and Sheffield took buses to Northern Ireland to make connections with youth groups. A contingent from the Southall Youth Movement went to the World Youth Festival in Cuba in 1978.[20] The AYM logo was a Black fist, the instantly recognisable symbol of the Black Panthers. This wasn't appropriation but rather recognition of the shared struggle, unconfined by borders.

After three years of defending the streets, in 1979 came another major moment for Southall and the SYM.

In April of 1979 the National Front organised an election meeting the month before the general election, to be held in Southall's town hall. On St George's Day of all days. The IWA was active in trying to get the meeting moved from the area, as it saw it as unnecessarily provocative given that Southall wasn't exactly a National Front stronghold.

The IWA organised a community-wide meeting to discuss a plan of action, and people from all religions, organisations and groups showed up.[21] There were divided opinions as to what to do on the day of the National Front meeting: stay away or confront them? In the end, it was decided to organise a half-day strike accompanied by a sit-down protest from 5 p.m. on the streets around the town hall before the meeting was due to start at 7.30 p.m. And there was widespread agreement to stage a march the day before the meeting from Southall to the council offices in Ealing to present a petition against the gathering. On Sunday 22 April, 4,000 people marched, from all parts of the community, and around 7,000 had signed the petition.[22] There was a heavy police presence, many on horseback, under the auspices of protection for the protestors, but that didn't stop them arresting twenty-three of the protestors.[23]

The SYM didn't join the Sunday march, and a sit-down protest was all well and good but as one participant said, 'our leaders wanted a peaceful sit-down but what can you do with a peaceful sit-down here? We had to do something, the young people.'[24] That something turned out to be quite something, with clashes between police and civilians that would make Grunwick look tame.

On Monday 23 April, rumours circulated that the police were going to escort the National Front to the venue early to avoid the protestors. SYM members left their headquarters on Featherstone Road around midday to walk to the Broadway, where the town hall was, and the first SYM members were arrested within the hour.

Businesses and shops started closing from 1 p.m. as they had agreed to do. People filed onto the streets as police tried to block access to the town hall by cutting off the four streets that led to it, leading people to congregate as close as they could get from the surrounding areas. The sit-down protest on the streets that the IWA and co. had organised took place for a time, but no one was sitting for very long as the police tried to clear the crowds.

Numbers vary but somewhere between 3,000 and 5,000 people showed up that day in Southall to protest, and a similar number of police officers were present, including ninety-four on horseback and members of the Special Patrol Group (of Grunwick and Brick Lane infamy).[25] Supporters came from outside Southall too, including Blair Peach, a white, thirty-three-year-old New Zealand-born teacher who taught in east London, and some of his friends. As an active member of the Anti-Nazi League, supporting events like this was commonplace for him.

While supporters had brought friends, the police came with vans, riot shields, dogs and helicopters. The protest soon turned violent under the guise of crowd control. Eyewitnesses report seeing the police drive vans into the crowds, charge with horses and openly hit people with batons. One man had kidney damage from being kicked by a horse, another was so badly injured he had to have his testicles removed.[26] People scattered in every direction to escape the onslaught, running into gardens, down side streets and into the park. 'It was like a pitched battle,' Purewal says.[27] Racist abuse was hurled around, the police calling the protestors 'black bastards, black whores, wogs and niggers'.[28] National Front signs could be seen drawn into the condensation on windows of waiting police vans, presumably drawn by police officers themselves.[29] This had all happened by 4 p.m., hours before the National Front meeting was even due to begin.

The police stormed the community building that housed the collective People Unite, known as the home of reggae band Misty in Roots. The building was being used as a make-shift medical treatment facility for the day, but that didn't stop the police smashing up the place, damaging the musical equipment and smacking people on the head. The manager of Misty in Roots, Clarence Baker, was hit so hard he fell into a coma. A doctor treating people that day in the centre said, 'someone somewhere must have said this was OK. Someone somewhere was prepared to see people killed on a demo in Britain.'[30]

Unfortunately, those words were prophetic. On Orchard Avenue, a police officer hit Blair Peach on the head.[31] At least fourteen people witnessed the act. The Atwal family took Peach in as he was disoriented from the blow, but he died a few hours later in hospital. A pathologist's report said he died from a single blow to the head, which crushed his skull.[32]

Finally, the National Front arrived under police escort, a small group in the end, no more than sixty.[33] They were escorted into the town hall protected by lines of police officers, wearing smug smiles and waving, showing the peace sign or raising their fists in victory at the crowd. As they were inside, calling for Southall to be razed to the ground, ironically it wasn't actually the National Front that was the threat.

At least 1,000 people were injured that day and more than 700 were arrested. The arrestees were mostly Brown and teenagers. The majority were not charged; some were dumped on the outskirts of Southall and told to make their way home. Of the 342 charged, many were convicted for possession of weapons or disturbing the peace. When they got to a police station, charge sheets had been pre-prepared and their names already written on them.

It's hard not to see the whole event as a way to try and quash the Southall Youth Movement and other local organisations, as many of those who were arrested were SYM members.[34] The police and courts used crafty techniques to prevent any further demonstrations and maximise prosecutions. Some of those charged were tried more than twenty miles away from Southall in Barnet, where it would be all the harder to organise pickets or protests. The type of charges that were brought meant that there would only be a magistrate's hearing rather than trial by jury. The magistrates 'bound over' witnesses, which meant that someone would go to testify in court and end up somehow being implicated themselves.[35] Not only implicated but they had to pay a sum of money as a guarantee and promise to be on their best behaviour, usually for a year. And this was all without actually being charged. Magistrates demonstrated a clear preference for police testimony over any other witnesses, in one instance favouring the testimony of one police officer against seven other witnesses, who included a doctor and a paramedic.[36] Meanwhile, the media painted the events as a 'riot'.

Southall wouldn't be defeated though. Members of the community soon created a Southall Defence Committee with organisations such as the SYM, the IWA and Southall Rights to help the defendants and monitor and publicise cases.[37] Despite the distance to Barnet, members of the various organisations were in the courtroom every day for seven months to take notes while others organised solicitors and raised funds.[38]

'We are not petty criminals,' reads a bulletin of the Southall Defence Committee, 'but people who protested against the filth and lies of a racist organisation. We fought for our dignity and respect. So we demand that all the charges be dropped that have been thrust upon us.'[39] There was a two-day fundraising concert in July organised by People Unite with Aswad, the Clash and Misty in Roots on the billing. The leaflet for the event read 'Southall Kids Are Innocent'.

The campaigning saw the conviction rate of the charged drop from 79 per cent to 52 per cent, a huge achievement.[40] They called upon lawyer Gareth Peirce to defend a number of those charged, and she would prove to be a loyal ally to the AYM.

Fifteen thousand people turned out for Blair Peach's funeral. Anti-racists cried out for an inquiry, for someone in the police force to be brought to justice. The police conducted an internal investigation but the results weren't made public, and no one was charged. It became publicly known that it was probably one of six SPG officers who inflicted the blow, but there was apparently little evidence to go on. The inquest was a sham; the coroner stopped evidence from being made public. In the end, the jury declared 'death by misadventure'.

But the community didn't forget. In 1980, a year after Peach's murder, they protested on the streets chanting the names of the six SPG officers – one of whom had probably killed Blair Peach.[41]

*

The Southall Youth Movement wasn't the only one with its work cut out. One of the most active AYMs was in Bradford. As a southerner, the most I knew about Bradford growing up was from its fleeting appearance in the 1999 film *East is East*. Formerly known as 'Woolopolis' for its importance to the wool trade, in the heyday of the Empire it was one of the richest cities in the world. More recently, it was named the second least romantic place in the UK by a Hotels.com poll.*[42]

Bradford is also known for giving us Zayn Malik from One Direction, and for winning the coveted title of Curry Capital of Britain for six consecutive years, making Bradford, for many, the undisputed curry capital of the UK.[43] (This is a hot-button issue and I can hear some of you gasping in disbelief, but can we all agree that there are numerous towns and cities with great South Asian food and focus on the more important things to hand, please?)

As in the rest of the UK, the National Front had a presence in Bradford and its members liked to stalk the areas where Brown people lived, like Manningham, a suburb of the city. And as in other places, there was a disconnect between the tactics of the older generations versus the younger ones. In 1976 the National Front organised a march through Manningham, but the counter-demonstration was organised in the city centre. Some of the young people, realising the futility of a counter-march in an entirely different location to the actual march, decided to go back to Manningham. They broke through the police presence and the day ended in clashes with the National Front and twenty-four arrests.[44]

---

* Scunthorpe came bottom of the list.

The Bradford Asian Youth Movement was formed in 1978 to counter these attacks on the community and state repression.[45] The serial killer known as the Yorkshire Ripper was in full force at the time and the police used that as an excuse to stop young Brown and Black people, even though it was known that the Ripper was white.[46]

Fascism and police brutality weren't the only targets of the AYMs; they also campaigned against the violence of the immigration system. Of the many immigration cases, one of the most successful for the Bradford AYM was the case of Anwar Ditta.

Ditta lived in Rochdale, and she attended a meeting in Longsight Library in Manchester, in November 1979, which was convened to discuss the cases of Nasira Begum and Nasreen Akhtar, who were threatened with deportation. Ditta could relate to immigration issues. She was born in the UK, but after her parents separated she was sent to live in Pakistan with relatives. There, she married and had three children.

She and her husband decided to move to the UK in 1975, making the tough decision to leave the children behind until they could get settled. They had been married via Islamic law, which they thought would not be valid under British law, and so listed their marital statuses as 'bachelor' and 'spinster' on their entry forms.[47] Once in Rochdale, they got married again, so that it would be recognised by the state. In September 1976, now with a fourth child in the family and settled, they applied for their other three children to join them.

In February 1978, a year and a half after they had applied, they finally got invited to an immigration interview. More than a year after that, in May 1979, their application was denied.[48]

The government wasn't convinced that the three children actually belonged to Anwar Ditta. In fact, the Home Office suspected that Ditta had never been in Pakistan and that the Anwar Ditta on the Pakistani marriage certificate was a *different* Anwar Ditta who so happened to marry her husband.[49] Ditta appealed. She sent photos, birth certificates and had the hospital confirm that she had given birth to four children. Her father swore an affidavit that she had been in Pakistan.[50] She offered to do blood tests.

It was in the midst of this appeal that she ended up in Longsight Library. When the convenors asked at the end of the meeting if anyone else had any immigration issues to raise, she stood up and told her story.

Her story moved and angered the crowd. Many organisations took up Ditta's case, forming the Anwar Ditta Defence Campaign, with the AYM Manchester, AYM Bradford and Ditta herself at the helm. They protested, picketed Conservative Party offices, sent petitions with thousands of signatories, and got the South Manchester Law Centre on board to help with the appeal. Ditta spoke at 400 events in less than eighteen months. That's roughly one event every 1.4 days. She spoke at law centres, student unions and the Leicester Women's Festival.[51]

Ditta said, 'when a person commits a crime, for example murder, they only need one or two witnesses to convict him. I've got more than ten or twenty witnesses who can prove they are my children, but the Home Office doesn't bother to ask them.'[52] She implored her Liberal Party MP Cyril Smith to look into her case, in writing and in person at a party committee meeting, and his response was, 'I don't know what all the fuss is about.'[53] Yes, this is Cyril Smith of child sexual abuse allegations. 'I just lost it,' Ditta said. Another party member asked why she didn't just 'go back to where she comes from'. 'Shall I go back to Birmingham, then?' she responded. Despite the lack of support from some, high-profile support was won for the campaign, including from celebrities such as Vanessa Redgrave.

It was all to no avail, her appeal was rejected in July 1980. That didn't stop the campaign. Ditta wrote to Cyril Smith again; he responded, 'I am sorry – I do not feel able to assist further, in view of past history. I am sure your "friends" will do all they can.'[54] The campaign caught the attention of people at Granada TV who made the show *World in Action*, and they investigated. They travelled to Pakistan to meet people in Anwar Ditta's area, and did blood tests, in the days before DNA was used regularly in immigration cases.

The evidence was damning against the Home Office, there was ample evidence to prove maternity, and the programme concluded that the immigration authorities had set Ditta 'an impossible task'.[55] The day after the show aired, Anwar Ditta's children were granted entry. After six years apart, the family was finally reunited, but it wasn't all celebrations; they had the hard task ahead of repairing a family that had been kept apart for so long.

Despite its success, the Bradford AYM soon fractured. Everything they did was self-funded or resourced. The first office premises was a squat, and Tariq Mehmood was Bradford AYM's one employee, paid from 25p membership dues. It was enough to give him the salary equivalent to someone working in industry in the area.[56] There was never any issue funding all the activities of the AYM as the membership was so dedicated.

Then the AYM came into a windfall as it received £3,000 from the Commission for Racial Equality. Suddenly, the AYM wasn't just accountable to its members, but to this state institution.[57] As it had for other organisations before it, this money divided the AYM between those who saw it as contradictory to take state funds while opposing the state, and those who saw it as a positive step. This was more money than the organisation had ever had, surely it could only be a good thing? Some members, including the AYM's one paid employee Mehmood, disagreed, and split from the AYM to form the United Black Youth League (UBYL) in 1981. Mehmood had experienced bussing and racist violence as a child arriving in the UK; he firmly believed that Britain continually exploited Brown people and consequently he did not trust in the establishment.[58]

This was 1981 and uprisings were happening all over the country (more on that in the next chapter). As they bubbled throughout the UK, a rumour was going around Bradford that the National Front was going to hold a march on 11 July and up to 300 people were expected.[59] This was par for the course by now, and the young people knew that it was also par for the course that the police wouldn't do much to protect them. They had seen what was happening around the rest of the UK, and previously in Bradford. So they took matters into their own hands. Members of the UBYL constructed petrol bombs in glass milk bottles, ready to use to protect themselves if needed.

On the day of the march, Brown, Black and white allies gathered together to defend the city. In the end, the march didn't take place and the petrol bombs weren't used, though some disputes with the police led to arrests of UBYL members, including four who would later become part of the 'Bradford 12'.[60] The arrests were no big deal though, it was standard practice, and they would surely be released soon. At least that's what the UBYL thought.

The thirty-eight petrol bombs were discarded near where they had been made, in some bushes on the grounds of a hospital. Six days later they were found by a gardener, who contacted the police. The police arranged a sting operation to try and catch who had made them; they got rid of the petrol and filled them with tea, and watched the area to catch the perpetrators when they came back for their bombs.[61] It was unsuccessful. The bombs had been dumped and the UBYL wasn't interested in retrieving them, but the suspects, two of whom had left fingerprints on the bottles, were arrested anyway.[62] Upon interrogation, one of the suspects crumbled and mentioned the names of seven other UBYL members.[63]

By the end of July, dawn raids had led to dozens of arrests in relation to the bombs, including Brown and Black men and at least one woman. Many had been marked by Special Branch.[64] Eventually eleven Brown men were charged with conspiracy to damage property by fire or explosion, and conspiracy to cause grievous bodily harm. They had been prevented from exercising their legal right to a solicitor or to have visitors during the first two days after their arrest, in which time they were made to give statements.[65]

The police put forward the idea that they were intending

to use the bombs on property and even against the police. The prosecuting lawyer said, 'it was only because the ring-leaders were arrested that things did not prove much worse'.[66] The charge of conspiracy meant not only that they faced a possibility of life imprisonment, but that this would not be a simple criminal trial but a political one: they were being called terrorists.

The UBYL saw the charges as the state's revenge for its involvement in high-profile campaigns such as Anwar Ditta's and that of Gary Pemberton, who had been framed by the police for assault.[67] White supremacists didn't receive such charges; when forty young white people threw a petrol bomb and attacked a Brown student, two of them were taken to court and charged with assault and stealing petrol.[68]

Later, another young Brown man was arrested and charged with the same offences. The 'Bradford 12' were complete. The twelve were: Ahmed Ebrahim Mansoor, Bahram Noor Khan, Giovanni Singh, Ishaq Mohammed Kazi, Jayesh Amin, Masood Malik, Pravin Patel, Sabir Hussain, Saeed Hussain, Tariq Mehmood, Tarlochan Gata-Aura and Vasant Patel. They ranged from eighteen years old to twenty-five.

The majority of the Bradford 12 were initially not granted bail, with the exception of three who agreed not to attend any political meetings as part of the bail conditions. Saeed Hussain had to have daily check-ins and stay inside at night as part of his bail conditions.[69] By 22 October 1981, a few months after their arrest, the rest were granted bail, with strict conditions seen as the equivalent of a gagging order or 'South African-style house arrest'.[70]

It was not going to be a quick process and the Bradford

12 would have to wait until 1982 for their trial. Meanwhile, lawyers Ruth Bundey and Gareth Peirce joined the campaign, as well as Michael Mansfield and Ian Macdonald of Mangrove Nine fame.

It is impossible to ignore the parallels with the Mangrove Nine trial of a decade earlier:

- An obvious ploy to take down an organisation that the police had been monitoring? Check
- Disproportionate charges as a deterrent to other groups? Check
- Sensationalist reporting and statements from the prosecution to show the police as the victims? Check

Like the Mangrove Nine, a campaign was mounted to free the Bradford 12. Eight hundred people showed up at a meeting in support of them. Every court appearance even before the trial proper was picketed by their supporters, including a hundred people who showed up at the initial Bradford City Court hearing on 12 August, and there were pickets outside the office of the director of public prosecutions in London.[71] There was a national demonstration on Saturday 12 December 1981 in Manningham Park, advertised with statements including 'state attack on black people must stop' and 'the only conspiracy is police conspiracy'.[72]

There was so much support for the Bradford 12 but in-fighting among groups meant that there was no unified campaign. The July 11th Action Committee was formed, then the Bradford 12 Defence Campaign and the United Black Youth

Defence Committee. Notably, the AYM Bradford did not join any of the campaigns as an organisation, though many members supported the Bradford 12 in their individual capacity.

The campaigns urged people to set up their own local support committees, organise meetings and pickets, send funds for the campaign and write letters to the director of public prosecutions, home secretary, chief constable of the West Yorkshire Police and the lord chancellor. Multiple cities had their own defence campaigns (the London Support Group was organised from Southall), and there was even protest action as far as Los Angeles, organised by Black Women for Wages for Housework, who picketed the British Consulate.[73]

The various groups all recognised the implications of this trial for all oppressed people in the UK. The July 11th Action Committee said, 'their trial is our trial, Asians, West Indians and Africans must unite and struggle to win their freedom. We call upon white workers and unemployed to support us. Together we must say NO to political repression.'[74] Its HQ was Textile Hall in Bradford, which was fire-bombed in late August 1981. The police had been warned by an anonymous tip that it would be burned down but they said that it was not arson.[75]

The year 1982 rolled around and the trial was looming. The political nature of the trial was obvious from the beginning. Saeed Hussain's original solicitor even pulled out due to the political focus as he didn't want to put his 'professional independence' at risk.[76] Tariq Mehmood decided to defend himself, with the support of Ian Macdonald and the rest of the defendants. With a possible outcome of life in prison, he wanted to speak for himself at least.

The trial started on 26 April 1982 in Leeds, with 500 Bradford 12 supporters inside and outside the courtroom.[77] The trial was fraught with conflict from the beginning. The assigned jury was all white, mostly middle-class. The defence contested this make-up, just like Mangrove: how could a jury to hear the case of Brown people possibly not have called up any Brown or Black people?

The judge refused the initial application to change the jury, before acquiescing and combining two jury panels to diversify the options.[78] Each potential juror was asked four questions to vet them: did they or any immediate family member have any sympathy or allegiance to a group which disliked non-whites? Were they or any immediate family a member of the National Front, the British Movement or Column 88 (two other neo-Nazi organisations)? Did they have an immediate family member serving in the police? Did they or their family experience any loss during the uprisings in Leeds or Bradford in 1981?[79] The final jury consisted of seven women, five men, and included five Brown and Black people and some working-class representation. The trial proper could finally begin.

The defendants had a united front for the trial. They all pleaded not guilty. For eleven of them this was on the basis that they were entitled to defend themselves against fascists given the state of affairs in the UK, and they didn't intend to use the bombs against the police and public property as they were accused of doing. They didn't deny making the bombs, but they disputed the alleged intention behind doing so. In short: self-defence was no offence. Jayesh Amin's defence was based on the fact that he wasn't even out on 11 July: he had just been at home watching cricket.[80]

There were too many defendants to all sit in the dock, so half of them sat in the dock while the rest sat with the solicitors.[81] As with all criminal cases, the prosecution went first to present its case. The prosecutor's case rested on confessions that some of the twelve had supposedly made, in which the 'real' purpose of the petrol bombs was apparently uncovered. Thirty-seven police officers confirmed that the statements reflected exactly what the defendants had said.[82]

The defence took issue with these statements. They argued that they were fabricated, with lines like 'further to my previous statement' and 'I would like to clarify the point which I did not mention before', which were not really in keeping with the parlance of a Bradford teen.[83] It also didn't help Officer Sidebottom's case when his own statement was found to include those exact turns of phrase.[84]

Another officer, Officer Maloney, had asked Sabir Hussain 196 questions during questioning without taking any notes but had supposedly written down everything later word for word. For the defence, Helena Kennedy then asked him, 'what was the first question I asked you today?'

'I can't remember,' answered Maloney.[85]

Gavel drop!

The other prong of attack in the prosecution's case was denying that there was any racism in Bradford, or more widely. Officer after officer denied any cause for concern, and purported not to know about a Home Office report from 1981, *Racial Attacks*, which said the exact opposite, that there was indeed a cause for concern as attacks on Black and Brown people had been increasing. The acting superintendent said he was proud of race relations.[86] Members of the public watching from the gallery literally gasped at the assertions.[87]

The judge even got so tired of the police statements that he asked, 'you have heard of Deptford, haven't you?', a reference to the New Cross fire from January 1981, covered in the next chapter, but for now know that it was shorthand for 'you can't possibly be that ignorant, can you?'[88]

By the end of the prosecution's case, the jury had seen a police force that seemed either wilfully ignorant of the realities of the communities they were meant to protect, or, more likely, a police force intent on lying to bolster their case.

Jayesh Amin was cleared of all charges at this point. It turns out that watching cricket is not conspiratorial after all.

It was now the turn of the defence. They worked to expose the conspiratorial behaviour of the police themselves. The West Yorkshire police had something of a reputation by this point of framing people, such as in the case of George Lindo, who was convicted for armed robbery on the basis of a false confession, which was overturned after a campaign. The police statements of the arrests weren't made until the 18 August, some three weeks after the arrests had been made, giving them plenty of time to fabricate their story.[89] According to the police, Tariq Mehmood had told them that 'coloured people are less intelligent than yourselves', to which he responded in the courtroom, 'are you trying to tell the jury that I would use those words about my people?'[90]

The defence called in people who could attest to what life was like for Brown and Black people in the UK and the deficiencies of the police. Witnesses came not just from Bradford but from all over the UK. The jury heard from magistrates, bus drivers, lawyers, community relations officers, AYM members, councillors, bookstore owners and Anwar Ditta.[91] There were a lot of people to contest the police assertion that racism was not A Thing. A firefighter from London described an arson attack in Walthamstow in which petrol was poured through the letterbox of a house and set alight, killing a Brown woman and her three children.[92]

The police pleading ignorance was even harder to digest when it came to light that Special Branch had been monitoring UBYL and had even searched the houses of Tariq Mehmood and Tarlochan Gata-Aura.[93] They seized materials including a Malcolm X book and political magazines such as the *New Statesman*, which they used as evidence in the trial.[94]

Nine of the remaining eleven defendants exercised their right not to submit to cross-examination, instead choosing to read out statements from the dock. They were advised to do this by their solicitors who were afraid of the pressure of cross-examination.[95] None of them refuted their part in the bomb production. Statement after statement admitted to making the bombs, or helping with the planning, and reinforced the point that they were made in self-defence. They all spoke of the fear they lived with on a daily basis.

Pravin Patel said, 'I have read articles on racial attacks not just in Bradford but other parts of the country ... When I have read things like this, I have had fear inside me thinking that my family or someone I love might be attacked or killed in a similar manner.'[96] Bahram Noor Khan was worried for his dad who had a shop near Manningham. Masood Malik recalls his brother talking about sealing their home's letterbox to prevent an arson attack. Saeed Hussain explained he started thinking politically from being treated differently at school and that:

> We have in this country certain people called politicians. My view is that there is no special category under which certain people come, we are all politicians. Politics is not about passing degrees at Oxford or Cambridge. Every ordinary day for every ordinary person is politics. Not being about to pay for the winter fuel bill – that's politics. Not being about to feed your family – that's politics. Not being able to afford school uniform for your children – that's politics. Living in slums in the damp – that's politics.[97]

They all said they would do it again.[98] Tarlochan Gata-Aura took to the stand, and over three days he also reinforced the idea that the bombs were for self-defence: 'After what happened in Southall, Deptford and Coventry where a man was stabbed to death in the street in daytime ... I could give you endless examples ... It would not be unique if such an attack took place ... my personal experience is that the police have not in fact defended our community.'[99]

Under cross-examination by the prosecution, he explained that they had intended simply to make a 'shield of fire ... maybe you don't know what it is to be black in this racist society. In such a situation, the only thing you can think of is measures you might take to defend yourself.'[100] *Race Today* called Gata-Aura's time on the stand the high point of the trial.[101]

The campaign for the Bradford 12 didn't wane during the trial. Leeds Crown Court was picketed almost daily, with a mass picket every Wednesday, and included individuals whom the Bradford 12 had helped in immigration cases, such as Nasira Begum.[102] Chants of 'Free the Bradford 12' could be heard in the court as people gathered outside, watched by 'pairs of wary police officers'.[103] The campaign also organised an investigation to gather evidence of all the racist attacks that had taken place to counter the prosecution's denial of racism.[104]

The defence's case was over and closing arguments had been made. The prosecution implored the jury to think about 'what sort of society do we want to live in?' and from 10.30 a.m. on Tuesday 15 June the jury had to do just that.[105] They had to decide on two things: were the petrol bombs legal given the lack of police protection of the community? And did the police indeed make up evidence? The judge warned them that what they decided would set a precedent one way or another and a wrong verdict could 'lead to chaos and confusion in the country'.[106]

On the morning of 16 June, after a day of discussions, the jury declared that the remaining Bradford 12 were not guilty. The jury had decided that they wanted to live in a society in which everyone should be protected, and, if protection was not forthcoming, that it was reasonable for someone to protect themselves.

Self-defence was no offence.

The result elicited tears, clapping and cheering in the courtroom, which the judge ended up ignoring when it was clear he couldn't stop the celebrations.[107]

Tariq Mehmood said of their acquittal, 'the police made a mountain out of a molehill and in so doing made a monument to our beliefs: the right to self-defence by a community under attack'.[108] The Bradford 12 Defence Committee said, 'these defendants have shown that fascist hooligans cannot rule Britain's streets'.[109] During the pub celebrations afterwards, one of the female jurors revealed a 'Free the Bradford 12' T-shirt she was wearing under her clothes.[110]

It wasn't all jubilation though, Mehmood and some others realising that this might be the beginning and not the end. 'The police were made to look stupid in court ... and they don't like that,' said Mehmood.[111] Not only that, but the judge was right, the decision of the jury had major implications. Though defending oneself was legal under certain circumstances, there was now a precedent for self-defence as an argument.

Did this mean that anyone could make petrol bombs and claim self-defence? It was unclear if the same claim could be used by groups such as the National Front. Junior Rashid, a member of the AYM, said, 'what happens if twelve fascists with some sort of weapons are charged, and they claim they've got them for self-defence? Will they be off the hook?'[112] As it was, the self-defence is no offence argument actually helped in other cases of people fighting racism. It was used in the case of the Newham 8 in 1983 after students were arrested for protecting themselves.[113]

On a less positive note, the case also led to the government getting rid of the right of defendants to make a statement from the dock, or just stay silent and not be subject to cross-examination on the stand. This right had protected people in many circumstances, such as those whose health would suffer, people with a language barrier, or those who would be easily confused by leading questions.[114] It was also the only safe way for defendants to tell stories of police corruption.

The UBYL didn't survive the trial and campaign. The toll of having its leadership removed, campaigning, and police actions was far too much for the relatively new group. But AYM branches continued into the late 1980s and even 1990s.

Gareth Peirce, who defended half of the Bradford 12, continues to defend the rights of victims of state racism, such as in 2021 in the case of the West Midlands 3, in which three British Sikh activists faced extradition to India to face charges for an attack for which there was no evidence.

Tariq Mehmood of the Bradford 12 is a writer and filmmaker.

Back in Southall, Clarence Baker, the manager of the band Misty in Roots who had been in a coma ever since 23 April 1979, when the police attacked him, woke up after three months. To a country where Thatcher was now prime minister. The People Unite building was demolished a few months after the demonstration.

In 2010, thirty-one years after Blair Peach's death, the Metropolitan Police released the internal Cass report written at the time. It confirmed what everyone knew, that Peach was 'almost certainly' killed by one of six SPG officers.[115] It also states that three of the officers clearly conspired to obstruct the investigation and recommends actions be taken against them. Searches of SPG officers' lockers had found crowbars, knives, a lead-weighted leather stick and Nazi regalia.[116]

The response by the police, which accompanied the newly

released material, said, 'this of course is and has always been a grave concern to the Met'.[117] The government finally apologised to Blair Peach's family after the report was released.[118] It also came to light as part of the 'Spy Cops' scandal that Peach's partner, Celia Stubbs, was spied on for nearly twenty years as she campaigned for justice.[119] No one has ever been charged with Peach's death.

A primary school named in honour of Blair Peach sits on Beaconsfield Road in Southall. And three blue plaques adorn the outside of Southall town hall in honour of Gurdip Singh Chaggar, Blair Peach, and Misty in Roots and People Unite. They were all stolen after the murder of George Floyd in 2020 led to new Black Lives Matter marches across the world, but they are now back in their rightful place once more.

# Chapter Eleven

# 1981

'Thirteen dead and nothing said.'[1]

Slogan following the New Cross fire

Black People's Day of Action, 2 March (1981)

*© Vron Ware. Courtesy of Autograph, London.*

What does January usually look like for you? For me, after the
fog of New Year's Eve regret has lifted and the tinge of sadness

that Christmas is over has faded, January is usually full of new hope. New Year, New Me. New Year, New Possibilities. I don't write resolutions but it is a time of reflection on the year gone by, and to dream about what I want to do and who I want to be over the next twelve months. It's a pretty magical time. That is, until mid-January, and then it becomes the longest and dreariest month of the year.

January 1981. Unemployment was rising and had already hit 8.9 per cent.[2] Black and Brown people woke up in the new year to unemployment often far higher than that, along with inadequate housing and ongoing police discrimination. 'There's No One Quite Like Grandma' was number one in the charts, soon to be replaced by John Lennon's 'Imagine'. Thatcher had been in power for nearly two years, and so far Britain's first female prime minister was proving to be as dangerous as her male predecessors. But, progress, right?

Not to be deterred by the January blues, on the night of Saturday 17 January in south London, between sixty and one hundred teenagers and young adults got together for the joint birthday party of teenagers Yvonne Ruddock and Angela Jackson at 439 New Cross Road. The party continued into the early hours of Sunday morning. People talked, danced, laughed and, I imagine, flirted, as is likely to happen at a party. Classic teenage stuff. Sometime around 5.30 a.m., the house caught fire. It spread quickly and the stairs collapsed, trapping many partygoers on the upper floors. Some jumped out of the window to try and escape. Some didn't get out.

Thirteen young Black people died from the fire, either that night or in the following weeks from severe injuries. They were: Andrew Gooding, Gerry Francis, Glen Powell, Humphrey

Brown, Lillian Henry, Lloyd Hall, Owen Thompson, Patricia Johnson, Patrick Cummings, Paul Ruddock, Peter Campbell, Yvonne Ruddock and Steve Collins.

Birthday girl Yvonne Ruddock and her brother Paul both died. Nearly thirty people were seriously injured.

The initial assessment from the police was that it was likely an arson attack. Yet another firebomb. Firebombing and arson had become so common this was a realistic possibility, and someone had seen a man outside acting suspiciously before driving off in a white van. The police soon backtracked from this theory and instead argued that a fight at the party caused the fire. Some of the survivors of the fire, mere teenagers, were interrogated and bullied into making statements to that effect.[3] The victims were being treated as suspects.

The relationship between the Black community and the police was already tense countrywide due to the widespread use of the 'sus' laws, the clashes at the Notting Hill Carnival in 1976, and events from the year before in St Pauls, Bristol, where there had been a showdown between the police and the Black community. The same St Pauls from Chapter Three, the district with high numbers of Black residents as at first it was the only place that they could find accommodation because it was so run-down.

On 2 April 1980, the police raided the Black and White Café in Bristol on suspicion that it was selling alcohol without a licence. Similar to the Mangrove, the Black and White Café was frequently raided. On this particular occasion, the police were met with a lot of aggrieved Black locals who gathered outside to defend the café and it escalated into a clash between police and the Black community, with burned-out police cars, fire engine and Lloyd's Bank branch, and more than a hundred arrests.[4] Even though it happened in a different city, the Black community in London felt the impact of St Pauls, and the treatment of the New Cross fire victims was a devastating blow to a community already tired and frustrated about racist policing and their second-class citizen status.

The media stayed quiet after the New Cross fire, barely acknowledging one of the biggest tragedies ever to befall the Black community in the UK. It is customary for politicians to make statements and send condolences to families in tragic times, but Prime Minister Margaret Thatcher was silent. The local MP didn't say anything for weeks either. In contrast, a fire a few weeks later in Dublin, which killed more than forty people, led to an immediate outpouring of condolences from public figures, including Thatcher. Some lives mattered more than others.

A few days after the New Cross fire a meeting was held at the Moonshot club, a Black community centre in Lewisham, which had itself been firebombed in 1977. Members of the *Race Today* Collective, the Black Parents' Movement and Black Youth Movement (formerly the Black Students' Movement) organised the meeting to discuss a response to the New Cross tragedy. It was intended to be a planning committee get-together, maybe 40 people maximum, in advance of a public meeting, but ended up attracting around 300 people.[5]

The meeting was tense, emotions running high after the fire. Some people suggested fighting fire with fire.[6] Farrukh Dhondy, from the *Race Today* Collective, attended with a white woman who was asked to leave as her presence was seen as provocative to some.[7] Others thought that Asians shouldn't be present either, though Mrs Ruddock who lost two children in the fire was herself Asian.[8]

It was clear that the fire had seriously affected the community, and a New Cross Massacre Action Committee, Fire Fund and Fact-Finding Commission were all formed at the meeting that day. The fund would raise money for the bereaved families and even Black prisoners at Wormwood Scrubs donated money.[9] The Fact-Finding Commission would interview the survivors and bereaved families, knowing that the police investigation was patchy at best, inaccurate and misleading at worst.[10] The bereaved parents were encouraged to set up their own group too.

The Action Committee was led by John La Rose (of New Beacon Books) and Darcus Howe (of the Mangrove Nine), and included organisations such as the Black Parents Movement, Black Youth Movement, *Race Today* Collective and the Black Unity and Freedom Party. They organised a public gathering for the following Sunday, which 2,000 people attended from all over the country.[11] Like the events in St Pauls in 1980, the fire and its mishandling by the state had not just affected a small part of London. The meeting ended with a police-approved vigil outside 439 New Cross Road, where gatherers stayed on and blocked the busy A2 road for hours.[12] They would not be ignored.

The next day, the committee hatched a plan for a national demonstration on a scale like no other ever seen in the UK. This one would be different to all the other marches that had gone before.

Marches were usually held on a weekend, following a well-trodden path that ended in Trafalgar Square or Hyde Park, and inconveniencing no one other than tourists. But not this one. This march was deliberately planned for a Monday, 2 March, so as to attract maximum attention and cause maximum disruption, as it was much harder to be buried in obscurity if you marched through London on a workday. The route was different from the usual marches too: this one would go over Blackfriars Bridge into the City of London, which no protest had done since the Chartists, a working-class movement, in 1848.

The Action Committee planned carefully throughout February 1981, meeting weekly and touring the country to spread the word about the march and distribute leaflets and posters, sometimes attending more than one meeting a day. Solidarity being what it was, Anwar Ditta also spoke at the meeting in Manningham alongside Darcus Howe and George Lindo, who we saw in the previous chapter had been wrongfully imprisoned.[13] People were mobilised wherever they were, from churches to youth groups to dances to colleges. Howe would report back to the *Race Today* offices with his views on the reception from people, the likelihood that people would organise to attend the march, and details of key contacts.[14] The route of the march was discussed and agreed with the police.

Meanwhile the committee also wrote to the prime minister and the Queen to express its disappointment and anger at the lack of response, and committee member Sybil Phoenix eventually got a response about five weeks later. Thatcher told Phoenix to pass on her condolences to the families but there were no personalised condolences.[15] The families did receive one personalised letter though, from a National Front organiser, Brian Bunting, who said, 'what a great day last Sunday, when I heard about the fire and all those niggers going up in flames'.[16]

On Monday 2 March 1981, one of the organisers from the *Race Today* Collective, Leila Hassan Howe (she was married to Darcus Howe), went to the meeting point at 8.30 a.m. and felt apprehensive; it was raining and they were asking people to forfeit a day's paid work to march on a Monday, would it work out?[17] She needn't have worried. By the time the march set off at 11 a.m., half an hour earlier than planned to avoid any police disruption, there were already thousands of people gathered.

The bereaved parents were at the front of the march as it made its way past the scene of the fire on New Cross Road, through Peckham and the heart of Black south London to reach Blackfriars Bridge. They collected protestors along the way; people left their offices and schoolchildren jumped over fences and walked out of school en masse to join in.[18] Dhondy went with around twenty young Bengalis from the East End who wanted to show their support.[19] Having the march on a working day didn't stop turnout: it would actually be the biggest march to date of the Black community.

Marchers carried thirteen red banners bearing the names and dates of birth and death of each of the deceased. Others carried photos of the teenagers who were their children, friends and community members. Darcus Howe shouted through a megaphone, 'this is the Black People's Day of Action. This is the Black insurrection'.[20] Anger and resistance coursed through the streets with shouts of 'Thirteen dead and nothing said', and placards carrying slogans like 'Ain't no stopping us now we are on the move', 'Mrs Thatcher sends sympathy to Ireland but not for thirteen young blacks in London, England'. And 'Blood aga run if justice na come', which was echoed in the name of a film made by Menelik Shabazz of the day's events, called *Blood Ah Go Run*. Others carried umbrellas to keep off the heavy rain.

The police were waiting for the march at Blackfriars Bridge and didn't want to let it pass, even though they had approved the route beforehand. Disrupting the sacred City of London was a step too far after all. Standing a few lines deep in riot gear the police tried to push the protestors back. The protestors at the front pushed right back, leading to some confrontations. Eventually the police fell back and the marchers made it across, having won the 'Battle of Blackfriars Bridge' and feeling elated.[21] They marched through the heart of British media, down the narrow Fleet Street, shouting 'Fleet Street liars!' to show their disdain for the media's allegiance to the state and the police. Some journalists shouted racial abuse at the protestors as they walked past, making monkey noises and throwing banana skins.[22]

The march ended in Hyde Park, twelve miles and eight hours after it started. Action Committee leader John La Rose and a delegation of parents who lost their children in the fire broke off from the main march to go to the Houses of Parliament, Scotland Yard and Downing Street to hand in 'The Declaration of New Cross', part of which read:

The authorities have ignored for three decades the pain, the rage and outrage of the black communities around the country at the racial murders, injuries and threats to our existence. Threats have come even from the highest authorities in the land ... We warn the country and the world that there will be no social peace while blacks are attacked, killed, injured and maimed with impunity on the streets or in our homes.[23]

Around 20,000 people marched that day. That's right, 20,000. Around 90 per cent were Black, and had come from all over the country and even France. Everyone turned out for the Black People's Day of Action. It was *the* march to end all marches. An anonymous account of the day from the time said, 'the demonstrators clogged the arteries of the city; curdling its blood, stopping its heart, they brought the capital to a stunned standstill'.[24] Poet and activist Linton Kwesi Johnson was one of the stewards on the day and he said, 'it was the most powerful, most spectacular expression of black political power'.[25]

After the Day of Action, you would think it would be hard to continue to ignore the New Cross tragedy. However, the media focused on the Day of Action itself and painted it as a 'riot'. The *Sun* had 'Day the Blacks Ran Riot in London' plastered over its pages.[26] The *Daily Express* front page said, 'Rampage of a Mob'.[27] Inflammatory headlines were almost invariably accompanied by images from the clashes on Blackfriars Bridge and accounts of the actions of a small group of people who had broken away from the protest to rob a jewellery store.

The inquest into the fire deaths started in April. Ian Macdonald and Michael Mansfield of Mangrove Nine fame, and Gareth Peirce from the Bradford 12 trial, represented the parents. By this point, the police were not putting forward any theories that involved a racist angle and had abandoned the theory that the fire was started after a fight. They believed it was either arson from outside, or arson or an accident from the inside.

The inquest was riddled with unusual practices, such as the coroner not taking any notes during the proceedings as witnesses gave their statements. It is the coroner who summarises evidence for the jury at the end of the inquest, which one can only imagine is much harder to do from memory. The jury returned an open verdict; they could not decide how the fire was started. The New Cross Massacre Action Committee had called for a week-long picket during the inquest and appealed its decision, and the High Court agreed that the summary provided by the coroner was inaccurate, but refused to overturn the jury's decision.

Thatcher's response to the Black People's Day of Action and the deteriorating relationship between the police and the Black community was to launch a harsh crackdown. Y'know, the obvious response to police brutality being more police brutality. One of the main targets of Thatcher's attention was Brixton, because according to Met Assistant Commissioner Wilford Gibson there were around ninety robberies a week in the Brixton area, four times as many as most areas of London.[28] It was also an area in which around half of the young Black men were unemployed.[29]

Named 'Operation Swamp 81' in honour of Thatcher's 1979 statement about the 'swamp' of migrants, police action was launched at the beginning of April to use the 'sus' laws to come down harshly on crime in Brixton. Plain-clothes officers, uniformed officers and members of the Special Patrol Group all took part in the operation, which led to official figures of 943 stops in six days, and 118 arrests.[30] Later, the Brixton Defence Campaign would put that figure at around 2,000 stops.[31]

Operation Swamp 81 was deemed a success by the police. Maybe they would rethink that after what happened next.

A week after the launch of Operation Swamp 81, a few months after the New Cross fire, police officers were assisting a Black man in Brixton who had been stabbed in the back and was found staggering down the street. It was a Friday afternoon, 10 April 1981. Police attended to the man in their car as they waited for an ambulance to arrive.

Onlookers saw the man in the police car and assumed he was being accosted, as was so common to see in the area, especially over the previous week. They attacked the car and threw bottles at it, demanding the release of the man. Police reinforcements arrived and the group was soon dispersed.

The next day, Saturday 11 April, there was a heavy police presence throughout Brixton; at least 150 officers including uniformed and plain-clothes officers patrolled the streets.[32] All the way down Railton Road, on Atlantic Road and Coldharbour Lane.

Shortly after 4.30 p.m. the police stopped a Black man outside S & M Car Hire, and arrested him. People rushed to the man's aid and scuffled with the police. The scuffle then soon turned into full-on clashes between police and protestors. The crowds grew with Brixton residents and others from surroundings areas to around 5,000 people, both Black and white. Police reinforcements were brought in from around London and may have been up to 7,000 strong over the course of the night.[33]

The police used truncheons and riot shields against the protestors, and the protestors threw whatever they could get their hands on. They kicked down walls outside houses to use the bricks as ammunition.[34] They threw scaffolding, bats and poles at the police. Windows were smashed, cars were overturned and set ablaze. Soon after, petrol bombs started whizzing through the air, and pubs known to have racist landlords were set alight. Shops were broken into, and the electricity went out on at least one road.[35]

Protestors, both Black and white, continued clashes with the police for hours, into the early hours of Sunday morning.

The home secretary and Metropolitan Police commissioner visited Brixton on Sunday to cries of 'why haven't you been here before?', before fighting broke out again on Sunday night, smaller in scale than the previous night.[36]

By Monday 13 April, the uprising was over. Brixton was smouldering. The embers of destroyed buildings and vehicles were still smoking and building rubble and broken glass lined the streets. There was ten million pounds' worth of property damage done.[37] Two hundred and eighty-two people were arrested, nearly 150 businesses were damaged, over 100 cars were damaged or completely destroyed.[38]

The mood was a mixture of giddy jubilation, and trepidation and despair. For Farrukh Dhondy, there was a feeling that something would happen now; it seemed like a positive result.[39] The catharsis that came from fighting back against the police and the pride from uniting as a community were soon clouded for some. As author Alex Wheatle says, 'there was a bit of despair after the riots as we realised we had laid waste to our community'.[40] The destruction was so widespread that in the aftermath residents were advised to boil drinking water as the damage to water and sewage pipes could lead to contamination.[41]

The police were surprised by what had happened – there were even suspicions that the disturbance had been coordinated by outsiders – but anyone paying attention wasn't surprised.[42] 'It's been coming a long time,' the director of the Brixton-based Abeng Centre said. 'I don't think it's a setback for race relations in this area. A lot of us have been saying this would happen for years and no one has been paying attention.'[43]

As usual, the media tended to focus on the impact on the police and downplayed the legitimate grievances that contributed to the uprising. Articles with headlines such as 'Injured PCs describe ordeal of bricks, bottles and flames' were more common than ones that talked to Brixton residents to understand the actions from their perspective.[44]

A quick time-out to discuss terminology. If you have heard of what happened in 1981 at all, you will probably have heard it referred to as a 'riot' while I use the term 'uprising'. What do you think of when you read the word 'riot'? Unprovoked, unruly violence? Opportunism by criminals? Looting?

And what do you think of when you read 'uprising'? Resistance with an underlying legitimate grievance? Rebellion against an authority? So does it really matter what word we use? Yes, yes it matters very much. 'Riot' has been used to describe what happened in 1981, and it was also used thirty years later in 2011 after the killing of Mark Duggan led people to take to the streets. As has been noted in the case of the USA, when white people fight back it is called a rebellion, when Black people are involved, it is called a riot.[45]

Now I understand that this is an emotive and divisive topic. For some, 'riot' may accurately describe what they see as mere criminal activity, and for sure there are some people who use uprisings such as Brixton as a cover for opportunistic crime, and those actions cannot be condoned. Not everyone takes part for the same reasons, and innocent bystanders can lose out. This is supported by the language used by the media, almost always the language of 'riot'.

But we have to ask what else is going on, what leads people to push back, to rise up, to put everything they have on the line when they know they will have to deal with the harsh consequences. In 2011, then sixty-eight-year-old Darcus Howe was interviewed by the BBC and assertively responded when asked if he had taken part in riots himself: 'I don't call it rioting – I call it an insurrection of the masses of the people ... I have never taken part in a single riot. I have been part of demonstrations that have ended up in a conflict. Have some respect for an old West Indian Negro, and stop accusing me of being a rioter.'[46]

Resistance is not always pretty, and 1981 shows the good, the bad and the ugly of resistance. Both 'riot' and 'uprising' are loaded terms and very clearly show you someone's politics. Be like Darcus Howe: interrogate the use of the word 'riot'.

OK, back to 1981. Local and national politicians called for a public inquiry into the causes of the events. By Tuesday,

Lord Scarman, who had investigated the Grunwick strike a few years earlier and concluded that the factory should recognise the union and reinstate the workers, was assigned to conduct an inquiry of the causes of the weekend's events. Meanwhile Thatcher condemned what happened and denied that unemployment had anything to do with the uprisings.[47] 'Nothing that has happened in unemployment would justify those riots,' she said.[48] 'No one should condone the violence. No one should condone the events ... they were criminal, criminal.'[49] The government would continue to do what it was doing for unemployment nationwide and refused to invest any extra in the area.

Many of the young Black people who were arrested after the uprising faced imprisonment, some even deportation. The community soon rallied round in the form of the Brixton Defence Campaign, with the Brixton Black Women's Group and Black People Against State Harassment leading the effort and working with organisations such as the *Race Today* Collective and the Brixton Legal Defence Group.

Through mobilising the community, they raised money for legal fees, and supported defendants in and out of court. They urged people to set up twenty-four-hour Race Attack Centres wherever they lived to document racist attacks and demonstrate against them.[50] The New Cross fire wasn't seen as an isolated incident, it was seen as the last attack in a long line of racist killings, at least thirty-one around the country since 1976.[51]

They also called for a boycott of the Scarman inquiry as they knew it wouldn't be conducted with the community's best interests in mind and believed that it would be used to further prejudice the defendants. They failed to stop it outright as they couldn't prove the inquiry would be biased.[52]

Some of their worst fears were borne out. Sentencing of those arrested after the uprising felt harsh; a nineteen-year-old teenager who had stolen four pairs of trousers and some other clothes in Brixton was imprisoned for thirty days.[53]

Out of the ashes also emerged another, somewhat different, campaign, to collect material that commemorated and celebrated Black British history and culture. Spearheaded by activist, poet, historian and educationalist Len Garrison, he and other activists and teachers set about housing and documenting items of importance to Black Britain to inspire members of the community, especially young people. This became the Black Cultural Archives which continues as a unique and vital institution to this day.

Police brutality, high unemployment, poor housing and feelings of abandonment by the state were not isolated to an area of south London, as Bristol had shown a year earlier almost to the day. The uprising in Brixton and how it had been responded to by the state led to both anger and confidence among young Black and Brown communities across the country and it was just the beginning of what was to be a summer of resistance. Warning calls for measures to address the root causes of the uprisings went unheeded by the government, and even those who had predicted further unrest may have been surprised at the level it reached.

Southall was still reeling from the murder of Blair Peach, or rather, the 'death by misadventure' of Blair Peach, and the continued presence of the National Front on its streets. A band popular with skinheads and National Front supporters, the 4-Skins (I defy you not to chuckle), was scheduled to play the Hambrough Tavern on a main street, the Broadway, on 3 July 1981. The band's lead singer and manager had both been members of the neo-Nazi British Movement.[54] Given that the gig didn't seem like a very good idea, the Southall Youth Movement asked the landlord to cancel the event. The police were also contacted but it was still going ahead, so the only option left was to stop it by force.[55]

Young people in Southall marched to the Hambrough Tavern. On the way they saw windows that had been smashed in by concertgoers arriving on foot. Other fans arrived by coach, taunting the community from the security of their windows as they rolled past. At the pub, the Southall residents were met by rows of police, with the National Front supporters who didn't make it inside the pub cowering behind them. A stand-off ensued between the 500-strong crowd of Southall residents, 300 skinheads and the police.[56]

The police were there to protect the concertgoers and premises. By now, the concertgoers inside the pub were taunting the Southall locals outside but they weren't going to budge. The residents pushed back against the police, destroying a low brick wall opposite the Tavern to provide throwing material, and using whatever they could get their hands on to create a barricade between them and the police and skinheads, even using police cars. Some got into the pub and a brawl ensued. They made petrol bombs and threw them in the direction of the pub and police.

They set the Hambrough Tavern alight and it burned to the ground as people chanted Blair Peach's name.[57]

After three hours of clashes, the National Front scattered from the area as the police pushed the youngsters away from the pub and down the Broadway.

The next day, the wall opposite the pub was just rubble, there were overturned cars, the Tavern was a shell, but it was a 'shrine of celebration' says Balraj Purewal, former SYM member, who we met in the previous chapter.[58] There was an overwhelming sense of pride at what they had done; they had been fighting against the fascists and police for five years since the murder of Gurdip Singh Chaggar and finally felt a sense of victory.

Not everyone felt that sense of pride, though. Some community leaders met with Thatcher and publicly praised the police.[59] The police reaction was, predictably, to increase their presence in the area. There was a police officer every 45 metres.[60] A week later, on 10 July 1981, there were clashes again between the police and young people in Southall.

Like in 1979, SYM members and other young people who were arrested were supported legally and financially by the rest. In light of the events, it seemed like monitoring police racism and misconduct would be helpful, and inspired by the Black Panthers in the USA the Southall Monitoring Group was set up to do just that.[61] It soon became a go-to organisation to coordinate campaigns, including contributing to the Bradford 12 campaign.

The same day as the Hambrough Tavern was burned down in Southall, Toxteth in Liverpool, known to residents by the postcode Liverpool 8 or L8, saw the start of one of the biggest uprisings in the UK that year.

Liverpool has one of the oldest Black communities in the UK. Its unique Black British community has lived in the area for generations, compared to many of the Black and Brown communities who could trace their migration to after the Second World War. This didn't mean Black people there were accepted as British and afforded the same rights and opportunities that many white Brits had. In 1981, unemployment among the young Black population was estimated to be anywhere between 70 and 80 per cent, and four times that of white folk.[62]

On 3 July a Black man riding a motorcycle was stopped by police, suspected of having stolen it. 'Sus' in action again. This soon garnered the attention of others who were hanging out in the area, and as the crowd grew in number so did the number of police. After some confrontation, a Black man, Leroy Cooper, was arrested and word soon spread about the incident.

Police presence was increased in the L8 postcode, and clashes soon followed. Night after night the police, white protestors and the Black community clashed. A local resident and participant in the uprising said, 'they'd been putting us down and oppressing us for a long time and I certainly don't remember the word mercy appearing in the police handbook when dealing with us people in Toxteth. This was payback, this was our turn . . .'[63]

Protestors armed themselves with whatever they could find, including rocks, poles, and a bulldozer, excavator and even milk floats; they would prop bricks on the accelerator pedals and direct them towards the police.[64]

By Monday, given the unprecedented extent of the

uprisings, the chief constable of Merseyside police authorised the use of CS tear gas to try and disperse the crowd. This was the first time tear gas was used on the mainland. Seventy-four canisters and cartridges were used, supposedly not directly at the crowds, but the warning labels advised against use if there was anyone within 300 yards (274 metres).[65] And they were certainly used at closer proximity than that.

At the end of July there were another two days of clashes between police and residents. This time, the police drove into the crowds to disperse them. Protestor David Moore, who had a disability, was unable to get away from an oncoming police vehicle and was hit and killed. The police officers in the van were acquitted of manslaughter.[66] One man reportedly had his penis cut by a police officer who said, 'I'll make sure you have no little bastards.'[67] Once the uprising was over, 500 people had been arrested and at least 70 buildings gutted by fire.[68]

One of the most sombre reflections on the events stated that afterwards, 'the streets were not so different from before. Liverpool 8 has long been an area of dereliction, of vacant lots and boarded empty shops. The lifetime of residents, the entire experience of youngsters has been this desolate landscape.'[69] Though the area may have remained rubble-strewn, more community activism also came out of this rubble; the Liverpool 8 Housing Association was formed in 1982 and still operates today as the Steve Biko Housing Association, and Liverpool Black Sisters went from strength to strength.

This chapter could be made up of vignettes of every rebellion that took place in 1981, but that would get repetitive and be very long. There is one more to highlight, though, and that is Moss Side in Manchester.

The grievances in Moss Side were similar to elsewhere in the country, with mistreatment by the police a major gripe. One young Black man said of the police: 'they pick you up for anything . . . they ask you what you have in your pockets, stand still and if you try to explain yourself you can't.'[70]

According to activist and academic Professor Gus John, Moss Side could have erupted at any time. In March 1981, shortly after the Black People's Day of Action had taken place in London, a store of illegal weapons and cannabis was found at the Moss Side police station. What the police intended to do with the cache was known only to the police, but it alarmed the Black community who were used to having drugs planted on them.[71] The weapons magically disappeared soon after they were discovered.

Events in Moss Side were supposedly sparked when a group of men were leaving the popular Black Nile Club in the early hours of Wednesday 8 July, and were taunted by two white men who told them Manchester could never be like Toxteth or Brixton because people would never resist in the same way. As if to prove them wrong, this led to a night of property damage followed by arrests. To protest the arrests, on the night of 8 July around 1,000 people, both Black and white (mainly of Irish descent), attacked Moss Side police station, pelting the windows with bricks and attacking police cars.[72]

The next night, the chief constable summoned Manchester's version of the Special Patrol Group, the Tactical Action Group, all 900 of them, to bring order to scenes he described as 'close to anarchy' and 'lunacy'.[73]

Once the 'lunacy' was over, 500 people were arrested.[74]

Moss Side residents had their own defence campaign as in Brixton and other areas. To counter the biased narrative they saw in the media and the ongoing inquiry into the events, they published and distributed their own leaflets at public meetings, hand-delivered press releases to the media, and worked with the other defence committees around the country to share information.[75] They also supported those charged with offences by identifying witnesses and collecting statements. The inquiry's *Hytner Report* brushed over issues such as police harassment and proposed that improving the police complaints system was the best way forward.[76]

Professor John says that in the aftermath of the uprising, young people felt 'a greater sense of their own power'.[77] And even if the message they were trying to give hadn't been fully heeded by the authorities, they had been seen.

These were not isolated incidents. Uprisings bubbled all over the country: Bolton, Leeds, Leicester, High Wycombe, Walthamstow, Bristol, Coventry and multiple locations in London. I can't even name them all here. On 10 July 1981, there were more clashes. Unrest reached Brixton and Southall again, Handsworth, Preston, Hull, Woolwich and Newcastle. On the morning of 10 July there were dawn raids on houses in Brixton and the police arrested 150 people.[78]

All marches were banned in London for a month by the home secretary to prevent more unrest, with the exception of the wedding procession for Prince Charles and Lady Diana's wedding on 29 July.

What can these four particular events – the Brixton,

Southall, Toxteth and Moss Side uprisings – tell us about life in 1981? Quite simply, people were pissed off, tired, and fast running out of options to express themselves. Each uprising was triggered by a unique event but the underlying grievances were basically a checklist that could be copied and pasted over and over. They weren't copycat uprisings. They were a collective, cathartic scream for change.

A heady mix of police brutality, unemployment and a constant low-quality, second-rate standard of life drove the uprisings, though once again the reasons were not believed by many. Chief constable of Manchester, James Anderton, said 'in our opinion this is in no sense a race riot. We are treating this as a very serious crime.'[79]* Police tactics accordingly became more brutal: the use of CS tear gas, driving vans into crowds, 'snatch squads' to target individuals in a crowd and saturation policing (densely populating an area with police).

Inside the courtrooms, tactics were updated as well to reduce the likelihood of trial by jury, which meant that charges that were popular at the time of the Mangrove Nine, such as conspiracy, affray and riot, were avoided by the police so that cases would stay in magistrates' courts.[80] As well as the constant repetition that this was nothing but crime, other popular theories were that trouble was always stoked by outsiders and not the residents of an area. Politicians and police officials alike constantly expressed their surprise at what was happening, which you can only imagine was some very wilful cognitive dissonance and not pure ignorance.

---

* James Anderton was coincidentally friends with none other than Sir Cyril Smith, the MP who refused to support Anwar Ditta in her immigration case as we saw in the previous chapter.

These were unequivocally uprisings against the state, the government and its police force. Even the burning of the Hambrough Tavern in Southall was not just motivated by a desire to get rid of the National Front once and for all, but against the police who had failed in their duty to protect the community and instead protected the fascists. This was a stand-off between the Black and Brown (and many white) communities and the state.

In the aftermath of the uprisings the local papers were full of fears that it would happen in other places, with headlines such as 'Let's make sure it doesn't happen here' and 'Could the riots happen here?'[81] Throughout the events, the media focused on what it framed as the depravity and criminality of those involved. The numbers of injured police officers were splashed all over the front pages, but it is seemingly impossible to get a reliable estimate of injured protestors, or even hear the perspective of the participants.

One analysis of media coverage of the events in Liverpool 8 and the aftermath found that only 10 per cent of articles actually quoted a resident from the area.[82] There was, however, an interview with the skinheads that had been in Southall on 3 July 1981 under the headline, 'We weren't looking for trouble . . .'[83] This approach is still seen in later discussions of the events: in 2011, one reporter described the 'battering' that police took.[84] The reasons for the uprisings were irrelevant; the media, like the government, were slow to learn lessons from Bristol and Brixton.

After hearing from fifty witnesses, including twenty-three Brixton locals and twenty-one police officers, reading numerous statements and visits to uprising hotspots around the country, the *Scarman Report* was published on 25 November 1981. It concluded that, contrary to popular belief, the uprising in Brixton was indeed a spontaneous eruption and not orchestrated by some outside forces. It also said that: '"Institutional racism" does not exist in Britain: but racial disadvantage and its nasty associate, racial discrimination, have not yet been eliminated. They poison minds and attitudes: they are, and so long as they remain will continue to be, a potent factor of unrest.'[85]

Scarman recognised 'racial disadvantage' in housing, employment and education, and how the social conditions led to grievances that preceded the uprisings, and saw them as priority number one to fix even above relations between the Black community and the police; but he refused to acknowledge that there could be deeper problems that led to the racial disadvantage in the first place. He categorically refused that the grievances caused or legitimised any of the actions in Brixton and placed the blame for the deterioration of police–community relations as much in the laps of community leaders as the police.[86]

On the police, Scarman subscribed to the bad apple theory – 'racial prejudice does manifest itself occasionally in the behaviour of a few officers on the streets' – and his recommendation for how to get them out of the fruit bowl was better screening during recruitment, instant dismissal in cases of racial prejudice, a better complaints system and more training.[87] Oh, and more Black recruits of course.

The response in the Black community was mixed. Some people were hopeful given that Scarman had actually gone into Brixton and spoken to people at schools and hubs such as the Railton Road Youth and Community Centre, while others had had no confidence in the process from the beginning.[88] The report was well received by the government, at least publicly. Thatcher's internal response was, 'I'm afraid the report seems highly critical of the police.'[89] It was actually anything but: Scarman didn't advocate for less policing, he actually recommended that hard policing tactics such as water cannons, stop and search, and groups like the Special Patrol Group still be used.

Scarman also essentially recommended that a Black middle class be created to make Black people feel more involved in society.[90] He said that there was a need for 'the encouragement of black people to secure a real stake in their own community, through business and the professions . . . if future social stability is to be secured'.[91] The idea was that creating this middle class would give Black people more to lose if an uprising was ever to loom again, thereby reducing any radical tendencies.

What followed in the rest of the 1980s served to do just this, and chipped away at the radical groups that had proliferated over the 1970s. One manifestation of this was the election of the first Black and Brown MPs in modern times in 1987: Diane Abbott, Paul Boateng, Bernie Grant and Keith Vaz.

Thatcher's government changed policing in some minor ways recommended by Scarman. The focus shifted to community policing, that is, the 'local bobby' known to the community, to build trust. And the complaints procedure was improved and liaison committees spread. But behind the scenes, the police were also fully trained in paramilitary techniques used by forces in Northern Ireland and Hong Kong, the techniques that they had dabbled in during the uprisings.[92] Unsurprisingly, this didn't help to foster harmony and peace.

In 1985, there were uprisings again after a Black woman, Cherry Groce, was shot and disabled by police in her home, and another Black woman, Cynthia Jarrett, died in a police raid on her home. Brixton rose up in protest against the shooting of Groce, and the Broadwater Farm estate in Tottenham rose up for Jarrett and endured months of opposition from the police.[93] Birmingham saw an uprising too, triggered by a conflict over a parking ticket. It's not that policing hadn't changed in the four years since 1981, it's that it had changed for the worse.

Other policies under Thatcher also served to reinforce the prevailing inequalities in society. 'Urban' policies focused on the physical regeneration of cities and fell short in the three areas of housing, education and employment, as recommended by Scarman. Thatcher was advised by ministers to leave Liverpool to rot after the uprisings, but she appointed a 'minister for Merseyside' and pumped money into the city.[94] Similarly, building projects in Manchester and the London Docklands area, orchestrated by Urban Development Corporations, emerged at that time. These facelifts weren't necessarily with a focus on improving housing conditions or other inequalities that contributed to the uprisings, and the jobs created were often out of the reach of the local population.[95]

In housing, more council houses were improved in 1984 compared to 1978, but this still didn't go far enough.[96] The

'Right to Buy' scheme was introduced, allowing tenants of council housing to buy their houses at a discounted rate, which helped to create an increase in the average house price over the decade of 171 per cent.[97] It was thought that this would help to create the Black middle class that Scarman had pushed for, but Black people often lived in council flats, which were not sold off to the same extent as council houses.[98]

For unemployment, a Youth Training Scheme came in during 1983, which provided on-the-job training for school leavers at a miserly wage and primarily served to keep the unemployment figures artificially lower than they would have been otherwise.[99] Between 1983 and 1995, more than 4 million people participated.[100] The scheme was eventually made compulsory since there would be no unemployment benefits for young people who didn't participate.[101]

The scheme didn't benefit young Black people as much as it did young white people; the former often ended up on 'mode B schemes', in training which had few employment prospects, while the latter were in 'mode A schemes' with major employers who were more likely to hire them afterwards.[102] It was found in 1995 that as many as half of all young people who had participated did not find a job at the end of the training.[103] But still, no institutional racism in the UK, right?

Not unlike today, different sectors also tried to increase diversity within their ranks. The Scott Trust had a bursary scheme for under-represented groups in journalism, which powerhouse Gary Younge attributes to him getting into the industry.[104]

*

The final death toll of New Cross was actually fourteen, not thirteen. Two years after the event one of the survivors, Anthony Berbeck, died in what was believed to be suicide. It was thought the psychological burden had been overwhelming. Many of the other survivors haven't had the easiest of lives. Wayne Haynes escaped the fire through a window but suffered burns to a third of his body and was disabled as a result of his jump to safety.[105]

Calls for a second inquest into the fire were eventually answered in 2004, but with the same result: an open verdict. It was conceded that the fire was probably deliberate, but that it likely wasn't a firebomb. The survivors and their families still have no closure.

The Brixton Defence Campaign was around for a few years. It supported other campaigns around the country, such as that for the Bradford 12, and organised national conferences on the anniversary of the Brixton uprisings. The New Cross Massacre Action Committee organised public meetings on the anniversary of the fire.

Many buildings in Liverpool 8 have remained boarded up ever since 1981.

The National Front didn't return to Southall after 1981. The Southall Monitoring Group, which was set up to keep tabs on the police, still exists today, now as The Monitoring Group, and has been involved in critical campaigns including that related to the murder of Stephen Lawrence.

Two important pieces of legislation went through in 1981. The 'sus' law was repealed, to be replaced with the Criminal Attempts Act and then the Police and Criminal Evidence Act in 1984, which effectively brought it back. The 1994

Criminal Justice and Public Order Act and 2000 Terrorism Act expanded the scope. Secondly, the British Nationality Act 1981 reworked and restricted who would be considered a British citizen, making it harder to get that status, and still informs a lot of migration law today.

And so, we have come to where we began in Chapter One. It should be clear by now how we got to this point, what drove Black and Brown people to rise up against the daily realities of state oppression, and the hopelessness they saw in their future. But 1981 was decades ago now (though if you are an eighties child, like I am, then perhaps that pains you to admit). What has happened since 1981? How has racism and resistance changed? And what can we take with us from all of these movements as we face and confront racism today?

# Conclusion

# So, What Happened Next?

'If those who have do not give, those who haven't must take.'[1]

AMBALAVANER SIVANANDAN,
Director of the Institute of Race
Relations 1973–2013

So, what happened next? Is everything OK: did racism end? We know the answer to that, and at times reading what happened forty or fifty years ago feels plucked out of a newspaper from present-day Britain, but change is incremental and our struggles are different. We have to hope – and we have to organise – fuelled by righteous anger and buoyed by the knowledge of the shoulders we stand on.

I didn't stop this book in 1981 because it was the end of racism and resistance to racism from Black and Brown people. I could have gone on to 1985 and discuss in more detail the shooting of Cherry Groce by the police and the death of Cynthia Jarrett, or 1993 and the murder of Stephen Lawrence and the family's tireless campaigning for justice, or 2001 and the Bradford uprising to protect the city from the National Front (again), or 2011 with the killing of Mark Duggan by police and the uprisings that followed, or to Black Lives Matter in 2020.

I stopped this book in 1981 as it was a defining moment in the UK's history of race and racism. The year 1981 was the logical culmination of the fights in the workplace, schools, courtrooms and streets in the decades before. It was the last prong in a multi-prong approach to be heard. This is not to say the uprisings were organised or premeditated, they weren't, they were spontaneous outrage in action. They were, however, an understandable outcome given the state of affairs.

I also stopped in 1981 because, in my quest to understand the UK of today through learning about the past, events leading up to and including 1981 were the key I needed to unlock the answers.

One of the reasons I wrote this book was to understand the UK I was born into as a Brown woman, and now I do understand it better. I understand all the things that have happened since the 1980s, which once led me to shake my head and ask, 'How could this happen?' Now I greet them with, 'Yep, makes sense.' My constant surprise at the news was a result of my ignorance of what came before, and I no longer feel surprised as I understand the inner workings of the UK a lot more.

This understanding has led to a great deal of sadness and wrestling with what I thought I knew of the UK, but I also feel so much more certain of my place in it. Armed with this understanding I am better able to make sense of society, to place events in their rightful context. Rather than have facts loose and unorganised like the odds-and-ends drawer in my kitchen, they now look rather like my well-organised cutlery drawer. I understand the pathology of racism in a way I didn't before.

So what did I learn? Perhaps most chillingly I have learned that the biggest perpetrator of racism in the UK was not the National Front member on the street, but actually the state. From elected politicians, to laws (especially immigration laws), to the police force, healthcare and even the education system, the state was the biggest perpetrator and supporter of racism. Not to be outdone, it was followed closely by the media.

But I have also learned that Black and Brown people have continuously shown that they aren't for messing with. Armed with knowledge and experience of imperialism and radical politics from the colonies and beyond, early migrant communities were not simply bodies to be exploited for cheap labour. They had aspirations and ideals, and they would fight for those in the UK as they had done in the Caribbean, sub-Saharan Africa or South Asia.

Add to this the new generation who had only known life in the UK. The integrationist, assimilationist policies of the older Brown communities weren't universally accepted by the new generation. And the relegation of Black people to menial, low-paid jobs would not be tolerated by the younger generation. They were every part as British as Tom, Dick and Harry down the street and would be taken seriously. Time and time again Black and Brown people showed that they were here to stay, here to fight. They could withhold their labour and grind workplaces to a halt, union support be damned. They could defend themselves and protect each other against the fiercest racist attacks, police support or not.

From the courtroom to the workplace and from school to the street, Black and Brown people showed that they were to be taken seriously and would fight for what was right. It wouldn't always be easy and there would be divisions and arguments, and misogyny and homophobia to boot, but it would be done. Thanks to the actions of Black and Brown people, bussing was stopped, virginity testing was exposed, innocent people walked free, and neo-Nazis were ousted from neighbourhoods. Families were housed, children were actually educated, workplaces were forced to change discriminatory practices and lives were saved from a premature ending through covert population control. Thanks to those who fought in the 1960s to 1980s, the UK we live in today is better than it was in many ways.

Like me, you might be wondering how we got from the collective organising of the 1960s to 1980s to the current state of affairs where racism is still pervasive and yet action is largely individual or in silos. What happened after 1981 set the UK on the path we know today and therefore is probably far more familiar to you and me. From 1981 onwards, institutional, structural racism, built into policies and organisational culture, became entrenched to become what we know today. It has been validated by co-opting Black and Brown people into those very organisations. Throughout the 1980s the radical possibilities of the previous decades diminished along with the prospects for solidarity.

One manifestation of this was the need to identify as a specific ethnic or national group to access state funding. No longer could 'Black' mean 'politically Black' and encompass all oppressed ethnic minorities. It couldn't even mean all Black people, but you had to specify between 'African' or 'Caribbean'. It was not enough to be 'Asian', you had to be 'Indian', 'Pakistani' or 'Bengali'. It didn't stop there, you had to be 'Punjabi' or 'Gujarati', and religious groupings were also encouraged; tick the box for 'Sikh', 'Muslim' or 'Hindu'. And there were further subcategories for gender. This pried apart the carefully constructed solidarities that had been formed and pitted groups of people against one another to compete for scarce resources.[2]

Whether this was part of a thought-out conspiracy on the part of the government or just an unintended consequence of trying to appear like they were doing something, which inadvertently worked in the government's favour, is debated.[3] As we've seen with the movements, whether or not to accept state funding was always a contentious choice – including for the IWA, AYM, Black women's groups and supplementary schools – and it became more damaging than ever to the wider cause of anti-racism in the 1980s and beyond.

Another key change in the 1980s was the ballooning of the anti-racism industrial complex. Community leaders and other would-be radicals were given jobs and co-opted into the state structures for working with communities, which dampened potential radical tendencies and took the sting out of the bee.

Working within the system was seen by some as the best way forward to create change, and it often is still seen that way. From the first four Black and Brown MPs elected in 1987, by the 2019 general election we saw the most diverse Parliament ever, with 10 per cent of MPs from an ethnic minority background.[4] At the time of writing, the Conservative cabinet has seven Black and Brown members out of thirty. That's 23 per cent for those of you who like percentages. That's compared to 12 per cent of the English and Welsh population who are Black or Brown.[5]

But I have learned enough about the machinations of racism in the UK that I am suspicious of this emphasis on representation as progress. This diverse government is the one that published the *Sewell Report* in 2021, which said that 'we no longer see a Britain where the system is deliberately rigged against ethnic minorities', while at the same time the government: has ever-more stringent immigration laws, strips Shamima Begum of her citizenship, passes the Nationality and Borders Bill to potentially take citizenship away from even more people, oversees Black people disproportionately dying in police custody, condones Islamophobia, organises the deportation of thousands of people a year, allows Windrush compensation applicants to die waiting, provides no justice for Grenfell, and knows that Black and Brown people were disproportionately dying from COVID-19 and did nothing apart from notice it was happening.[6] The same ones who saw the rise in hate crime rise after Brexit and during COVID-19 and did nothing.[7] As activist Farrukh Dhondy says, it is 'Uncle Tom's cabinet'.[8]

This doesn't mean that a diverse Labour government would be any better. What has been striking as I've written this book, and maybe as you've been reading it, is that it is almost impossible to tell who was in power in the 1960s to 1980s looking at actions and policies alone. I had to keep looking up who was governing during any particular event until I realised it didn't really matter. Dare I say, it still doesn't matter.

This is not to say that diversification and representation aren't helpful at all. I would much rather that there are Black and Brown people in Parliament and public institutions than none at all, but they are not the panacea that they are made out to be. Just look at the views espoused by Kemi Badenoch, or someone I am ashamed to share my name with, Priti Patel. Put all the Black and Brown people you like in government, even as chancellor or as prime minister, but it won't guarantee that life will get better for Black and Brown people and racism in Britain will be magicked away.

Crucially, while we have a first-past-the-post system with career politicians funnelled through the private school→ Oxbridge→Westminster pipeline, an unelected second house, a monarchy, and tools such as the police, all under- pinned with a capitalist, extractive logic that sees people as expendable tools to be used in the pursuit of ever greater profit and higher GDP, then it doesn't really matter who's in power as they will all operate within the same norms. Both, all, parties are just wolves sharing each other's sheep outfits. That we think otherwise is one of the greatest illusions we've been fed by the media and the state since 1981.

So community solidarity has been prised apart, would-be- critics have been co-opted, and participation in the broken system has been sold as the solution. Since 1981, racism has become ever more elusive and it can be hard to discern some- times as there can be fewer 'concrete' examples at which to point. The policies become ever more coded, they shapeshift and change names and forms. It's that special British form of subtle racism.

It is often left to the hunches we get, the instinct that we are being discriminated against but you can't quite put your finger on it. Maybe it wasn't racism, maybe they were just having a bad day? It's not racism, those are just the rules. Racism likes to gaslight us into believing it is all in our heads, that we are the ones with the chip on our shoulder, that we are the ones who make 'everything about race'. It would serve us well to keep in mind these words from a young person in the Brick Lane area in 1978:

> The white establishment in this country wants to make chapatis of us ... you know how to make chapatis? First you knead the dough, then you sprinkle water on it, then you knead it again and flatten it with a rolling-pin. Here the National Front and the police do the kneading and kick us around. Then the Labour Party and the community workers step in and sprinkle some water to cool things down. They are two parts of the same process: suppressing black militancy.[9]

I can't lie to you, this quest has been long and often physically and emotionally draining. I sometimes wish I still had the same capacity to be surprised by racism as it has become almost saddeningly run-of-the-mill. But this quest has also contradictorily been inspiring and empowering. I have learned that now, as then, we have the answer to what creates change: collective action.

Collective action is magic. Groups of people working towards the same ends are hard to ignore. While a one-person strike isn't likely to change much, tens of thousands of people or a general strike will force change. Organising as groups around shared aims is the only thing that will change anything. Of that I am more convinced than ever.

Withholding labour, changing our consumer behaviour, demonstrating, uprising, consistently disrupting the status quo in as many ways as possible are the most powerful ways to get the attention of those who would have you be seen and not heard, and preferably not seen either. We've had the tools all along, we have just been lacking examples of how they have been used by people who look like us.

Similarly, just as collective action trumps individual action, so does directing action towards changing structures rather than individuals within those structures. While it is important that individual police officers are held to account for horrific deeds they do, such as taking selfies with the bodies of murdered Black sisters Nicole Smallman and Bibaa Henry, or that someone is held to account for the many failures that led to Grenfell, it is meaningless without discussion of more radical change.

What happens when the next police officer does something horrific? What about the hundreds who aren't held to account for things like deaths in police custody? What about the other buildings like Grenfell inhabited by Black and Brown people that have inappropriate cladding that still hasn't been changed? They are symptoms of the illness, not the cause. Racism isn't just reproduced through individual actions, it is a mindset, a logic of its own, and it is that which needs to be the target of our actions. Pulling down statues and renaming schools or streets who bear the names of colonists will not alone fix the problems we have.

This sits in contrast to our often-individualised approach today. 'White guilt', 'allyship' and 'white privilege' are the terms of the day. It's important for individuals to look at the ways in which we perpetuate all the -isms – it is important for all of us and not just white people – but it's also important for us to ask where we got these ideas from and how we change that too.

The movements of the 1960s to 1980s weren't focused on changing the mindset of National Front members to not be racist. In Brick Lane, the Bengalis didn't try to convince the National Front that they were worthy of being in the UK because of what they had achieved and contributed to the economy since being there. No one expected Sergeant Ridgewell or PC Pulley to suddenly realise the error of their ways and buy a copy of C. L. R. James's *The Black Jacobins* from New Beacon Books.

The focus was always on the bigger picture. The structures and policies that allowed this to keep happening time and time again. The trigger was immediate, but the cause was always much larger than the event. We need to channel those whose shoulders we stand on, to imagine a radical future that isn't just about tweaking the current system. I don't have the answers to what that looks like, that too needs to be a collective effort. That said, defunding the police may be a good start.

The movements were also concerned with what was right rather than what was always strictly legal. Some of the actions

I describe were illegal then, like the self-defence actions of the Bradford 12, or would be illegal now, like the type of secondary picketing seen at Grunwick. The movements remind us to think critically about the law and what risks we are willing to take to break the law.

This is not a blanket condoning of illegality, but neither is it a blanket condemnation of actions that are deemed illegal. The law is like other tools of control, it is not neutral, and sometimes it must be bent or broken in order to highlight its biases and faults. It is person-made, or, let's face it, largely white man-made, and we must always ask ourselves: whose interests are served by this law?

If collective action weren't so powerful, then Thatcher wouldn't have undermined union power in the 1980s. If collective action weren't so powerful, then the government at the time of writing wouldn't have introduced the 2022 Police, Crime, Sentencing and Courts Act to restrict 'highly disruptive protest tactics' which 'have caused a disproportionate impact on the hardworking majority seeking to go about their everyday lives'.[10] This means it is now easier for the police to intervene in and stop marches and demonstrations, ultimately restricting the ability to protest freely. Someone protesting who is essentially deemed too loud according to the police can face hefty punishment. There is a minority who greatly benefit from racism, classism and misogyny. The rest of us, the majority, are all adversely affected and have more in common than we are often led to believe.

I said at the beginning that this is not a 'how-to' guide. This is a storybook, a history book, and has unexpectedly turned into a call to arms. But there is one thing that screams out time and time again from these pages, and that is solidarity in collective action. It is what those generations did so much better than we do, to support each other and recognise that our fates are intertwined.

This isn't to denounce the differences either, as there must be space in movements for different needs, but we must go beyond the divide-and-conquer tactics that have manipu-lated us into silos, which have led Indians in the UK to think we're better than 'them' and that has let anti-Blackness run rampant. We need to come together to share stories and experiences and rally around what we can. Intersectionalities and all. White people are not the problem, white supremacy is, racism is, and we too support that system, and we need to look inwards, and have those conversations in our communi-ties, and imagine new communities.

The people described in these movements are not flaw-less, not 'heroes' in the traditional sense: they had their own prejudices and their own politics, which served at times to undermine what they tried to do in frustratingly obvious ways, like when a character in a horror film goes into the basement in the middle of the night. The longest-running immigrant association in the UK, the Indian Workers' Association, had so much in-fighting about political affilia-tion and campaigning tactics that it split into two, and then three, separate groups. But I like that they are flawed humans, because so am I. And if they can be flawed and still resist and often find ways to put aside their prejudices for the greater good, that gives me more hope that we can find a way to move forward together, just as we are.

So we organise, warts and all, and focus on the bigger

picture and not just individuals. We also keep educating ourselves. We read about Empire, and more books about post-war Britain. We talk to our parents and grandparents and encourage them to share their stories, and even give their documents and testimony to an archive.* We support radical publishers and independent bookstores because we know the power that comes from the written word.

We support supplementary schools, and critical independent media. We gather knowledge like magpies, to be able to see through the smoke and mirrors and understand that the system is working exactly as intended, and that more Black teachers here, or a diversity and inclusion scheme there, will ultimately not help us.

The truth is that I don't know what to do exactly, but I know that we can each do something. We have to do something. We may not have white privilege (well, some of you may do) but we may have class, gender, ableism, heterosexuality or other privileges that give us a platform. We use what we can.

You now know the history of what has led to where we are today and understand the often-malignant roots of the seemingly benign policies we have. You now know that you are not imagining things when you sense racism is afoot. My hope is

---

* Encourage your parents and grandparents to dig into their belongings from the 1960s–1980s, their photos, old newspapers or magazines, letters, anything and everything, and contact an archive (you can see the list of archives I consulted at the back as a starting point) to see if it could be added to a collection. There is so much of historical value hidden away in wardrobes or attics, and if more of these stories are to be told, it relies on us to help bring them to light. It is especially important that we hear more female voices and experiences from the time, as the narrative and stories are skewed male.

that armed with the knowledge of how the state et al. have not only just allowed but facilitated and constructed systems of oppression, you feel better equipped for intersectional anti-racist actions in your own life. And with the knowledge of how racism has been fought in all arenas, from the quiet radicalism of publishing to protests of tens of thousands of people, I hope you share my feeling that change today is not only possible but probable.

We stand on the shoulders of those who came before us. We stand on the shoulders of individuals such as Jayaben Desai, Altheia Jones-LeCointe, Winston Trew and Darcus Howe, but more than that we stand on the shoulders of the tens of thousands of individuals whose names we will never know. Thanks to them, we have everything we need: determination, smarts, and a whole lot of fight. And thanks to each other we don't have to do it alone. There is vast power, wisdom and strength in our solidarity, and much joy to be had as well. We mustn't forget about joy. So let's be bold in taking the torch from the elders and carrying on the struggle. The struggle is not over. It will never be over. It will continue to change and morph, and we will be ready.

This is not The End.

# Other movements, campaigns and organisations

## Groups then

I have only been able to include a small number of movements and organisations from the time. In case you would like to do your own research some more are listed below. This is by no means a definitive list. It is my hope that the movements I have detailed in this book and others become common knowledge in the UK and that this list is a helpful starting point to those of you who want to help with that too.

- Action Committee Against Racialism
- Afro-Asian Caribbean Conference
- Association for the Advancement of Coloured Peoples
- Awaz
- Bangladeshi Divided Families Campaign
- Black Parents Movement
- Black People Against State Harassment (BASH)
- Black People's Alliance

- Black People's Committee Against State Brutality
- Black Students Action Collective
- Black Students Movement
- Black Unity and Freedom Party
- Campaign Against Racial Discrimination (CARD)
- Caribbean Artists Movement (CAM)
- Committee of Afro-Asian-Caribbean Organisations (CAACO)
- Coordinating Committee Against Racial Discrimination (CCARD)
- Council of African Organisations
- Inter-Racial Friendship Coordinating Council (IRFCC)
- Joint Council for the Welfare of Immigrants (JCWI)
- Min Quan
- Movement for Colonial Freedom
- National Association for Asian Youth
- Organisation for Sickle Cell Anaemia Research (OSCAR)
- Pakistani Workers' Association
- Racial Action Adjustment Society
- Teachers Against Racism
- West Indian Development Council
- West Indian League
- West Indian Standing Conference
- West Indian Workers' Association

## Groups now

There are a lot of movements, groups and organisations currently fighting the good fight against racism and wayward capitalism and/or promoting vital Black and Brown history. A few of these organisations are listed here in case you want to get involved. Some are exclusively Black and Brown led or largely Black and Brown led. Again, this is not a definitive list as there are many local and regional organisations not included, and many campaigns for individuals affected by police violence or negligence. And please note that inclusion here does not mean an endorsement of the organisation.

- Abolitionist Futures
- Action for Race Equality
- The Alliance for Inclusive Education
- Altab Ali Foundation
- The Anti-Racist Educator
- Believe In Me CIC
- Black Activists Rising Against Cuts (BARAC UK)
- The Black Child Agenda
- The Black Curriculum
- Black History Walks
- Black Lives Matter
- Black Protest Legal Support UK (BPLS)
- Black South West Network
- Black Thrive Global
- BLAM UK
- Blueprint for All
- BME National

- brap
- Campaign Against Racism Group
- Caribbean and African Health Network
- Cherry Groce Foundation
- The David Oluwale Memorial Association
- Decolonise The Curriculum
- Decolonising Contraception
- Don't Divide Us
- End Violence and Racism Against East and Southeast Asian Communities
- Equality 4 Black Nurses
- Five X More
- 4Front Project
- The Free Black University
- Harambee Organisation of Black Unity
- Hope Not Hate
- Impact of Omission
- INQUEST
- Justice 4 Grenfell
- Kids of Colour
- Migrant Rights Network
- The Monitoring Group (formerly Southall Monitoring Group)
- Mothers 4 Justice Ubuntu
- National Association of Black Supplementary Schools
- The Network for Police Monitoring
- Nijjormanush
- No More Exclusions
- Northern Police Monitoring Project

- Nubian Jak Community Trust
- Olmec
- Operation Black Vote
- Parents Action and Resource Centre
- Positive Action in Housing
- Race Equality Foundation
- Race Equality Matters
- Race on the Agenda
- Racial Justice Network
- Runnymede Trust
- Solve: The Centre for Youth Violence and Conflict
- Southall Black Sisters (and other Black and Brown domestic violence focused charities include London Black Women's Project and the umbrella organisation Imkaan)
- Stand Against Racism and Inequality (SARI)
- Stand Up To Racism
- Stephen Lawrence Day Foundation
- StopWatch
- Stuart Hall Foundation
- Swadhinata Trust
- Tottenham Rights
- United Friends and Family Campaign
- Women of Colour Global Women's Strike
- Young Historians Project
- The Zahid Mubarek Trust

# Acknowledgements

To the elders, thank you. Without you who knows what kind of life we would have today. Your sacrifices are seen and appreciated. I hope I have done the stories justice.

Thank you to the interviewees who took the time to share a piece of themselves with me – Ansar Ahmed Ullah, Farrukh Dhondy, Stella Dadzie and Winston Trew. It was an absolute honour to speak with you.

To my agent, Abi Fellows, pitching this book to you remains one of the most terrifying and exhilarating experiences of my life so far and I am so unbelievably lucky to get to work with you. Thank you for understanding the book instantly, for your patience with a newbie, and for your uncanny ability to say just what I need to hear, when I need to hear it. And thank you to the amazing team at the Good Literary Agency.

Thank you to Sharmaine Lovegrove for championing this book from the very beginning when you should have had your feet up before having twins. And a huge thanks to Maisie Lawrence for getting the vision of this book so completely, and for your keen editorial eye, which took it to the next level. Thanks to Amy Baxter for managing the editorial process so smoothly. And thank you to everyone from Dialogue Books and Little, Brown who worked to get this book published, an absolute dream come true.

Thank you to the Women's History Network for awarding me the role of an Independent Research Fellow 2021–2022, which provided valuable financial support to do archival research.

A huge thank you to all the dedicated archivists who were as excited about the research as I was and found sources I hadn't even heard of to help me in my research. I loved geeking out with you. Thank you to Paul Trevor for granting rights to use your magnificent photo for the cover, and the organisations and photographers for the photos inside.

To my English and history teachers at Dormers Wells who instilled a love of both subjects from early on – Mr Guntrip and Miss Benson – do get in touch if you read this, I'd love to thank you personally. Thank you to my wonderful professors at university, John and Jay, for always seeing potential in me.

I am forever grateful for my phenomenal family, friends and writing community.

Leanne, thank you for believing so completely in the book, and me, from the very beginning. When the seeds of an idea were germinating and I sheepishly told you about it you didn't laugh at me or sound sceptical and I'm not sure I ever would have pursued it had it not been for that conversation. You always have my back and I am ridiculously lucky to have you in my life; I'm not sure I will ever find the words to let you know just how much.

I am so grateful to you, Kristin, for being one of my biggest cheerleaders. Everyone needs a Kristin in their lives. You have been my sounding board, my unconditional support and my safe space throughout the process.

Bethany, you absolute star. You have been there from the early days as a fountain of enthusiasm and practical and emotional support. Thank you, Aleisha, for all the love and support and screaming WhatsApp messages from afar. Thank you to Ruth for all the excitement, talking to you always spurred me on to keep going when it felt like a chore.

As I have learned so completely now, everyone needs a community, and my writing community sustains me. Thanks to all my Penguin Write Now 2020 pals, you are absolute tops! Our WhatsApp group continues to be my most joyous and supportive corner of social media. A special thank you to Lucy, you always stopped me from spiralling and helped me think of helpful ways forward when I couldn't always see them through the fog of frustration.

To my writing group, Nicole and Poonam, a massive thank you, it is not a platitude to say that I could not have done this without you. You inspire me with your writing and the gentle and insightful way you have handled my words have turned this nervous wreck of a writer into slightly less of a nervous wreck. We did it!

I am also so lucky to have a family who lift me up. To my cousins who are like sisters: you are simply some of my very favourite people and you inspire me every day. You are so generous with your support and belief in me. Thank you, thank you, thank you! Thanks to Chachi for fuelling my archival research with trifle.

Thank you to my Mum and Dad, some of the first shoulders I stood on, for your sacrifices, for your support of me and for always encouraging and facilitating my love of reading and learning. The many library, bookstore and museum visits are some of my fondest childhood memories.

Brother, your fanboying of this book means more to me than you'll ever know, we may be grown but big brother's opinion still holds a lot of sway! Thank you for being a sounding board and having my back.

Thank you to my unwavering support, my husband. Thank you for our life together and making changes to it to help me write this book. Thank you for helping me work through ideas when they got sticky, making sure I celebrated every win along the way no matter how small, and for pulling me out of my writing hole when I had gotten too deep. And thanks for not being offended when I didn't trust your biased opinion of my work.

And lastly, thank you to my daughter for accompanying me for so much of this process. You gave me another reason to write this book.

# Notes

**Archives visited**
    Ahmed Iqbal Ullah Race Relations Archive
    Bishopsgate Institute
    Black Cultural Archives
    British Library
    George Padmore Institute
    Gunnersbury Park Museum
    Institute of Race Relations
    Lambeth Archives
    London Metropolitan Archives
    The National Archives
    Tower Hamlets Local History Library and Archives
    Working Class Movement Library

## Introduction

1. Labour Party, *Manifesto*, 1997, http://labour-party.org.uk/manifestos/1997/1997-labour-manifesto.shtml [accessed January 2021].
2. Left Book Club, '40 years on from the 1981 uprisings: Setting the streets on fire', Pluto Press webinar, 17 November 2021.
3. J. Burnett, 'Racial violence and the Brexit state', Institute of Race Relations, 2016, https://irr.org.uk/app/uploads/2016/11/Racial-violence-and-the-Brexit-state-final.pdf.
4. R. Styles, 'EXCLUSIVE: Harry's girl is (almost) straight outta Compton: Gang-scarred home of her mother revealed – so will he be dropping by for tea?', *Daily Mail*, 2 November 2016, https://www.dailymail.co.uk/news/article-3896180/Prince-Harry-s-girlfriend-actress-Meghan-Markles.html [accessed January 2021].
5. United Nations Human Rights Office of the High Commissioner, 'UN human rights experts says deaths in custody reinforce concerns about "structural racism" in UK', 27 April 2018, https://www.ohchr.org/EN/NewsEvents/Pages/DisplayNews.aspx?NewsID=22997&LangID=E [accessed January 2021].
6. A. Leach, A. Voce and A. Kirk, 'Black British History: the row over the school curriculum in England', *Guardian*, 13 July 2020, https://

www.theguardian.com/education/2020/jul/13/black-british-history-school-curriculum-england [accessed January 2021]; K. Proctor, '"Tone deaf" ministers reject BAME review of English curriculum', *Guardian*, 30 July 2020, https://www.theguardian.com/education/2020/jul/30/exclusive-tone-deaf-ministers-reject-bame-review-of-english-curriculum [accessed January 2021].

## Chapter One: So, What Happened?

1.  G. Younge, 'Ambalavaner Sivanandan obituary', *Guardian*, 7 February 2018, https://www.theguardian.com/world/2018/feb/07/ambalavaner-sivanandan [accessed January 2021].

2.  C. Brown, 'Whitelaw offers armoured vans', *Guardian*, 14 July 1981, p. 1.

3.  '1570–1750 estimated population', 1841census.co.uk, https://1841census.co.uk/1570-1750-estimated-population/ [accessed January 2021]; P. Fryer, *Staying Power: The history of black people in Britain* (Pluto Press, reprint 2018, original 1984), p. 70.

4.  Fryer, p. 74.

5.  R. Visram, *Asians in Britain: 400 Years of History* (Pluto Press, 2002), p. 18.

6.  Ibid., p. 39.

7.  The railway is often cited as a 'positive' outcome of the British Empire. For more on this see for example: S. Tharoor, '"But what about the railways . . . ?" The myth of Britain's gifts to India', *Guardian*, 8 March 2017, https://www.theguardian.com/world/2017/mar/08/india-britain-empire-railways-myths-gifts [accessed January 2021].

8.  V. Kant, 'India and WWI: Piecing together the impact of the Great War on the subcontinent', *LSE Blogs*, 2016, http://eprints.lse.ac.uk/66602/1/blogs.lse.ac.uk-India%20and%20WWI%20Piecing%20together%20the%20impact%20of%20the%20Great%20War%20on%20the%20subcontinent.pdf [accessed January 2021]; S. Bourne, 'How Black Soldiers Helped Britain in the First World War', *Black History Month*, 2020, https://www.blackhistorymonth.org.uk/article/section/bhm-heroes/how-black-soldiers-helped-britain-in-first-world-war/ [accessed January 2021].

9.  D. Olusoga, *Black and British: A forgotten history* (Macmillan, 2016),
    p. 431.

10. Ibid., p. 452.

11. Ibid., pp. 452–3.

12. Ibid., p. 451.

13. Ibid., pp. 454–5.

14. M. Goodfellow, *Hostile Environment: How immigrants became scapegoats* (Verso, reprint 2020, original 2019), p. 54.

15. S. Nasta, F. Stadtler and R. Visram, 'South Asians in Britain: World wars', British Library, 2017, https://www.bl.uk/asians-in-britain/articles/world-wars [accessed January 2021]; C. Brennan, 'Soldiers of the Caribbean: Britain's forgotten war heroes', *BBC News*, 13 May

2015, https://www.bbc.com/news/uk-32703753 [accessed January 2021]; Olusoga, p. 428.

16. L. McDowell, 'How Caribbean migrants helped to rebuild Britain', British Library, 2018, https://www.bl.uk/windrush/articles/how-caribbean-migrants-rebuilt-britain [accessed January 2021].

17. Approximately 80,00 migrants under the 'European Volunteer Workers' scheme, 150,000 Polish migrants through the Polish Resettlement Act of 1947, and 30,000 refugees from the Hungarian Revolution of 1956. 'When the war was over: European refugees after 1945', Briefing paper 6: Coming to Britain, University of Nottingham, 2012, https://www.nottingham.ac.uk/postwar-refugees/documents/briefing-paper-6-coming-to-britain.pdf; K. Burrell, 'Polish soldiers and refugees in World War II Britain', Our Migration Story, https://www.ourmigrationstory.org.uk/oms/polish-soldiers-and-refugees-in-world-war-ii-britain- [accessed January 2021]; K. Lowe, 'Five times immigration changed the UK', *BBC News*, 20 January 2020, https://www.bbc.com/news/uk-politics-51134644 [accessed January 2021]; C. Kenny, 'Britain's shrinking, ageing Irish population', *Irish Times*, 9 March 2019, https://www.irishtimes.com/life-and-style/abroad/britain-s-shrinking-ageing-irish-population-1.3817868 [accessed January 2021].

18. Reading Museum, '4. Caribbean resettlement', https://www.readingmuseum.org.uk/4-caribbean-resettlement [accessed March 2022].

19. Transport for London, *Generations: Celebrating 50 years of Caribbean recruitment* (Group Publishing, 2006), p. 34.

20. B. Bryan, S. Dadzie and S. Scafe, *The Heart of the Race: Black women's lives in Britain* (Verso, reprint 2018, original 1985), 'Chapter 1: Labour Pains: Black Women and Work'.

21. 'Notting Hill Race Riot', *Witness History*, BBC World Service, 25 August 2017, https://www.bbc.co.uk/programmes/w3csv254 [accessed January 2021].

22. A. Travis, 'After 44 years secret papers reveal truth about five nights of violence in Notting Hill', *Guardian*, 24 August 2002, https://www.theguardian.com/uk/2002/aug/24/artsandhumanities.nottinghillcarnival2002 [accessed January 2021].

23. 'Police "knocking everybody off" at Notting Hill', *Manchester Guardian*, 18 September 1958, p. 2.

24. Office for National Statistics, 'Gross Domestic Product: Year on Year growth: CVM SA %', 2020, https://www.ons.gov.uk/economy/grossdomesticproductgdp/timeseries/ihyp/pn2 [accessed January 2021].

25. UCL Social Research Institute, 'CLOSER, Television ownership in private domestic households', https://www.closer.ac.uk/data/television-ownership-in-domestic-households/ [accessed January 2021].

26. S. Jones, 'The cost of living then: 20p a pint, and a Mini for £600', *Guardian*, 5 March 2004, https://www.theguardian.com/uk/2004/mar/05/health.drugsandalcohol [accessed January 2021]; £63,000 is

the rounded amount from January 2023, conversion done with the Bank of England inflation calculator, bankofengland.co.uk/monetary-policy/inflation/inflation-calculator.

27.  W. Dahlgreen, 'Britain "was greatest in the sixties"', YouGov, 2016, https://yougov.co.uk/topics/lifestyle/articles-reports/2016/05/10/britain-was-greatest-sixties [accessed January 2021].

28.  D. Owen, *Ethnic Minorities in Great Britain: Patterns of population change, 1981–91* (National Ethnic Minority Data Archive, Centre for Research in Ethnic Relations, University of Warwick, 1995), p. 1.

29.  Campaign Against Racism and Fascism and Southall Rights, *Southall: The birth of a black community* (Russell Press, 1981), p. 8.

30.  Fryer, p. 382.

31.  A. Kundnani, 'Black British History: Remembering Malcolm X's visit to Smethwick', Institute of Race Relations, 10 February 2005, https://irr.org.uk/article/black-british-history-remembering-malcolms-visit-to-smethwick/ [accessed January 2021].

32.  S. Blinder and L. Richards, *UK Public Opinion toward Immigration: Overall Attitudes and Level of Concern*, Migration Observatory briefing (COMPAS, University of Oxford, 2020).

33.  *Britain's Racist Election*, Channel 4, 4 March 2015, https://www.channel4.com/press/news/britains-racist-election [accessed January 2021].

34.  D. Brown, 'A new language of racism in politics', *Guardian*, 27 April 2001, https://www.theguardian.com/uk/2001/apr/27/race.world2 [accessed January 2021].

35.  R. Waters, *Thinking Black: Britain, 1964–1985* (University of California Press, 2019), p. 110; V. Hunter, 'Michael X (1933–1975)', BlackPast.org, 24 October 2018, https://www.blackpast.org/global-african-history/michael-x-1933-1975/ [accessed January 2021].

36.  'On This Day, 1965: New UK race law "not tough enough"', *BBC News*, 8 December 1965, http://news.bbc.co.uk/onthisday/hi/dates/stories/december/8/newsid_4457000/4457112.stm [accessed January 2021].

37.  'Immigration from the Commonwealth', *Hansard*, HL Deb 2 August 1965, vol. 269, col. 23–32, https://api.parliament.uk/historic-hansard/lords/1965/aug/02/immigration-from-the-commonwealth [accessed January 2021].

38.  J. Hunte, *Nigger hunting in England?* (West Indian Standing Conference, 1966), p. 12.

39.  C. McGlashan, 'Coloured immigrants set up vigilantes', *Observer*, 15 August 1965, p. 3.

40.  M. Collins, 'The National Front at 50', *HOPE Not Hate Magazine*, 23 November 2017, https://www.hopenothate.org.uk/2017/11/23/national-front-50/ [accessed January 2021].

41.  R. Hansen, 'The Kenyan Asians, British Politics, and the Commonwealth Immigrants Act, 1968', *Historical Journal*, 42:3 (1999), p. 810.

42.  Ibid., p. 821n.

43.  E. Powell, 'Speech at Birmingham', 20 April 1968, https://enochpowell.net/fr-79.html [accessed January 2021].

44.  E. Powell, 'Speech to London Rotary Club, Eastbourne', 16 November 1968, https://enochpowell.net/fr-83.html [accessed January 2021].

45.  Staff Reporter, 'Immigrant control march', *The Times*, 30 September 1968, p. 2.

46.  'David Oluwale's death in 1969 helped "reshape Leeds"', *BBC News*, 19 April 2019, https://www.bbc.com/news/uk-england-leeds-47946556 [accessed January 2021].

47.  UN General Assembly, 'United Nations Declaration on the Elimination of All Forms of Racism and Discrimination', 1964, https://digitallibrary.un.org/record/203994 [accessed January 2021].

48.  D. Wyatt, 'On Margaret Thatcher's funeral day her "favourite song" "(How Much Is That) Doggie in the Window?" marks 60 years since topping the charts', *Independent*, 17 April 2013, https://www.independent.co.uk/arts-entertainment/music/news/margaret-thatcher-s-funeral-day-her-favourite-song-how-much-doggie-window-marks-60-years-topping-charts-8576233.html [accessed January 2021].

49.  K. O. Morgan, 'Britain in the Seventies – Our Unfinest Hour?', *Revue Française de Civilisation Britannique*, XXII-Hors série (2017); 'On This Day, 1972: UK unemployment tops one million', *BBC News*, 20 January 1972, http://news.bbc.co.uk/onthisday/hi/dates/stories/january/20/newsid_2506000/2506897.stm [accessed January 2021].

50.  Labour Party, *Manifesto*, 1979, http://labour-party.org.uk/manifestos/1979/1979-labour-manifesto.shtml [accessed January 2021].

51.  Owen, p. 1.

52.  S. Ashe, S. Virdee and L. Brown, 'Striking back against racist violence in the East End of London, 1968–1970', *Race & Class* (Institute of Race Relations, 2016), p. 39.

53.  D. Rosenberg, 'The racist killing of Altab Ali 40 years ago today', openDemocracy, 2018, https://www.opendemocracy.net/en/shine-a-light/remembering-altab-ali/ [accessed January 2021].

54.  Fryer, p. 391.

55.  C. Uche, 'The British Government, Idi Amin and the Expulsion of British Asians from Uganda', *Interventions*, 19:6 (2017), pp. 818–36.

56.  K. Paul, *Whitewashing Britain: Race and citizenship in the postwar era* (Cornell University Press, 1997), p. 182.

57.  'Ugandan Asians advert "foolish", says Leicester councillor', *BBC News*, 8 August 2012, https://www.bbc.com/news/uk-england-leicestershire-19165216 [accessed January 2021].

58.  N. Shrapnel, 'Ugandan Asians' best interests', *Guardian*, 8 August 1972, https://www.theguardian.com/theguardian/2009/aug/08/amin-uganda-refugee-commons [accessed January 2021].

59.  'Racial Expulsion', *The Times*, 14 August 1972, p. 13.

60.  J. Callaghan, 'Leader's speech, Blackpool', BritishPoliticalSpeech,

1976, http://www.britishpoliticalspeech.org/speech-archive. htm?speech=174 [accessed January 2021].

61.  M. Thatcher, 'Speech to Conservative party conference', Margaret Thatcher Foundation, 1978, https://www.margaretthatcher.org/document/103764 [accessed January 2021].

62.  Office for National Statistics, 'Explore 50 years of international migration to and from the UK', 2016, https://www.ons.gov.uk/peoplepopulationandcommunity/populationandmigration/internationalmigration/articles/explore50yearsofinternationalmigrationtoandfromtheuk/2016-12-01 [accessed January 2021].

63.  G. Sturge, 'Migration Statistics', Briefing Paper, House of Commons Library, Number CBP06077, 2 December 2020, p. 13.

64.  'On This Day, 1972: Miners' strike turns off the lights', *BBC News*, 16 February 1972, http://news.bbc.co.uk/onthisday/hi/dates/stories/february/16/newsid_2757000/2757099.stm; 'On This Day, 1972: UK unemployment tops one million', *BBC News*, 20 January 1972, http://news.bbc.co.uk/onthisday/hi/dates/stories/january/20/newsid_2506000/2506897.stm [accessed January 2021].

65.  Waters, p. 169.

66.  T. Branigan, 'Race to identify "first" black police officer', *Guardian*, 26 July 2004, https://www.theguardian.com/uk/2004/jul/26/race.ukcrime [accessed January 2021].

67.  Fryer., p. 394.

68.  A. Wilson, *Finding a Voice: Asian women in Britain* (Daraja Press, reprint 2018, original 1978), p. 59.

69.  Fryer, p. 395.

70.  Home Office, 'Racial discrimination', 9 September 1975, pp. 3–4, http://filestore.nationalarchives.gov.uk/pdfs/small/cab-129-184-c-93.pdf [accessed January 2021].

71.  Runnymede Trust, 'Race Relations Act 1976', http://runnymedetrust.org/histories/race-equality/48/race-relations-act-1976.html [accessed January 2021].

72.  H. Taylor, '"Rivers of Blood" and Britain's Far Right', *Political Quarterly*, 89:3 (July–September 2018); L. Audickas, N. Dempsey and P. Loft, 'Membership of UK political parties', House of Commons Library, Briefing Paper number SN05125, 2019.

73.  Office for National Statistics, 'Labour disputes in the UK: 2018', 2019, https://www.ons.gov.uk/employmentandlabourmarket/peopleinwork/workplacedisputesandworkingconditions/articles/labourdisputes/2018 [accessed January 2021].

74.  A. Travis, 'National archives: Fear of fights at cemetery gates during 1979 winter of discontent', *Guardian*, 30 December 2009, https://www.theguardian.com/uk/2009/dec/30/liverpool-gravedigger-strikes [accessed January 2021].

75.  'TV Interview for Granada *World in Action* ("rather swamped")', Margaret Thatcher Foundation, 1978, https://www.margaretthatcher.org/document/103485 [accessed January 2021].

76.  'Guardian Century, Two million – before it gets rough', *Guardian*,

28 August 1980, https://www.theguardian.com/century/1980-1989/
Story/0,,108182,00.html [accessed January 2021]; 'The Thatcher
years in statistics', *BBC News*, 9 April 2013, https://www.bbc.com/
news/uk-politics-22070491 [accessed January 2021].

77. M. Lesh, 'The radical neoliberal programme which can revitalise the
Conservatives', *Conservative Home*, 9 October 2019, https://www.
conservativehome.com/platform/2019/10/matthew-lesh-the-radical-
neoliberal-programme-which-can-revitalise-the-conservatives.html
[accessed January 2021].

78. The Equality Trust, 'How has inequality changed?', https://www.
equalitytrust.org.uk/how-has-inequality-changed [accessed January
2021].

79. Owen, p. 2.

80. L. Churchill, 'The St Paul's Riot 37 years on', *BristolLive*, 3 April
2017, https://www.bristolpost.co.uk/news/bristol-news/st-pauls-
riots-37-years-17634 [accessed January 2021].

81. Fryer, p. 402.

## Chapter Two: Indian Workers' Association

1. S. Richards and P. Saba (transcription, editing and markup),
'Remembering Comrade Joshi', *Encyclopedia of Anti-Revisionism On-
Line*, first published in *Class Struggle*, June 1983, https://www.
marxists.org/history/erol/uk.hightide/joshi.htm [accessed February
2021].

2. Details about Anant Ram's life in this section from: D. S. Tatla,
'This Is Our Home Now: Reminiscences of a Panjabi Migrant in
Coventry an Interview with Anant Ram', *Oral History*, 21:1 (Spring
1993).

3. £1,700 is the rounded amount from January 2023. Conversion done
with the Bank of England inflation calculator, bankofengland.co.uk/
monetary-policy/inflation/inflation-calculator.

4. R. Visram, *Asians in Britain: 400 Years of History* (Pluto Press,
2002), p. 271.

5. India Office, 'Intelligence report on the Indian Workers'
Association', British Library: File 273/42 – Indian Workers' Union or
Association: reports on members and activities, 1942, Shelfmark:
IOR/L/PJ/12/645.

6. Ibid.

7. Visram, p. 272.

8. *Indian Workers' Association (IWA): 60 Years of Struggles and
Achievements*, digital:works, online documentary, 2016.

9. Campaign Against Racism and Fascism and Southall Rights,
*Southall: the birth of a black community* (Institute of Race Relations
and Southall Rights, 1981), p. 9.

10. A. Sivanandan, *A Different Hunger: Writings on Black Resistance*
(Pluto Press, reprint 1991, original 1982), p. 3.

11. S. Josephides, *Towards a History of the Indian Workers' Association*
(Centre for Research in Ethnic Relations, University of Warwick,
1991), p. 2.

12. T. Gill, 'The Indian Workers' Association Coventry 1938–1990: political and social action', *South Asian History and Culture*, 4:4 (2013), p. 560.
13. Ibid.
14. Ibid.
15. Josephides, p. 29.
16. Campaign Against Racism and Fascism and Southall Rights, p. 12.
17. Ibid., p. 41.
18. 'Asians deny factory "colour bar in reverse"', *Guardian*, 25 November 1968, p. 5.
19. Campaign Against Racism and Fascism and Southall Rights, p. 13.
20. *The Struggle of Asian Workers in Britain* (Race Today, 1983), p. 10; £170 is the rounded amount comparing 1965 to January 2023, conversion done with the Bank of England inflation calculator, bankofengland.co.uk/monetary-policy/inflation/inflation-calculator.
21. J. Dewitt, *Indian Workers' Associations in Britain* (Institute of Race Relations, 1969), p. 145.
22. *Indian Workers' Association (IWA)*.
23. B. Purewal, *Indian Workers' Association: 60 years of struggles and achievements 1956–2016* (The Asian Health Agency, 2016), p. 24.
24. *Indian Workers' Association (IWA)*.
25. Ibid.
26. H. Punja, 'The need for unity: an interview with Vishnu Sharma', *Race & Class*, 58:1 (2016), p. 108.
27. '"Danger point" in school', *Guardian*, 16 October 1963, p. 1.
28. Campaign Against Racism and Fascism and Southall Rights, p. 31.
29. Ibid., p. 32.
30. O. Esteves, 'Babylon by Bus? The dispersal of immigrant children in England, race and urban space (1960s–1980s)', *Paedagogica Historica*, 54:6 (2018), p. 754.
31. Ibid., p. 752.
32. London Borough of Ealing Education Committee, 'Coach travel for immigrant school children', Gunnersbury Park Museum and Library, 2006.178/bb(ii).
33. Department of Education and Science, *The Education of Immigrants*, Circular 7/65 (1965), educationengland.org.uk/documents/des/circular7-65.html [accessed February 2021].
34. Campaign Against Racism and Fascism and Southall Rights, p. 32; P. Harrison, 'The Patience of Southall', *New Society*, 4 April 1974, p. 11.
35. Campaign Against Racism and Fascism and Southall Rights, p. 32.
36. B. Bebber, '"We Were Just Unwanted": Bussing, Migrant Dispersal, and South Asians in London', *Journal of Social History*, 48:3 (2015), p. 645.
37. Esteves, p. 759.
38. Ibid., p. 755.
39. Campaign Against Racism and Fascism and Southall Rights, p. 47.
40. Esteves, p. 759.

41. Bebber, p. 648.
42. Ibid., p. 647.
43. Esteves, p. 760.
44. Campaign Against Racism and Fascism and Southall Rights, p. 46.
45. Harrison.
46. Campaign Against Racism and Fascism and Southall Rights, p. 32.
47. Bebber, p. 646.
48. Ibid., p. 651.
49. Esteves, p. 753.
50. B. S. Purewal, *Panjabis of Southall: 70 years of struggles and achievements 1949–2019* (The Asian Health Agency, 2019), p. 60.
51. *Indian Workers' Association (IWA).*
52. M. Phillips, 'Virginity tests on immigrants at Heathrow', *Guardian*, 1 February 1979, p. 1.
53. A. Wilson, *Finding a Voice* (Daraja Press, second edition 2018, original 1978), pp. 89–90.; Punja, p. 109.
54. Phillips, 'Virginity tests on immigrants at Heathrow'.
55. M. Marmo and E. Smith, 'Uncovering the "virginity testing" controversy in the National Archives: The intersectionality of discrimination in British immigration history', *Gender & History*, 23:1 (2011), p. 147.
56. IWA Southall, 'Review – Report (August 1977–August 1979)', Institute of Race Relations, 01/04/04/01/12/050.
57. 'Immigrants (gynaecological examination)', *Hansard*, HC Deb 5 February 1979, Vol. 962, cc1–2w.
58. Ibid., c539w.
59. M. Marmo and E. Smith, 'Is there a desirable migrant? A reflection on human rights violations at the border: the case of "virginity testing"', *Alternative Law Journal*, 35:4 (2010), p. 224.
60. M. Phillips, 'I knew about virginity tests, says former Minister', *Guardian*, 2 February 1979, p. 1.
61. Marmo and Smith, 'Is there a desirable migrant?', p. 224.
62. 'Mrs B. L. Kakar: Claim for compensation', National Archives, FCO50/675.
63. I. Guest, 'Britain in UN row over virginity tests', *Guardian*, 6 March 1979, p. 29.
64. 'This immigration control must stop', National Archives, HO418/29.
65. Marmo and Smith, 'Uncovering the "virginity testing" controversy', p. 154.
66. Ibid., p. 148.
67. 'Letter from the Treasury Chambers to the Home Office, Ex gratia payment to Mrs Kakar, 5 March 1980', National Archives, FCO50/675.
68. Ibid.
69. M. Phillips, 'Indian woman in virginity test row "will reject Home Office cash offer"', *Guardian*, 19 June 1980, p. 26; see documents at the National Archives, FCO50/675, related to Mr Kakar's case.
70. 'Immigrants (gynaecological examination)', *Hansard*, HC Deb 9 February 1979, Vol. 962, cc312-3W.

71. A. Ballantyne, 'Immigration report reveals raw deal for blacks', *Guardian*, 13 February 1985, p. 8.
72. Punja, p. 109.
73. Gill, p. 566.
74. Tatla, p. 72.

## Chapter Three: Bristol Bus Boycott

1. M. Dresser, *Black and White on the Buses: The 1963 colour bar dispute in Bristol* (Bookmarks Publication, reprint 2013, original 1986), p. 25.
2. K. Andrews, 'Guy Reid-Bailey: the man who sparked the Bristol bus boycott and then fought to desegregate housing', *Guardian*, 17 December 2020, https://www.theguardian.com/world/2020/dec/17/guy-reid-bailey-the-man-who-sparked-the-bristol-bus-boycott-and-then-fought-to-desegregate-housing [accessed April 2021].
3. Dresser, p. 36.
4. J. Kelly, 'What was behind the Bristol bus boycott?', *BBC News*, 27 August 2013, https://www.bbc.com/news/magazine-23795655 [accessed April 2021].
5. S. Anthony, 'The UK's Most Woke Cities: The most progressive places in which to live and work', *Bankrate*, 6 August 2019.
6. Bristol Museums Black History Steering Group, 'Bristol's Black History', Bristol Museums, https://www.bristolmuseums.org.uk/stories/bristols-black-history/ [accessed April 2021].
7. D. Olusoga, *Black and British: A forgotten history* (Macmillan, 2016), p. 104.
8. R. Mukena, 'Taking a look back at the history of St Paul's', *BristolLive*, 21 October 2019, https://www.bristolpost.co.uk/news/bristol-news/taking-look-back-history-st-3450661 [accessed April 2021].
9. Dresser, p. 11.
10. Dresser, p. 7.
11. P. Goldblatt and J. Morrison, 'Initial assessment of London bus driver mortality from COVID-19', Institute of Health Equity, http://www.instituteofhealthequity.org/resources-reports/london-bus-drivers-review/london-bus-driver-review-phase-1-rapid-review.pdf, p. 13; Office for National Statistics, 'Which occupations have the highest potential exposure to the coronavirus (COVID-19)?', 2020, https://www.ons.gov.uk/employmentandlabourmarket/people inwork/employmentandemployeetypes/articles/whichoccupation shavethehighestpotentialexposuretothecoronaviruscovid19/2020-05-11 [accessed April 2021].
12. Dresser, p. 12.
13. P. Fryer, *Staying Power: The history of black people in Britain* (Pluto Press, reprint 2018, original 1984), p. 382.
14. Ibid.
15. J. Kelly, 'What was behind the Bristol bus boycott of 1963?', *BBC News*, 27 August 2013, https://www.bbc.com/news/magazine-23795655 [accessed April 2021].

16. Dresser, p. 34.
17. Kelly.
18. T. Mazumdar, 'What was behind Bristol bus boycott?', *Newsnight*, 28 August 2013, https://www.bbc.com/news/av/uk-23863577 [accessed February 2023].
19. Ibid.
20. Dresser, p. 38.
21. Mazumdar.
22. Kelly.
23. 'Roy Hackett interview', Bristol Archive Records, http://www.bristolarchiverecords.com/people/people_Roy_Hackett.html [accessed April 2021].
24. P. Stephenson and L. Morrison, *Memoirs of a Black Englishman* (Tangent Books, 2011), p. 12.
25. K. Andrews, 'Paul Stephenson: the hero who refused to leave a pub – and helped desegregate Britain', *Guardian*, 1 October 2020, https://www.theguardian.com/society/2020/oct/01/paul-stephenson-the-hero-who-refused-to-leave-a-pub-and-helped-desegregate-britain [accessed April 2021].
26. Stephenson and Morrison, p. 48.
27. K. Ajala, 'The Seven Saints of St Pauls: Memorials and Black Joy in Bristol', Bristol Museums, https://www.bristolmuseums.org.uk/stories/the-seven-saints-of-st-pauls-memorials-and-black-joy-in-bristol/ [accessed April 2021].
28. Dresser, p. 16.
29. Stephenson and Morrison, p. 52.
30. Bristol estimate from: Dresser, p. 11. Total number from: GB Historical GIS/University of Portsmouth, Bristol UA/City through time, 'Population Statistics | Total Population', *A Vision of Britain through Time*, https://www.visionofbritain.org.uk/unit/10056676/cube/TOT_POP [accessed April 2021].
31. Stephenson and Morrison, p. 51.
32. Ibid., p. 57.
33. Dresser, p. 24.
34. K. Andrews, 'Roy Hackett: the civil rights hero who stood in front of a bus – and changed Britain forever', *Guardian*, 6 August 2020, https://www.theguardian.com/society/2020/aug/06/roy-hackett-the-civil-rights-hero-who-stood-in-front-of-a-bus-and-changed-britain-for-ever [accessed April 2021].
35. Stephenson and Morrison, p. 54.
36. Dresser, p. 23.
37. Ibid., p. 24.
38. Special Correspondent, 'Bus boycott by West Indians', *The Times*, 3 May 1963, p. 11.
39. 'Road transport operators (racial discrimination)', *Hansard*, HC Deb 15 May 1963, Vol. 677, cc149–50w.
40. English Heritage, 'Learie Constantine', https://www.english-heritage.org.uk/visit/blue-plaques/learie-constantine/ [accessed April 2021].

41. Parliamentary Correspondent, 'Bus colour bar to end', *The Times*, 8 May 1963, p. 12.
42. Ibid.; 'Colour bar ends on buses', *Guardian*, 8 May 1963, p. 1.
43. Stephenson and Morrison, p. 57.
44. Ibid., p. 53.
45. Dresser, p. 17.
46. Stephenson and Morrison, p. 59.
47. J. Chappell, 'Racial Discrimination in Employment? The Bristol Bus Boycott of 1963', university unknown, student thesis, p. 22.
48. Dresser, p. 27.
49. Our Correspondent, 'Church statement "lamentable"', *The Times*, 7 May 1963, p. 5.
50. Dresser, p. 29.
51. Our Special Correspondent, 'Bus boycott by West Indians'.
52. Ibid.
53. Stephenson and Morrison, p. 56.
54. K. Andrews, 'Paul Stephenson: the hero who refused to leave a pub – and helped desegregate Britain'.
55. Ibid.
56. Chappell, p. 20; Dresser, p. 26.
57. Dresser, p. 26.
58. Ibid., p. 30.
59. Ibid., p. 21.
60. Our Correspondent, 'Compromise on buses colour bar sought', *The Times*, 7 May 1963, p. 5.
61. 'Industrial Colour Bar, *The Times*, 7 May 1963, p. 13.
62. Dresser, p. 45.
63. Our Correspondent, 'Bus crew colour bar ends', *The Times*, 29 August 1963, p. 6.
64. 'Teachers TV, Post-war Britain: race relations', *TES*, 22 February 2018, https://www.tes.com/teaching-resource/teachers-tv-post-war-britain-race-relations-6085169 [accessed February 2023].
65. Manchester Central Library, 'Fight for the turban', http://www.archivesplus.org/history/fight-for-the-turban/ [accessed April 2021].
66. W. Noble, 'The man who insisted on wearing a turban on the tube', *Londonist*, 6 March 2018, https://londonist.com/london/transport/when-london-underground-sent-a-staff-member-home-for-wearing-a-turban [accessed April 2021].
67. R. Collins, 'The turban-wearing British bus driver who changed the law', *BBC News*, 30 April 2019, https://www.bbc.com/news/uk-england-birmingham-47853718 [accessed April 2021].
68. 'Trooping the Colour: Guardsman first to wear turban', *BBC News*, 9 June 2018, https://www.bbc.com/news/uk-england-leicestershire-44413296 [accessed April 2021]; 'Trooping the Colour: Leicester soldier dismisses criticism', *BBC News*, 13 June 2018, https://www.bbc.com/news/uk-england-leicestershire-44466263 [accessed April 2021].
69. 'QuickTake, Bristol bus boycott: Remembering the first black bus driver in Bristol', Bloomberg, 2020.

70. Dresser, p. 46.
71. Ibid.
72. G. Halladay, 'The first coloured conductor thinks it's so nice', *Bristol Evening Post*, 17 September 1963.
73. Dresser, pp. 48, 50.
74. Stephenson and Morrison, p. 51.
75. English Heritage.
76. St Pauls Carnival, 'An update for 2021', 2021, https://www.stpaulscarnival.net/news/2021/3/5/an-update-for-2021 [accessed April 2021].
77. M. Ingoldby, 'Interview with Roy Hackett', 2011, https://memaps.club/bbb/archive/audio-interviews/roy-hackett/ [accessed April 2021].
78. Triodos Bank, 'Seven Saints of St Pauls', 2020, https://www.triodos.co.uk/articles/2020/seven-saints-of-st-pauls [accessed April 2021].
79. Ibid.
80. K. Andrews, 'Guy Reid-Bailey: the man who sparked the Bristol bus boycott and then fought to desegregate housing', *Guardian*, 17 December 2020, https://www.theguardian.com/world/2020/dec/17/guy-reid-bailey-the-man-who-sparked-the-bristol-bus-boycott-and-then-fought-to-desegregate-housing [accessed April 2021].
81. Ibid.
82. UWE Bristol, 'The Paul Stephenson Bursary', https://www.uwe.ac.uk/courses/funding/scholarships-and-bursaries/paul-stephenson-bursary [accessed April 2021]; A. Ballinger, 'This is why Paul Stephenson a Bristol legend just won a Pride of Britain award', *BristolLive*, 7 November 2017, https://www.bristolpost.co.uk/news/bristol-news/paul-stephenson-who-is-bristol-707262 [accessed April 2021]; Z. Drewett, 'Petition to replace Edward Colston statue with man who led Bristol Bus Boycott', *Metro*, 8 June 2020, https://metro.co.uk/2020/06/08/10000-call-replace-edward-colston-statue-bristol-bus-boycott-leader-12820101/?ico=more_text_links [accessed April 2021].
83. Mukena.
84. Excluding London. Department for Transport, 'Annual bus statistics: England 2019/20', 28 October 2020, https://assets.publishing.service.gov.uk/government/uploads/system/uploads/attachment_data/file/929992/annual-bus-statistics-year-ending-march-2020.pdf [accessed February 2023].
85. A. Postans, 'First Bus STILL having a "huge problem" recruiting drivers', *BristolLive*, 11 March 2019, https://www.bristolpost.co.uk/news/first-bus-still-having-huge-2626335 [accessed April 2021].
86. Bristol City Council, 'The Population of Bristol', September 2020, https://www.bristol.gov.uk/documents/20182/33904/Population+of+Bristol+September+2020.pdf/69aa0aa1-290a-ccf2-ec4f-13a7376b41a8.
87. Mazumdar.
88. N. Phillips, 'Bristol bus boycott: Meet the faces behind the UK's own 1963 civil rights movement', *Sky News*, 12 October 2020, https://

news.sky.com/story/bristol-bus-boycott-meet-the-faces-behind-the-uks-own-1963-civil-rights-movement-12086127 [accessed April 2021].

89. E. Beeston, 'Replace the Colston Statue with a Black Individual, petition', change.org, https://www.change.org/p/bristol-city-council-replace-the-colston-statue-with-a-black-individual [accessed April 2021]; J. Phillips, 'Get a monument to Roy Hackett erected in place of Colston in Bristol City Centre, petition', change.org, https://www.change.org/p/marvin-rees-get-a-monument-to-roy-hackett-erected-in-place-of-colston-in-bristol-city-centre [accessed April 2021].

## Chapter Four: Black Power and the Mangrove Nine

1. A.-M. Angelo, '"Black oppressed people all over the world are one": The British Black Panthers' Grassroots Internationalism, 1969–73', *Journal of Civil and Human Rights*, 4:1 (2018), p. 66.

2. Universal Coloured People's Association, *Black Power in Britain* (Universal Coloured People's Association, 1968), p.5., artsandculture.google.com/asset/-wGCabbYRjn5YQ?childAssetId=OAGymY_bbkiz6g [accessed May 2021].

3. R. Waters, *Thinking Black: Britain, 1964–1985* (University of California Press, 2019), p. 26.

4. Angelo, p. 65.

5. B. Knight, '"They were afraid of us": The legacy of Britain's Black Panthers', Al Jazeera, 7 December 2020, https://www.aljazeera.com/features/2020/12/7/they-were-afraid-of-us-the-legacy-of-britains-black [accessed May 2021].

6. Author interview with Farrukh Dhondy, 31 March 2022.

7. Waters, p. 42.

8. Author interview with Farrukh Dhondy.

9. Universal Coloured People's Association.

10. Angelo, p. 75.

11. D. Aitkenhead, 'Linton Kwesi Johnson: "It was a myth that immigrants didn't want to fit into British society. We weren't allowed"', *Guardian*, 27 April 2018, https://www.theguardian.com/books/2018/apr/27/linton-kwesi-johnson-brixton-windrush-myth-immigrants-didnt-want-fit-british-society-we-werent-allowed [accessed May 2021].

12. Ibid.

13. Waters, p. 59.

14. Angelo, pp. 72, 76.

15. Ibid., p. 70.

16. Ibid., p. 81.

17. Author interview with Farrukh Dhondy.

18. Angelo, p. 66.

19. R. Bunce and P. Field, *Darcus Howe: A political biography* (Bloomsbury, 2015), p. 108.

20. 'Battle for Freedom at the Old Bailey' flyer, National Archives, DPP 2/5059.

21. A. John-Baptiste, 'The Mangrove Nine: Echoes of black lives matters from 50 years ago', *BBC News*, https://www.bbc.co.uk/news/extra/jGD9WJrVXf/the-mangrove-nine-black-lives-matter [accessed May 2021].
22. Bunce and Field, p. 100.
23. John-Baptiste.
24. 'Frank Crichlow's complaint to the Race Relations Board, 23 December, 1969', National Archives, CK 2/690.
25. Bunce and Field, p. 100.
26. J. Steele, 'End for Special Branch after 122 years', *Daily Telegraph*, 9 September 2005.
27. T. Thompson, 'Inside the lonely and violent world of the Yard's elite undercover unit', *Guardian*, 14 March 2010, https://www.theguardian.com/uk/2010/mar/14/undercover-police-far-left-secret [accessed May 2021]; C. Woodman, 'The infiltrator and the movement', *Jacobin*, 23 April 2018, https://jacobinmag.com/2018/04/uk-infiltration-secret-police-mi5-special-branch-undercover/ [accessed May 2021].
28. Associated Press, 'MI5 files reveal details of 1953 coup that overthrew British Guiana's leaders', *Guardian*, 26 August 2011, https://www.theguardian.com/world/2011/aug/26/mi5-files-coup-british-guiana [accessed May 2021].
29. Bunce and Field, p. 27.
30. E. Lubbers, 'Black Power – 4. The Black Power desk', Special Branch Files Project, 17 September 2019, http://specialbranchfiles.uk/black-power-4-black-power-desk/ [accessed May 2021].
31. B. Knight, 'Behind the Lens ft. Neil Kenlock', *Tell A Friend*, podcast, series 3, episode 20, 9 August 2020, https://podcasts.apple.com/gb/podcast/behind-the-lens-feat-neil-kenlock/id1438462126?i=1000487610732.
32. 'Demonstration/political statement from Action Group for the Defence of the Mangrove', National Archives, HO 325/143.
33. 'Marcher "had not violence in mind"', *The Times*, 12 November 1971.
34. Bunce and Field, p. 106.
35. D. Howe, *From Bobby to Babylon: Blacks and the British Police* (Race Today Publications 1988, reissued Bookmarks Publications 2020), p. 53.
36. Bunce and Field, p. 108.
37. Ibid., p. 109.
38. Howe, p. 54.
39. Ibid., p. 55.
40. Our Own Reporter, '17 police hurt in race fight', *Guardian*, 10 August 1970, p. 1; P. Evans, '19 held in clash with police', *The Times*, 10 August 1970, p. 1.
41. P. Evans, 'Outsiders blamed for weekend race clash', *The Times*, 14 August 1970, p. 3.
42. 'March planned by "Black House"', *Daily Mail*, 11 August 1970, p. 5.
43. J. Spicer, 'Why the drive for more coloured police flopped', *Daily Mail*, 4 February 1970, p. 5.

44. '3 charged after demonstration', *The Times*, 15 October 1970, p. 6.
45. Bunce and Field, p. 120.
46. Ibid., p. 116.
47. Ibid., p. 118.
48. Ibid., p. 117.
49. Ibid., p. 101.
50. Ibid., p. 101.
51. 'Aim of Black Power march was to enlist sympathy', *The Times*, 18 November 1971, p. 24.
52. John-Baptiste.
53. Author interview with Farrukh Dhondy.
54. Bunce and Field, p. 115.
55. 'Petition', *International Times*, 1:114 (7–21 October 1971), p. 4.
56. Our Own Reporter, 'All-black jury plea rejected', *Guardian*, 7 October 1971, p. 6.
57. D. Pien, 'Mangrove Nine Trial 1970–1972', BlackPast.org, 2 July 2018, https://www.blackpast.org/global-african-history/mangrove-nine-trial-1970-1972/ [accessed May 2021].
58. 'Two coloured jurors for "all-black" trial', *Daily Mail*, 8 October 1971; Bunce and Field, p. 125.
59. Standard Reporter, 'Barrister calls for an all-black jury', *Evening Standard*, 5 October 1971, p. 7.
60. 'Shouts of "pigs" at police from crowd, witness says', *The Times*, 12 October 1971, p. 2.
61. 'PC denies drawing his truncheon in fight', *The Times*, 15 October 1971.
62. 'Demo "erupted into a riot"', *Daily Mail*, 9 October 1971, p. 21.
63. 'Black Power case man in clash with judge', *The Times*, 21 October 1971, p. 5.
64. 'Mangrove Nine Trial', *International Times*, 1:119 (16–30 December 1971), p. 3.
65. Author interview with Farrukh Dhondy.
66. John La Rose notebook, George Padmore Institute, LRA02/01/01/03.
67. Bunce and Field, p. 132; 'Judge gives new warning in Black Power trial', *The Times*, 19 November 1971, p. 4.
68. 'Police brutality in Notting Hill denied', *The Times*, 13 October 1971, p. 4.
69. 'PC says restaurant is a "den of iniquity"', *The Times*, 19 October 1971, p. 2.
70. John-Baptiste.
71. Bunce and Field, p. 129.
72. 'Mangrove case: "Hit by plain-clothes men" claim', *The Times*, 10 November 1971, p. 3.
73. 'Race worker says he took no part in the violence', *The Times*, 16 November 1971, p. 3.
74. V. Hines, 'Racists in setback', *International Times*, 1:96 (28 January–10 February 1971), pp. 3, 10.
75. 'Aim of Black Power march was to enlist sympathy', *The Times*, 18 November 1971, p. 24.

76. 'Woman says police threw her into a van', *The Times*, 25 November 1971, p. 5.
77. 'Mangrove Nine Trial', *International Times*, 1:119 (16–30 December 1971), p. 3.
78. Bunce and Field, p. 129.
79. Ibid.
80. Ibid.
81. Ibid., p. 130.
82. Author interview with Farrukh Dhondy.
83. Our Own Reporter, 'Picket at court arrested', *Guardian*, 8 December 1971, p. 6.
84. 'Mangrove trial "passion"', *The Times*, 2 December 1971, p. 3.
85. J. Cunningham, 'Short order for the law', *Guardian*, 17 December 1971, p. 13.
86. Ibid.
87. 'Mangrove trial jury told "keep your cool"', *The Times*, 15 December 1971, p. 4.
88. R. Hillel and V. Iglikowski-Broad, 'Rights, resistance and racism: the story of the Mangrove Nine', National Archives, 21 October 2015, https://blog.nationalarchives.gov.uk/rights-resistance-racism-story-mangrove-nine/ [accessed May 2021].
89. R. E. Wild, '"Black was the colour of our fight." Black Power in Britain, 1955–1976', University of Sheffield, PhD thesis, August 2008, p. 188.
90. 'Suspended sentences on four convicted at Mangrove trial', *The Times*, 17 December 1971, p. 5.
91. Author interview with Farrukh Dhondy.
92. 'Mangrove verdict', *International Times*, 1:120 (30 December 1971–13 January 1972), p. 2; John-Baptiste.
93. Wild, p. 188.
94. I. Thompson, 'The Mangrove 9 and the Radical Lawyering Tradition', *Verso*, 20 November 2020, https://www.versobooks.com/blogs/4920-the-mangrove-9-and-the-radical-lawyering-tradition [accessed May 2021].
95. 'House prices in All Saints Road, Notting Hill, West London, W11', Right Move, https://www.rightmove.co.uk/house-prices/w11/all-saints-road.html?locationIdentifier=STREET%5E2335801&index=25 [accessed May 2021].
96. 'Suspended sentences on four convicted at Mangrove trial'.

## Chapter Five: The Fasimbas, the Oval Four and the Black Liberation Front

1. Black Liberation Front Working Platform, Young Historians Project, https://www.younghistoriansproject.org/blf-exhibition [accessed March 2022].
2. Author interview with Winston Trew, 24 March 2022.
3. J. Cunningham, 'Come the Revolution', *Guardian*, 10 March 1972, p. 14.

4.  For a glimpse of how dire it is today: N. Jerome, 'As a black literary agent, I despair at UK's lack of publishing diversity', *Guardian*, 1 January 2022, https://www.theguardian.com/commentisfree/2022/jan/01/black-literary-agent-uk-publishing-diversity [accessed March 2022].
5.  Black History Walks, 'Books, violence and resistance: Eric Huntley', webinar, 16 April 2021.
6.  A. Payne, 'The Rodney riots in Jamaica: the background and significance of the events of October 1968', *Journal of Commonwealth & Comparative Politics*, 21:2 (25 March 2008), pp. 158–74.
7.  'Books, violence and resistance: Eric Huntley'.
8.  Ibid.
9.  A.-M. Angelo, '"Black oppressed people all over the world are one": The British Black Panthers' Grassroots Internationalism, 1969–73', *Journal of Civil and Human Rights*, 4:1 (2018), p. 89.
10. 'Books, violence and resistance: Eric Huntley'.
11. Bookshop Joint Action Committee summary of attacks 1977, George Padmore Institute, BPM 6/1/1/1.
12. Ibid.
13. Race Today Collective, 'We won't be terrorised out of existence', *Race Today*, 9:7 (November/December 1977), p. 148.
14. Author interview with Winston Trew.
15. 'A different kind of mugging', *Time Out*, 27 October–2 November 1972, London Metropolitan Archives, LMA 4463/B/17/01/002.
16. W. Trew, *Black for a Cause . . . Not Just Because . . .: The case of the 'Oval 4' and the story of Black Power in 1970s Britain* (Trew Books, third edition 2015, first edition 2010), p. 31.
17. Trew, p. 32.
18. C. McCrae, '"I felt my face getting tight and I could hardly breathe" – The story of Winston Trew and the Oval Four (Part I)', *Un:Just*, podcast, 26 June 2020, anchor.fm/unjust/episodes/I-felt-my-face-getting-tight-and-I-could-hardly-breathe---the-story-of-Winston-Trew-and-the-Oval-Four-Part-I-egnoor.
19. Trew, p. 53.
20. 'Court frees men in pick pocket attempt case', *The Times*, 31 July 1973, p. 3.
21. Afrika Speaks with Alkebu-Lan, 'Are YOU Black for a cause? Winston Trew and the story of the "Oval 4"', radio programme, 27 January 2020, https://www.mixcloud.com/AfrikaSpeaks/are-you-black-for-a-cause-winston-trew-and-the-story-of-the-oval-4-270120/ [accessed February 2013].
22. Letter from the Fasimbas to Bogle-L'Ouverture Publications, London Metropolitan Archives, LMA 4463/B/17/01/002.
23. Race Today Collective, dock brief, *Race Today*, December 1972, personal files of Winston Trew.
24. Oval Four flyer, London Metropolitan Archives, LMA 4463/B/17/01/002.
25. Trew, p. 38.
26. McCrae, '"I felt my face getting tight"'.

27. A flyer from the Fasimbas refers to it as the 'book of unsolved crimes'; Trew, p. 53.
28. Trew, pp. 41–2.
29. Author interview with Winston Trew.
30. Trew, p. 43.
31. Trew, p. 45.
32. Trew, p. 48.
33. Author interview with Winston Trew.
34. Ibid.
35. J. Ayto, 'Words from the 1970s', *Oxford English Dictionary*, 13 March 2019, https://public.oed.com/blog/words-from-the-1970s/ [accessed June 2021].
36. S. Hall et al., *Policing the Crisis: Mugging, the state and law and order* (Macmillan, 1978).
37. 'Three years for leader of "mugging" gang, *The Times*, 26 September 1972, p. 4.
38. Standard Reporter, 'London mugging: Judge talks of a city in fear', *Evening Standard*, 25 September 1972, p. 1.
39. Author interview with Winston Trew.
40. Trew, pp. 59–60.
41. Author interview with Winston Trew.
42. Ibid.
43. Trew, p. 61.
44. Author interview with Winston Trew.
45. Trew, p. 61.
46. Author interview with Winston Trew.
47. Ibid.
48. '"Revenge" cry as Tube gang trio jailed', *Evening Standard*, 8 November 1972, p. 12.
49. Trew, p. 70.
50. Author interview with Winston Trew.
51. Trew, p. 75.
52. M. Wall, 'Fasimbas – and a glossary of violence', *Evening Standard*, 16 February 1973, p. 8.
53. Ibid.
54. Ibid.
55. Oval Four flyer, London Metropolitan Archives, LMA 4463/B/17/01/002.
56. Author interview with Winston Trew.
57. 'Race Today Collective, dock brief', *Race Today*, unknown date, personal files of Winston Trew.
58. Author interview with Winston Trew.
59. Ibid.
60. Letter from Constantine 'Omar' Boucher to Jessica Huntley, 14 January 1973, London Metropolitan Archives, LMA 4463/B/17/01/002.
61. Author interview with Winston Trew.
62. Trew, p. 96.
63. Trew, p. 87; Our Own Reporter, 'Appeal Court frees four blacks', *Guardian*, 31 July 1973, p. 6.

64. S. K. Brooks and N. Greenberg, 'Psychological impact of being wrongfully accused of criminal offences: A systematic literature review', *Medicine, Science and the Law*, 61:1 (2021), p. 45.

65. D. Campbell, '"It shattered me": Winston Trew on the decades-long fight to clear his name', *Guardian*, 13 October 2019, https://www.theguardian.com/world/2019/oct/13/winston-trew-to-clear-his-name [accessed June 2021].

66. Author interview with Winston Trew.

67. R. E. Wild, '"Black was the colour of our fight." Black Power in Britain, 1955–1976', University of Sheffield, PhD thesis, August 2008, p. 87.

68. Ibid.

69. *Black for a Cause*, dir. S. Thompson, 2017.

70. D. Campbell, 'Man convicted of theft in 1976 cleared after Googling his arresting officer', *Guardian*, 17 January 2018, https://www.theguardian.com/uk-news/2018/jan/17/man-convicted-of-theft-in-1976-cleared-after-googling-his-arresting-officer [accessed June 2021].

71. D. Campbell, 'A real Line of Duty: the London police officer who "went bent"', *Guardian*, 1 May 2021, https://www.theguardian.com/uk-news/2021/may/01/a-real-line-of-duty-the-london-police-officer-who-went-bent [accessed June 2021].

72. H. Athwal, 'Too Black? The case of the Oval 4 revisited', Institute of Race Relations, 11 November 2010, https://irr.org.uk/article/too-black-the-case-of-the-oval-4-revisited/ [accessed June 2021]; author interview with Winston Trew.

73. Criminal Cases Review Commission, 'The commission refers the case of George Griffiths – a third Oval Four conviction', 14 November 2019, https://ccrc.gov.uk/commission-refers-the-case-of-george-griffiths-a-third-oval-four-conviction/ [accessed June 2021].

74. Criminal Cases Review Commission, 'The CCRC refers for appeal the conviction of the fourth and final member of the Oval Four', 13 January 2020, https://ccrc.gov.uk/the-ccrc-refers-for-appeal-the-conviction-of-the-fourth-and-final-member-of-the-oval-four/ [accessed June 2021].

75. C. McCrae, '"I'm innocent, I'm innocent, I'm innocent" – The story of Winston Trew and the Oval Four (Part II, Feat. Stephen Simmons and Jenny Wiltshire)', *Un:Just*, podcast, 13 July 2020, anchor.fm/unjust/episodes/Im-innocent--im-innocent--im-innocent---the-story-of-Winston-Trew-and-the-Oval-Four-Part-ii--feat--Stephen-Simmons--Jenny-Wiltshire-egnoos.

76. Author interview with Winston Trew.

77. D. Campbell, 'Final member of Oval Four has 1972 conviction overturned', *Guardian*, 24 March 2020, https://www.theguardian.com/law/2020/mar/24/final-member-oval-four-1972-conviction-overturned-constantine-omar-boucher [accessed June 2021].

78. Ibid.

79. F. Snead, "'If you are innocent, don't give up": Wrongly convicted man jailed as part of "Oval Four" has name cleared after nearly 50 years', *I*, 5 December 2019, https://inews.co.uk/news/uk/oval-four-winston-trew-wrongly-convicted-overturned-court-appeal-371337 [accessed June 2021].

80. Ibid.

81. Criminal Cases Review Commission, 'CCRC referral sees another "Stockwell Six" conviction quashed', 23 November 2021, https://ccrc.gov.uk/news/ccrc-referral-sees-another-stockwell-six-conviction-quashed/ [accessed February 2023].

82. Author interview with Winston Trew.

## Chapter Six: Black Education Movement

1. 'Education for liberation: a new purpose for schooling and education', George Padmore Institute, BPM 4/1/1/1.

2. P. Curtis, 'Opportunity locked', *Guardian*, 1 February 2005, https://www.theguardian.com/education/2005/feb/01/raceineducation.race [accessed July 2021]; *Subnormal: A British scandal*, dir. L. Shannon, BBC One, 2021.

3. Ministry of Education, *Special Educational Treatment* (His Majesty's Stationery Office, 1946), paragraph 25, http://educationengland.uk/documents/minofed/pamphlet-05.html [accessed August 2021].

4. Ibid., paragraph 49.

5. S.-M. Chan et al., *A recent history of primary and secondary education in England Part 1: 1944–1985* (ITT MFL, 2004), https://www.exeter.ac.uk/media/universityofexeter/collegeofsocialsciences andinternationalstudies/education/pgce/pre-coursedocuments/pre-coursedocuments2021-22/Secondary_MFL_-_History_of_Education_in_England_part_1.pdf.

6. For example: B. Yule et al., 'Children of West Indian immigrants – II. Intellectual performance and reading attainment', *Journal of Child Psychology and Psychiatry*, 16 (1975), pp. 1–17.

7. Ibid.

8. Ibid. The study on Turkish Cypriots is an Inner London Education Authority one quoted in this study.

9. Ministry of Education, *Education of the Handicapped Pupil 1945–1955* (Her Majesty's Stationery Office, 1956), paragraph 26, educationengland.org.uk/documents/minofed/pamphlet-30.html [accessed July 2021].

10. Excluding hospital schools. Ibid., paragraphs 9 and 48.

11. B. Coard, *How the West Indian Child Is Made Educationally Subnormal in the British School System* (McDermott Publishing, fifth edition 2021, original 1971), p. 56.

12. Coard, pp. 3–5. Emphasis added.

13. Ibid., p. 58.

14. Ibid., p. 6.

15. Ibid., p. 23.

16. *Subnormal: A British scandal*.

17. Ibid.

18. Our Home Affairs Correspondent, 'Injustice to children in subnormal schools', *The Times*, 5 May 1971, p. 2.
19. Coard, p. 62.
20. 'Letters to the Editor: Black and white marks for Mr Coard', *Guardian*, 8 May 1971, p. 10.
21. P. Evans, 'Big immigrant ratio in special schools', *The Times*, 19 December 1969, p. 2.
22. North London West Indian Association, 'Briefing Note', 23 April 1969, George Padmore Institute, BEM2/1/1/17. The NLWIA was affiliated to the West Indian Standing Conference.
23. Black Education Movement, George Padmore Institute, georgepadmoreinstitute.org/collections/the-black-education-movement-1965-1988 [accessed July 2021].
24. P. Evans, 'Race ratio question', *The Times*, 21 January 1970, p. 3.
25. G. Wansell, 'Board criticizes "subnormal" labelling', *The Times*, 22 February 1971, p. 3.
26. R. Bourne, 'Richard Bourne finds that not much is being done about reclassifying coloured ESN children who should be in ordinary schools', *Guardian*, 3 March 1971, p. 10.
27. Wansell.
28. 'NLWIA our reply to the Race Relations Board', 21 February 1971, George Padmore Institute, BEM1/2/6/10.
29. There are many studies that show this. Here is a snippet of the discussion: UCL, 'Setting pupils by attainment unlikely to boost attainment, but specific activity grouping might', 7 September 2018, https://www.ucl.ac.uk/ioe/news/2018/sep/setting-pupils-attainment-unlikely-boost-attainment-specific-activity-grouping-might [accessed July 2021]; National Education Union, 'Streaming and setting', 9 January 2019, https://neu.org.uk/streaming-and-setting [accessed July 2021].
30. S. Weale, 'Schoolchildren in lower attainment groups more likely to show emotional problems, study finds', *Guardian*, 26 November 2021, https://www.theguardian.com/education/2021/nov/26/children-harmed-by-school-streaming-into-lower-ability-groups-uk-study-shows [accessed March 2022].
31. A. Truefitt, 'London schools' banding system may be illegal', *Evening Standard*, 18 February 1970, p. 10.
32. Ibid.
33. A. Doulton, 'Haringey Comprehensive Schools', 13 January 1969, George Padmore Institute, BEM1/2/5.
34. NLWIA meeting flyer, 29 September 1969, George Padmore Institute, BEM1/2/4/10.
35. 'Proposals of the NLWIA concerning education in Haringey schools', George Padmore Institute, BEM2/1/1/101.
36. 'An appeal to Haringey Councillors from the Haringey Parents Group', George Padmore Institute, BEM1/2/3/28.
37. Consultative Council of Teachers, 'Review of Secondary Education', 10 March 1969, George Padmore Institute, BEM1/2/3/18–25.

38. P. Newell, 'At school we dance, tomorrow we ...', *Illustrated London News*, 18 May 1968, p. 21.

39. 'War Against Black Children' flyer, 24 January 1970, George Padmore Institute, BEM1/2/4/11.

40. 'Hearing today on "leaflet for blacks"', *Birmingham Daily Post*, 28 May 1970.

41. 'England's pioneering black head teachers', *BBC News*, 11 May 2018, https://www.bbc.com/news/uk-england-42649541 [accessed July 2021].

42. Coard, p. 61.

43. S. Jessel, 'Statistics back West Indian complaint of unfairness in schooling', *The Times*, 9 June 1971, p. 2.

44. Ibid.

45. Coard, p. 62.

46. P. A. J. Stevens, 'Researching race/ethnicity and educational inequality in English Secondary Schools: A critical review of the research literature between 1980–2005', *Review of Educational Research*, 77:2 (June 2007), p. 153.

47. J. D. Ingleby and E. Cooper, 'How teachers perceive first-year schoolchildren: sex and ethnic differences', *Sociology*, 8:3 (1974), pp. 463–73.

48. Ibid., p. 472.

49. P. Foster, 'Cases Not Proven: An Evaluation of Two Studies of Teacher Racism', *British Educational Research Journal*, 16:4 (1990); C. Y. Wright, 'Comments in Reply to the Article by P. Foster, "Cases Not Proven: An Evaluation of Two Studies of Teacher Racism"', *British Educational Research Journal*, 16:4 (1990); P. Foster, 'Case Still Not Proven: a reply to Cecile Wright', *British Educational Research Journal*, 17:2 (1991).

50. K. Andrews, *Resisting Racism: Race, inequality, and the Black supplementary school movement* (Institute of Education Press, 2013), p. 16.

51. Waters, p. 133.

52. 'Comprehension sheets', George Padmore Institute, BEM3/1/5/11/1 & 17.

53. 'Activity sheet', George Padmore Institute, BEM3/1/5/3/7.

54. Andrews, p. 45.

55. Andrews, p. 46.

56. Andrews, p. 42.

57. Akala, *Natives: Race and Class in the Ruins of Empire* (Two Roads, 2019), p. 125.

58. C. Seton, 'Independent study of poor school performance by blacks in Britain urged by committee', *The Times*, 31 March 1977, p. 3.

59. Ibid.

60. Committee of Enquiry into the Education of Children from Ethnic Minority Groups, *Education for All* (Her Majesty's Stationery Office, 1985); Rampton Report reproduced in the Swann Report, http://www.educationengland.org.uk/documents/swann/swann1985.html [accessed July 2021].

61. Ibid., Section 1.2.

62. Ibid., p. 768.

63. In the full report at least, the summary that was written by Swann and widely circulated avoided the term. See: 'Denying our colonial past', Socialist Labour Party, 19 April 2021, https://www.socialistlabourparty.org/post/denying-racism [accessed August 2021].

64. Committee of Enquiry into the Education of Children from Ethnic Minority Groups, p. 201.

65. D. Gillard, 'Education in England: A history', chapter 15, May 2018, http://www.educationengland.org.uk/history/chapter15.html#02 [accessed July 2021].

66. S. Strand and A. Lindorff, 'Ethnic disproportionality in the identification of Special Educational Needs (SEN) in England: Extent, causes and consequences', Department of Education, University of Oxford, 20 December 2018, http://www.education.ox.ac.uk/wp-content/uploads/2018/08/Executive-Summary_2018-12-20.pdf [accessed July 2021].

67. K. Jiwani, 'Supplementary schools case studies', Paul Hamlyn Foundation, May 2015, https://www.phf.org.uk/wp-content/uploads/2015/06/PHF----Education-Resources-Rpt-final.pdf [accessed July 2021].

68. Human Intelligence, 'The Cyril Burt Affair', 2018, https://www.intelltheory.com/burtaffair.shtml [accessed July 2021].

69. G. Tredoux, 'Defrauding Cyril Burt: A reanalysis of the social mobility data', *Intelligence*, 49 (March–April 2015), pp. 32–43.

70. N. Kelley, O. Khan and S. Sharrock, *Racial Prejudice in Britain Today* (NatCen, 2017).

71. R. Rees, T. Warner and J. Garry, *Migrants in Britain, c.800–present* (Pearson, 2021).

## Chapter Seven: Brixton Black Women's Group and OWAAD

1. P. Akpan, 'How the stories of Black women in the UK are being reclaimed', *Refinery29*, 10 October 2019, https://www.refinery29.com/en-gb/black-women-history-uk [accessed September 2021].

2. Y. Callahan, 'John Ridley erased black women in his series *Guerrilla* because of his interracial relationship', *Root*, 4 November 2017, https://www.theroot.com/john-ridley-erased-black-women-in-his-series-guerilla-1794206424 [accessed September 2021].

3. Striking Women, 'Women at work – post World War II: 1946–1970', https://www.striking-women.org/module/women-and-work/post-world-war-ii-1946-1970 [accessed September 2021].

4. Young Historians Project, 'Timeline of African women and the health service', https://www.younghistoriansproject.org/research-hub [accessed September 2021].

5. Sisterhood and After Research Team, 'Women's liberation: a national movement', British Library, 8 March 2013, https://www.bl.uk/sisterhood/articles/womens-liberation-a-national-movement [accessed September 2021].

6.  B. Bryan, S. Dadzie and S. Scafe, 'Chain reactions: Black women organising', *The Heart of the Race: Black women's lives in Britain* (Verso, reprint 2018, original 1985).

7.  T. Thomas, 'Beverley Bryan: the British Black Panther who inspired a generation of women', *Guardian*, 28 January 2021, https://www.theguardian.com/society/2021/jan/28/beverley-bryan-the-british-black-panther-who-inspired-a-generation-of-women [accessed September 2021].

8.  N. Thomlinson, *Race, Ethnicity and the Women's Movement in England, 1968–1993* (Palgrave Macmillan, 2016), p. 67.

9.  A. Quashie, 'Talking personal, talking political', *Trouble & Strife*, 19 (1990), reprinted in 'Spotlight on London's radical herstory: the Brixton Black Women's Group', *past tense* blog, 13 May 2020, https://pasttenseblog.wordpress.com/2020/05/13/spotlight-on-londons-radical-herstory-the-brixton-black-womens-group/ [accessed September 2021].

10.  Bryan, Dadzie and Scafe.

11.  M. T. Bogle, 'Brixton Black Women's Centre: Organizing on Child Sexual Abuse', *Feminist Review*, 28 (1988), p. 133.

12.  S. Lowry (ed.), 'Observatory', *Observer*, 31 August 1980, p. 33.

13.  'Brixton before the riots, part 3: the Brixton plan & squatting', *past tense* blog, 10 April 2021, https://pasttenseblog.wordpress.com/2021/04/10/brixton-before-the-riots-part-3-the-brixton-plan-squatting/ [accessed September 2021]; Remembering Olive Collective, *Do you remember Olive Morris?* (Aldgate Press, 2009), p. 12.

14.  'Brixton before the riots, part 3'.

15.  Remembering Olive Collective, p. 12.

16.  Ibid., p. 11.

17.  Ibid.

18.  Quashie.

19.  Ibid.

20.  Thomlinson, p. 88.

21.  OWAAD Constitution, Black Cultural Archives, DADZIE/1/1/4.

22.  Thomlinson, p. 80.

23.  Ibid.

24.  Additional notes to the OWAAD Constitution, Black Cultural Archives, DADZIE/1/1/3.

25.  Author interview with Stella Dadzie, 20 April 2022.

26.  Ibid.

27.  Interview with Mia Morris, 7 January 2009, Lambeth Archives, IV/279/2/5/1.

28.  Author interview with Stella Dadzie.

29.  Ibid.

30.  Thomlinson, p. 71.

31.  'The streets where they live', *Guardian*, 1 June 1979, p. 11.

32.  Brixton Black Women's Group, 'Black Women Organizing: Brixton Black Women's Group', *Feminist Review*, No. 17 (1984), pp. 84–85.

33.  C. Lambert, '"The objectionable injectable": recovering the lost

history of the WLM through the campaign against Depo-Provera', *Women's History Review*, 29:3 (2019), p. 523.

34. P. Chorlton, 'Birth control jab awaits the watchdogs' all-clear', *Guardian*, 20 February 1980, p. 2.
35. Lambert, p. 527.
36. Ibid., p. 525.
37. Ibid.
38. Brent Community Health Council, 'Black People and the Health Service', Institute of Race Relations, 32 HCCR.JN.
39. 'DP on TV', *FOWAAD!*, July 1979, Lambeth Archives, IV/279/3/1.
40. Lambert, p. 524.
41. Brent Community Health Council.
42. Lambert, p. 525.
43. Ibid., p. 532.
44. Ibid., p. 524.
45. 'Letters to the editor: Why Depo-Provera should not be given to nursing mothers', *Guardian*, 28 February 1980, p. 10.
46. K. von Henneberg and M. Rothschild, 'Contraceptive draws fire', *Multinational Monitor*, 1:7 (August 1980), https://multinationalmonitor.org/hyper/issues/1980/08/henneberg.html [accessed September 2021].
47. A. Veitch, 'Company deplores hospital drug use', *Guardian*, 27 April 1983, p. 2.
48. A. Chen, 'Depo-Provera under scrutiny', *Science News*, 123:8 (1983), p. 123.
49. A. Goodman and K. von Henneberg, 'The Grady Clinic study', *Multinational Monitor*, 6:2/3 (February/March 1985), https://multinationalmonitor.org/hyper/issues/1985/02/grady-clinic-study.html [accessed September 2021].
50. Interview with Jocelyn Wolfe, 2011, British Library, C1420/12.
51. Interview with Stella Dadzie, 2011, British Library, C1420/20.
52. Lambert, p. 534.
53. Black Cultural Archives, DADZIE/1/10.
54. 'Ban the Jab' campaign leaflet, Lambeth Archives, IV/279/1/14/17.
55. Ibid.
56. 'DP on TV'.
57. Black History Walks, 'Beyond the Black Panthers: Dr Beverly Bryan', webinar, 8 September 2021.
58. Fight against DP on Black Women, '3 months later' leaflet, Black Cultural Archives, DADZIE/1/10.
59. Interview with Mia Morris, 7 January 2009, Lambeth Archives, IV/279/2/5/1.
60. Author interview with Stella Dadzie.
61. J. Douglas, 'Black Women's Activism and Organisation in Public Health – Struggles and Strategies for Better Health and Wellbeing', *Caribbean Review of Gender Studies*, 13 (2019), p. 57.
62. 'Marketing abroad', *Multinational Monitor*, 6:2/3 (February/March 1985), https://multinationalmonitor.org/hyper/issues/1985/02/

marketing-abroad.html [accessed September 2021]; Von Henneberg and Rothschild.

63. Lambert; 'Marketing abroad'.
64. 'Marketing abroad'.
65. Bryan, Dadzie and Scafe.
66. 'Marketing abroad'.
67. Ibid.
68. Von Henneberg and Rothschild.
69. Ibid.
70. 'Marketing abroad'.
71. Von Henneberg and Rothschild.
72. P. Chorlton, 'Row goes on as contraceptive jab study is finished', *Guardian*, 25 February 1980, p. 2.
73. Lambert, p. 523.
74. A. Veitch, 'Abuse of contraceptive drug by doctors "no reason to ban it"', *Guardian*, 9 November 1982, p. 4.
75. 'Upjohn's Contraceptive Hit', *Multinational Monitor*, 3:7 (July 1982), https://www.multinationalmonitor.org/hyper/issues/1982/07/upjohn.html [accessed September 2021].
76. A. Veitch, 'Drug approval "based on unreliable data"', *Guardian*, 30 April 1983, p. 26.
77. A. Veitch, 'Company deplores hospital drug use', *Guardian*, 27 April 1983, p. 2.
78. A. Veitch, 'Contraceptive injection drug sanctioned', *Guardian*, 12 April 1984, p. 2.
79. Lambert, p. 523.
80. Thomlinson, p. 89.
81. Author interview with Stella Dadzie.
82. Quashie.
83. Thomlinson, p. 95.
84. Ibid., p. 89.; Interview with Mia Morris, 26 July 2010, British Library, C1420/08.
85. Quashie.
86. B. Zephaniah, '"If we did nothing we would be killed on the streets" – Benjamin Zephaniah on fighting the far right', *Guardian*, 28 February 2016, https://www.theguardian.com/books/2016/feb/28/if-we-did-nothing-we-would-be-killed-on-the-streets-benjamin-zephaniah-on-fighting-the-far-right [accessed September 2021]; 'Sari Squad – the Afia Begum campaign, *The Spectacle Blog*, 29 July 2016, http://www.spectacle.co.uk/spectacleblog/despite-tv/sari-squad-the-afia-begum-campaign/ [accessed September 2021].
87. FPA, 'Your guide to contraceptive injections: helping you choose the method of contraception that's best for you', August 2021.
88. N. Davis and N. McIntyre, 'Revealed: pill still most popular prescribed contraceptive in England', *Guardian*, 7 March 2019, https://www.theguardian.com/uk-news/2019/mar/07/revealed-pill-still-most-popular-prescribed-contraceptive-in-england [accessed September 2021].
89. FPA.

90. Ibid.
91. United Nations Department of Economic and Social Affairs, Population Division, *World Family Planning 2020 Highlights: Accelerating action to ensure universal access to family planning* (United Nations, 2020), https://www.un.org/development/desa/pd/sites/www.un.org.development.desa.pd/files/files/documents/2020/Sep/unpd_2020_worldfamilyplanning_highlights.pdf; J. A. Adetunji, 'Rising popularity of injectable contraceptives in sub-Saharan Africa', *African Population Studies*, 25:2 (December 2011).
92. 'Zimbabwe bans dangerous contraceptive, Depo-Provera', *Multinational Monitor*, 2:9 (September 1981), https://www.multinationalmonitor.org/hyper/issues/1981/09/zimbabwe.html [accessed September 2021].
93. Z. Stein et al., 'The right to know: women's choices, Depo-Provera and HIV', openDemocracy, 20 July 2012, https://www.opendemocracy.net/en/5050/right-to-know-womens-choices-depo-provera-and-hiv/ [accessed September 2021]; E. Spevack, 'The long-term health implications of Depo-Provera', *Integrative Medicine*, 12:1 (February 2013).
94. The *Lancet* even disagrees with itself. See R. Heffron et al., 'Use of hormonal contraceptives and risk of HIV-1 transmission: a prospective cohort study', *Lancet*, 12:1 (1 January 2012), https://www.thelancet.com/journals/laninf/article/PIIS1473-3099%2811%2970247-X/fulltext; Evidence for Contraceptive Options and HIV Outcomes (ECHO) Trial Consortium, 'HIV incidence among women using intramuscular depot medroxyprogesterone acetate, a copper intrauterine device, or a levonorgestrel implant for contraception: a randomised, multicentre, open-label trial', *Lancet*, 394:10195 (27 July 2019), https://www.thelancet.com/journals/lancet/article/PIIS0140-6736%2819%2931288-7/fulltext.
95. A. Kassam et al., 'Europe needs many more babies to avert a population disaster', *Guardian*, 23 August 2015, theguardian.com/world/2015/aug/23/baby-crisis-europe-brink-depopulation-disaster; J. Yeung and M. Maruyama, 'Japan births fall to record low as population crisis deepens', *CNN*, 1 March 2023, edition.cnn.com/2023/03/01/asia/japan-births-2022-record-low-intl-hnk/index.html [accessed March 2023].
96. United Nations Department of Economic and Social Affairs, Population Division, *Global Population Growth and Sustainable Development: Ten key messages* (United Nations, February 2022), https://www.un.org/development/desa/pd/sites/www.un.org.development.desa.pd/files/undesa_pd_2022_key_messages_global_population_growth.pdf [accessed February 2023].
97. G. Chamberlain, 'UK aid helps to fund forced sterilisation of India's poor', *Guardian*, 15 April 2012, https://www.theguardian.com/world/2012/apr/15/uk-aid-forced-sterilisation-india [accessed September 2021].
98. L. Davies, '"Use your £11bn climate fund to pay for family

planning," UK told', *Guardian*, 26 August 2021, https://www.
theguardian.com/global-development/2021/aug/26/use-your-11bn-
climate-fund-to-pay-for-family-planning-uk-told [accessed September
2021].

99. Office for National Statistics, 'Coronavirus and vaccine hesitancy,
    Great Britain: 13 January to 7 February 2021', 8 March 2021, https://
    www.ons.gov.uk/peoplepopulationandcommunity/
    healthandsocialcare/healthandwellbeing/bulletins/
    coronavirusandvaccinehesitancygreatbritain/
    13januaryto7february2021 [accessed November 2021].
100. Author interview with Stella Dadzie.
101. Interview with Gerlin Bean, 9 September 2009, Lambeth Archives,
     IV279/2/20/1a and b.
102. Remember Olive Collective, p. 13.
103. Google, 'Doodles, Olive Morris' 68th birthday', 26 June 2020,
     https://www.google.com/doodles/olive-morris-68th-birthday
     [accessed September 2021].

## Chapter Eight: Grunwick Strike

1.  H. Athwal, 'Brave and inspirational: the story of Grunwick',
    Institute of Race Relations, 8 March 2017, https://irr.org.uk/article/
    brave-and-inspirational-the-story-of-grunwick/ [accessed October
    2020].
2.  Trades Union Congress, 'Grunwick strikers changed the face of
    British trade unionism', 2019, https://www.tuc.org.uk/news/
    grunwick-strikers-changed-face-british-trade-unionism [accessed
    October 2020]; GMB Union, 'Grunwick: The Workers' Story',
    https://www.gmb-shop.org.uk/grunwick-the-workers-story-book
    [accessed October 2020].
3.  R. Pearson and A. Sundari, *Striking Women: Struggles and Strategies of
    South Asian Women Workers from Grunwick to Gate Gourmet*
    (Lawrence & Wishart, 2018), p. 107.
4.  Housing and Key Workers letter from London Borough of Brent
    Housing Service, 15 November 1977, Working Class Movement
    Library, EVT/GRUNWICK/6/6.
5.  Pearson and Sundari, p. 109.
6.  J. Dromey and G. Taylor, *Grunwick: The workers' story* (Lawrence &
    Wishart, second edition 2015), p. 50.
7.  Lord Scarman, *Report of a Court of Inquiry Under Lord Justice
    Scarman, OBE, into a Dispute Between Grunwick Processing
    Laboratories Limited and Members of the Association of Professional,
    Executive, Clerical and Computer Staff* (Her Majesty's Stationery
    Office, 1977), p. 16.
8.  S. Anitha and M. Parmar, 'On the picket line: Jayaben Desai from
    East Africa to Grunwick', Our Migration Story, https://www.
    ourmigrationstory.org.uk/oms/from-east-africa-to-grunwick-
    jayaben-desai [accessed October 2020].
9.  A. Qayyum et al., *Changes in the economy since the 1970s* (Office for
    National Statistics, 2019), ons.gov.uk/economy/economicoutputand

productivity/output/articles/changesintheeconomysincethe1970s/
2019-09-02 [accessed October 2020].

10.  R. Pearson, S. Anitha and L. McDowell, 'Striking Women', http://
www.leeds.ac.uk/strikingwomen/grunwick/quotes [accessed
October 2020].

11.  J. Desai, interviewed by C. Thomas for *The Great Grunwick Strike
1976–1978 – a history*, dir. C. Thomas for Brent Trades Union
Council, 2007, https://mrc-catalogue.warwick.ac.uk/records/GGS/1.

12.  A. Wilson, 'Jayaben Desai: Waking the generals', *Red Pepper*, 4
February 2011, https://www.redpepper.org.uk/jayaben-desai-
waking-the-generals/ [accessed October 2020].

13.  A. Sivanandan, 'Grunwick', *Race & Class*, 19:1 (1977).

14.  'Interview with Jayaben Desai', *Women's Voice*, 7 (July), Working
Class Movement Library, EVT/GRUNWICK/6/6.

15.  Desai, interviewed by Thomas.

16.  Ibid.

17.  P. Hepburn, 'Striker no. 1 hits out', *Sunday Mirror*, 26 June 1977, p. 5,
Working Class Movement Library, EVT/GRUNWICK/6/3 – Box 8.

18.  Desai, interviewed by Thomas.

19.  Scarman, p. 18.

20.  S. Lewis, 'How union membership has grown – and shrunk',
*Guardian*, 30 April 2010, https://www.theguardian.com/news/
datablog/2010/apr/30/union-membership-data [accessed October
2020]; S. Schifferes, 'The trade unions' long decline', *BBC News*, 8
March 2004, http://news.bbc.co.uk/2/hi/business/3526917.stm
[accessed October 2020].

21.  W. Sullivan, 'Race and trade unions: Black workers and trade unions
1945–2000', Britain at Work: Voices from the Workplace 1945–
1995, http://www.unionhistory.info/britainatwork/narrativedisplay.
php?type=raceandtradeunions [accessed October 2020].

22.  For more information see: B. Bunnsee, 'Women in struggle: The.
Mansfield Hosiery strike', *Spare Rib*, 21 (1974); 'Imperial
Typewriters strike project recalls "shameful" union', *BBC News*, 15
June 2019, https://www.bbc.co.uk/news/uk-england-leicestershire-
48586737 [accessed October 2020].

23.  Thorpe; J. Freeman, 'Trade unions 1970s Britain: The Social
Contract – a success or failure?', *James Freeman* blog, 2019,
jamesfreemanhistorian.org/decadeofdiscord/wp/2019/04/07/trade-
unions-1970s-britain-the-social-contract-a-success-or-failure/
[accessed October 2020].

24.  Dromey and Taylor, p. 42.

25.  *The Great Grunwick Strike 1976–1978*.

26.  'The Grunwick Strike 1976', *Working Class History*, podcast, 2018,
workingclasshistory.com/podcast/grunwick-strike-1976/.

27.  Dromey and Taylor, p. 2.

28.  Desai, interviewed by Thomas.

29.  *The Great Grunwick Strike 1976–1978*.

30.  M. Amin-Smith, *Grunwick Changed Me*, BBC Radio 4, 17 August
2016, bbc.co.uk/programmes/b07npvfh.

31.  A. Wilson, *Finding a Voice* (Daraja Press, second edition 2018, original 1978), p. 77.
32.  Dromey and Taylor, p. 70.
33.  Pearson and Sundari, p. 121.
34.  Letter from Roy Grantham to solicitors, 19 November 1976, Working Class Movement Library, EVT/GRUNWICK/4/11.
35.  Letter from Roy Grantham to Len Murray, 23 December 1976, Working Class Movement Library, EVT/GRUNWICK/6/6.
36.  Letter from Leonard Gristey to Ron Todd, 9 June 1977, Working Class Movement Library, EVT/GRUNWICK/6/6.
37.  Letter from Brent Trades Council, 29 October 1976, and letter from Leonard Gristey, 9 June 1977, Working Class Movement Library, EVT/GRUNWICK/6/6.
38.  Wilson, *Finding a Voice*, p. 78.
39.  Scarman, p. 12.
40.  The Freedom Association, 'History', https://www.tfa.net/history [accessed October 2020].
41.  Ibid.
42.  *The Great Grunwick Strike 1976–1978*.
43.  Wilson, *Finding a Voice*, p. 77.
44.  *The Great Grunwick Strike 1976–1978*.
45.  Dromey and Taylor, p. 106.
46.  C. Borrell and T. Jones, '84 arrests in clash of pickets and police', *The Times*, 14 June 1977.
47.  *The Great Grunwick Strike 1976–1978*.
48.  Interview with Gail Lewis, British Library, 15 April 2004, British Library, C1420/14.; Author interview with Farrukh Dhondy, 31 March 2022.
49.  'Special Branch Report Grunwick 30 June 1977', Special Branch Files Project, https://www.documentcloud.org/documents/2693933-1977-06-20-Special-Branch-Report-Grunwick [accessed February 2023].
50.  Bristol Radical History Group, 'Grunwick: The end of an era?', talk, 2010, https://www.brh.org.uk/site/events/grunwick-the-end-of-an-era/ [accessed October 2020].
51.  'Shouts of kill as PC is hurt', *Daily Telegraph*, 24 June 1977, Working Class Movement Library, EVT/GRUNWICK/6/3 – Box 8.
52.  'Notes of a meeting at Chequers on 26 June 1977: The Grunwick dispute', Special Branch Files Project, http://specialbranchfiles.uk/grunwick-dispute-files-overview/ [accessed February 2023].
53.  'On This Day: Home secretary jeered on the picket line', *BBC News*, 27 June 1977, http://news.bbc.co.uk/onthisday/hi/dates/stories/june/27/newsid_2520000/2520097.stm [accessed October 2020].
54.  A. Wilson, '"We are the lions, Mr Manager": Revisiting the Great Grunwick Strike', *Ceasefire*, 15 June 2016, https://ceasefiremagazine.co.uk/we-lions-mr-manager-revisiting-great-grunwick-strike/ [accessed October 2020].
55.  The Freedom Association, 'History'.
56.  Ibid.

57. 'Grunwick Gates: The entry to unionisation', *Race Today*, reprinted in P. Field, R. Bunce, L. Hassan and M. Peacock (eds), *Here to Stay, Here to Fight* (Pluto Press, 2019), p. 134.
58. Ibid., p. 135.
59. *The Great Grunwick Strike 1976–1978*.
60. Ibid.
61. 'Special Branch Report Grunwick 30 June 1977', Special Branch Files Project, http://specialbranchfiles.uk/grunwick-dispute-files-overview/ [accessed February 2023].
62. '4,000 police mobilized for Grunwick protest march', *The Times*, 11 July 1977.
63. *Stand Together!*, Newsreel Collective, 1977, The University of Warwick, mrc-catalogue.warwick.ac.uk/records/GGS/2/1.
64. T. Jones, 'Police arrest 70 as Grunwick battle leaves 70 hurt', *The Times*, 12 July 1977.
65. Wilson, *Finding a Voice*, p. 79.
66. *The Great Grunwick Strike 1976–1978*.
67. Ibid.
68. Grunwick Strike Committee letter from APEX, reference A/5/8 RAG/DAH, 7 October 1977, Working Class Movement Library, EVT/GRUNWICK/6/6.
69. Dromey and Taylor, p. 189.
70. Ibid., p. 193.
71. Desai, interviewed by Thomas.
72. Pearson, Anitha and McDowell.
73. 'Grunwick Revisited: Jayaben Desai Interviewed', *Race Today*, June/July 1987, p. 10, Working Class Movement Library, EVT/GRUNWICK/6/6.
74. Department for Business, Energy & Industrial Strategy, *Trade Union Membership, UK 1995–2019: Statistical Bulletin* (Office for National Statistics, 2020).
75. Grunwick Processing Laboratories APEX internal correspondence, 14 December 1978, Working Class Movement Library, EVT/GRUNWICK/6/6.
76. 'George Ward and family', *The Times*, 27 April 2008, https://www.thetimes.co.uk/article/george-ward-and-family-pljnbm93530 [accessed October 2020].
77. Steerpike, 'Jacob Rees-Mogg: "the SNP are now the real opposition"', *Spectator*, 9 December 2015, https://www.spectator.co.uk/article/jacob-rees-mogg-the-snp-are-now-the-real-opposition- [accessed October 2020].
78. The Freedom Association, 'Treat yourself to these wonderful Jacob Rees-Mogg cufflinks', https://www.tfa.net/treat_yourself_to_these_wonderful_jacob_rees-mogg_cufflinks [accessed October 2020].
79. J. Dromey, 'Power list reminds us of the heroic struggle of Grunwick strikers', *Labour List*, 14 December 2016, https://labourlist.org/2016/12/jack-dromey-power-list-reminds-us-of-the-heroic-struggle-of-grunwick-strikers/ [accessed February 2023].
80. Pearson, Anitha and McDowell.

81.  J. Dromey, 'Jayaben Desai obituary', *Guardian*, 28 December 2010, https://www.theguardian.com/politics/2010/dec/28/jayaben-desai-obituary [accessed October 2020].

82.  'Grunwick revisited: Arthur Scargill and Jayaben Desai', *Race Today*, reprinted in Field, Bunce, Hassan and Peacock, p. 138.

83.  Wilson, '"We are the lions, Mr Manager": Revisiting the Great Grunwick Strike'.

84.  TUC Equality Audit, *Black Workers and Unions* (TUC, 2014).

85.  Play: Townsend Theatre Productions, *We are the Lions, Mr Manager*, 2017.
     Exhibition: Grunwick 40, *Remembering the Grunwick strike 40 years on*, 2016.
     Song: J. Warshaw, 'Hold the Line Again (The Grunwick Strike)', 1975.

### Chapter Nine: Altab Ali and the Battle of Brick Lane

1.  Bethnal Green and Stepney Trades Council, *Blood on the Streets: A report by Bethnal Green and Stepney Trades Council on racial attacks in East London* (Bethnal Green and Stepney Trades Council, 1978), p. 56, Working Class Movement Library, H03.

2.  Corporate Research Unit, Tower Hamlets, 'Spitalfields and Banglatown Ward Profile', May 2014, https://www.towerhamlets.gov.uk/Documents/Borough_statistics/Ward_profiles/Spitalfields-and-Banglatown-FINAL-10062014.pdf [accessed September 2021].

3.  The City of London is wild. For starters, see G. Monbiot, 'The medieval, unaccountable Corporation of London is ripe for protest', *Guardian*, 31 October 2011, https://www.theguardian.com/commentisfree/2011/oct/31/corporation-london-city-medieval; M. Glasman, 'The City of London's strange history', *Financial Times*, 29 September 2014, https://www.ft.com/content/7c8f24fa-3aa5-11e4-bd08-00144feabdc0.

4.  Trust for London, 'London's Poverty Profile', 2020, https://www.trustforlondon.org.uk/data/poverty-borough/ [accessed September 2021].

5.  Corporate Research Unit, Tower Hamlets, 'Child poverty briefing', May 2018, https://www.towerhamlets.gov.uk/Documents/Borough_statistics/Income_poverty_and_welfare/2015_Child_Poverty_Briefing.pdf [accessed September 2021].

6.  *The Bengali East End: Histories of life and work in Tower Hamlets* (Tower Hamlets Local History Library and Archives, undated booklet), p. 28, https://www.ideastore.co.uk/assets/documents/bengali%20booklet%20FINALcropped1.pdf [accessed September 2021].

7.  Ibid., p. 4.

8.  D. Lamarche, *Bengalis in East London: A community in the making for 500 years* (Swadhinata Trust, 2017), p. 4, https://swadhinata.org.uk/wp-content/uploads/2017/08/BENGALIS-IN-EAST-LONDON-daniele-lamarche-AAU-edited.pdf [accessed September 2021].

9.  Ibid.

10. R. Visram, *Asians in Britain: 400 Years of History* (Pluto Press, 2002),
    p. 57.
11. Ibid., p. 234.
12. Lamarche, p. 3.
13. Visram, p. 225.
14. Ibid., p. 236.
15. Ibid., p. 239.
16. Ibid., p. 257.
17. *The Bengali East End*, p. 5.
18. Ibid.
19. Z. Masani, 'We'll take care of it ourselves', *Time Out*, 8–14 June 1979, p. 8, Tower Hamlets Local History Library and Archives, LCX00002 Class 300.2 Folder 2.
20. Ibid.
21. M. A. Salam, interviewed by J. Iqbal, 22 June 2006, Swadhinata Trust, https://www.swadhinata.org.uk/interviewee-profiles-full-transcripts-strand-2/ [accessed October 2021].
22. S. Ashe, S. Virdee and L. Brown, 'Striking back against racist violence in the East End of London, 1968–1970', *Race & Class*, 58:1 (2016), p. 39.
23. K. Leech, *Brick Lane 1978: The events and their significance* (Stepney Books, revised edition 1994, original September 1980), p. 7; Bethnal Green and Stepney Trades Council, p. 5.
24. D. Rosenberg, 'The racist killing of Altab Ali 40 years ago today', openDemocracy, 4 May 2018, https://www.opendemocracy.net/en/shine-a-light/remembering-altab-ali/ [accessed October 2021].
25. University of the West of England, 'The history of council housing', 2008, https://fet.uwe.ac.uk/conweb/house_ages/council_housing/print.htm?source=post_page-------------------------- [accessed September 2021].
26. B. Wheeler, 'A history of social housing', *BBC News*, 14 April 2015, https://www.bbc.com/news/uk-14380936 [accessed October 2021].
27. University of the West of England.
28. Ibid.
29. Bengali Housing Action Group, 'The right to decent housing', *Race Today*, 8:5 (May 1976), p. 104.
30. A. K. Azad Konor, *The Battle of Brick Lane 1978* (Grosvenor House, 2018), p. 15.
31. D. Beresford, 'An 80-minute protest heralds new era of East End', *Guardian*, 24 July 1978, p. 3.
32. C. Wall, 'Sisterhood and squatting in the 1970s: Feminism, housing and urban change in Hackney', *History Workshop Journal*, 83 (2017), p. 81.
33. *The Bengali East End*, p. 6.
34. Leech, p. 13.
35. Wall, p. 80.
36. Bengali Housing Action Group, p. 104.
37. 'East End Housing Campaign, December 1975', *Race Today*,

reprinted in P. Field, R. Bunce, L. Hassan and M. Peacock (eds), *Here to Stay, Here to Fight* (Pluto Press, 2019), p. 115.

38.  Ibid., p. 116.
39.  D. Pallister and L. Mackie, '"Ghetto" row grows after race attack', *Guardian*, 13 June 1978, p. 2.
40.  S. Ahmed, interviewed by J. Iqbal, A. Ahmed Ullah and C. Sen, 30 April 2006, Swadhinata Trust, https://www.swadhinata.org.uk/ interviewee-profiles-full-transcripts-strand-2/ [accessed October 2021].
41.  'East End Housing Campaign, December 1975', pp. 115–6.
42.  'Rising up against racism: London's forgotten Bangladeshi squatters', prod. N. Sivathasan, *BBC News*, 12 October 2021, https://www.bbc. com/news/av/uk-58878289 [accessed October 2021].
43.  Terry Fitzpatrick, 'Bengali Housing Action Group', Altab Ali Foundation, http://www.altabalifoundation.org.uk/articles/Bengali_ Housing_Action_Group%28TF%29.pdf [accessed September 2021].
44.  'Housing struggle: The tiger is on the loose', *Race Today*, March 1976, reprinted in Field, Bunce, Hassan and Peacock, p. 118.
45.  Ibid., p. 120.
46.  Interview with Terry Fitzpatrick.
47.  'Housing struggle', p. 119.
48.  A. S. Francis, 'Black Liberation Front, 1971–1993 – A blue print for activism today', *Editions Lifestyle*, 2021, https://editionbhm.com/ 2020/10/17/the-black-liberation-front-1971-1993/ [accessed December 2021].
49.  Azad Konor, p. 35.
50.  Bethnal Green and Stepney Trades Council, p. 37.
51.  Leech, p. 7.
52.  Azad Konor, p. 32.
53.  Salam, interviewed by Iqbal.
54.  Leech, p. 7.
55.  Ibid.
56.  M. Thatcher, 'TV Interview for Granada World in Action ("rather swamped")', Margaret Thatcher Foundation, 1978, https://www. margaretthatcher.org/document/103485 [accessed January 2021]; Runnymede Trust, 'Margaret Thatcher claims Britons fear being "swamped"', http://runnymedetrust.org/histories/race-equality/59/ margaret-thatcher-claims-britons-fear-being-swamped.html [accessed September 2021].
57.  S. Manzoor, 'The year rock found the power to unite', *Guardian*, 20 April 2008, https://www.theguardian.com/music/2008/apr/20/ popandrock.race [accessed September 2021].
58.  Azad Konor, p. 9.
59.  C. Rallings and M. Thrasher, 'Local elections handbook 1978: The 1978 local election results', The Elections Centre, https://www. electionscentre.co.uk/?page_id=3686 [accessed February 2023].
60.  D. Rosenberg, 'The racist killing of Altab Ali 40 years ago today', openDemocracy, 2018, https://www.opendemocracy.net/en/shine-a-light/remembering-altab-ali/ [accessed January 2021].

61.  Standard Reporter, 'Asian killed in East End knifing', *Evening Standard*, 5 May 1978, p. 5.
62.  'Police hunt the knife murderers', *East London Advertiser*, 12 May 1978, Tower Hamlets Local Library & Archive, LCX00003 Class 300.2 Folder 3.
63.  Rallings and Thrasher.
64.  Bethnal Green and Stepney Trades Council, p. 37.
65.  J. Hasan, interviewed by J. Iqbal, 7 April 2006, Swadhinata Trust, https://www.swadhinata.org.uk/interviewee-profiles-full-transcripts-strand-2/ [accessed October 2021].
66.  J. Hasan, 'Altab Ali and the "Battle of Brick Lane"', Altab Ali Foundation, http://altabalifoundation.org.uk/articles/Altab_Ali_&_The_Battle_Of_Brick_Lane(JH).pdf [accessed September 2021].
67.  B. Day and M. Jempson, *East London Advertiser*, 12 May 1978, Tower Hamlets Local Library & Archive, LCX00003 Class 300.2 Folder 3.
68.  C. Osborne, *Tower Hamlets – radical actions then and now: The fight for equality* (London Borough of Tower Hamlets, undated), p. 24, https://www.towerhamlets.gov.uk/Documents/Leisure-and-culture/Events/Altab_Ali_The_Fight_for_Equality.pdf [accessed September 2021].
69.  Leech, p. 9.; Azad Konor, p. 47.
70.  Day and Jempson.
71.  Hasan, interviewed by Iqbal.
72.  Salam, interviewed by Iqbal.
73.  M. Akash, *Altab Ali: Murder* (MA Publishing, 2021), p. 83; Bethnal Green and Stepney Trades Council, p. 56.
74.  'Street fury over "race" slaying', *East London Advertiser*, 19 May 1978, Tower Hamlets Local Library & Archive, LCX00003 Class 300.2 Folder 3.
75.  C. Nye and S. Bright, 'Altab Ali: The racist murder that mobilised the East End', *BBC News*, 4 May 2016, https://www.bbc.com/news/uk-england-london-36191020 [accessed September 2021].
76.  R. Jalal, interviewed by J. Iqbal and C. Sen, 11 March 2006, Swadhinata Trust, https://www.swadhinata.org.uk/interviewee-profiles-full-transcripts-strand-2/ [accessed October 2021].
77.  Azad Konor, p. 38.
78.  P. Wintour, 'Race, death and fear in London's East End', *New Statesman*, 19 May 1978, p. 665, Tower Hamlets Local Library & Archive, LCX00003 Class 300.2 Folder 3.
79.  Ibid.
80.  Leech, p. 9.
81.  T. Fishlock, 'Mob of youths attack Bengali area in East End of London', *The Times*, 12 June 1978, p. 1.
82.  S. Wall, 'The trail of terror', *East London Advertiser*, 16 June 1978, Tower Hamlets Local Library & Archive, LCX00003 Class 300.2 Folder 3.
83.  L. Mackie, 'Front followers are blamed for violence', *Guardian*, 12 June 1978, p. 1.
84.  O. Duke, 'United against the Nazis', *Express*, week ending 24 June

1978, p. 5, Tower Hamlets Local Library & Archive, LCX00002 Class 300.2 Folder 2; Staff Reporter, '2,000 march against East End violence', *The Times*, 19 June 1978, p. 2.

85. J. Taylor, 'Police avert East End clashes', *Guardian*, 19 June 1978, p. 2; S. Wall, 'It's peace – thanks to a little help from police', *East London Advertiser*, 23 June 1978, Tower Hamlets Local Library & Archive, LCX00002 Class 300.2 Folder 2.

86. Leech, p. 10.

87. G. Parry, 'Bengalis in talks after murder', *Guardian*, 26 June 1978, p. 1.

88. B. Gardner, 'Fears of East End race war', *Evening News*, 26 June 1978, Tower Hamlets Local Library & Archive, LCX00002 Class 300.2 Folder 2.

89. Bethnal Green and Stepney Trades Council, p. 57.

90. Akash, p. 40.

91. 'Lane tells Bengalis to stand firm', *Guardian*, 8 July 1978, p. 2.

92. 'MP urges inquiry into Brick Lane violence', *Guardian*, 2 August 1978, p. 4.

93. 'Lane tells Bengalis to stand firm'.

94. T. Fishlock, '12 arrested in East End protest', *The Times*, 17 July 1978, p. 3.

95. Tower Hamlets Trades Council and Hackney Legal Action Group, *Brick Lane 1978: The case for the defence*, London (Tower Hamlets Trades Council and Hackney Legal Action Group, 1978), Institute of Race Relations, 32 HR.hdk.

96. Ibid.

97. D. Beresford, '13 arrests in Brick Lane', *Guardian*, 17 July 1978, p. 20.

98. E. Bober, 'An effective demo', *Militant*, 4 August 1978, Tower Hamlets Local Library & Archive, LCX00002 Class 300.2 Folder 2.

99. O. Duke and N. Brett, 'Black Monday ...', *East Ender*, week ending July 23, Tower Hamlets Local Library & Archive, LCX00002 Class 300.2 Folder 2.

100. 'Asians hold protest strike as Mr Rees discusses racialism', *The Times*, 18 July 1978, p. 4; D. Beresford, 'Asians in sit-down protest over arrests', *Guardian*, 18 July 1978, p. 2.

101. B. Jones, 'Hundreds outside police station to demand prisoners release', *East Ender*, 22 July 1978, Tower Hamlets Local Library & Archive, LCX00002 Class 300.2 Folder 2.

102. 'Bengali workers on strike', *Race Today*, 10:6 (September/October 1978), pp. 125–7.

103. 'MP urges inquiry into Brick Lane violence', *Guardian*, 2 August 1978, p. 4.

104. *A Safe Place to Be*, dir. S. Heaven, BFI, 1980, https://player.bfi.org.uk/free/film/watch-a-safe-place-to-be-1980-online [accessed October 2021].

105. Hackney & Tower Hamlets Defence Committee and Anti-Nazi League, *Defend Brick Lane*, pamphlet, Tower Hamlets Local Library & Archive, LCX00002 Class 300.2 Folder 2.

106. 'Brick Lane call goes out as racists daub mosque', *Morning Star*, 19 August 1978, Tower Hamlets Local Library & Archive, LCX00002 Class 300.2 Folder 2.

107. Leech, p. 10; Bethnal Green and Stepney Trades Council, p. 60.

108. P. Chippindale, 'Front outrallies anti-Nazis', *Guardian*, 22 September 1978, p. 22.

109. M. Walker and P. Chippindale, '5,000 police keep Front and its opponents at bay', *Guardian*, 25 September 1978, p. 32.

110. Author interview with Ansar Ahmed Ullah, 28 March 2022.

111. Ibid.

112. Ibid.

113. Office for National Statistics, 'Percentage of people living in the most deprived 10% of neighbourhoods, by ethnicity', 16 June 2020, https://www.ethnicity-facts-figures.service.gov.uk/uk-population-by-ethnicity/demographics/people-living-in-deprived-neighbourhoods/latest; Office for National Statistics, 'Child poverty and education outcomes by ethnicity', Office for National Statistics, 25 February 2020, https://www.ons.gov.uk/economy/nationalaccounts/uksectoraccounts/compendium/economicreview/february2020/childpovertyandeducationoutcomesbyethnicity; Office for National Statistics, 'Unemployment, Ethnicity Facts and Figures', 29 January 2021, https://www.ethnicity-facts-figures.service.gov.uk/work-pay-and-benefits/unemployment-and-economic-inactivity/unemployment/latest [all accessed March 2022].

114. Author interview with Ansar Ahmed Ullah; Journey to Justice, 'Tower Hamlets, London: Women Unite Against Racism', https://jtojhumanrights.org.uk/local-stories/local-stories-posts/women-unite-against-racism/ [accessed March 2022].

115. Author interview with Ansar Ahmed Ullah.

116. V. Shaw, 'Average house prices in some parts of London have doubled since 2012 Olympics', *Independent*, 3 August 2021, https://www.independent.co.uk/money/average-house-prices-in-some-parts-of-london-have-doubled-since-2012-olympics-b1895716.html?r=63962 [accessed September 2021].

117. C. Alexander et al., 'Beyond Banglatown: Continuity, change and new urban economies in Brick Lane', Runnymede Trust, July 2020, p. 17, https://www.runnymedetrust.org/uploads/publications/pdfs/RunnymedeBanglatownReport.pdf [accessed September 2021].

118. Ibid.

119. N. Sivathasan, 'From korma to coconuts – the evolution of Indian cuisine in the UK', *BBC News*, 13 October 2019, https://www.bbc.com/news/av/stories-49993929 [accessed December 2021]; A. Gillan, 'From Bangladesh to Brick Lane', *Guardian*, 21 June 2002, https://www.theguardian.com/uk/2002/jun/21/religion.bangladesh [accessed October 2021].

120. Jalal, interviewed by Iqbal and Sen.

121. Ahmed, interviewed by Iqbal, Ahmed Ullah and Sen.

122. https://www.spitalfieldsha.co.uk.

123. https://bangladesh-youth-movement3.webnode.co.uk.
124. Azad Konor, p. 56.
125. Runnymede Trust, 'Altab Ali murdered in Whitechapel, London', https://www.runnymedetrust.org/histories/race-equality/71/altab-ali-murdered-in-whitechapel-london.html [accessed October 2021].
126. Nye and Bright.
127. Akash, p. 91.
128. Author interview with Ahmed Ansar Ullah.

## Chapter Ten: Asian Youth Movements

1. T. Ali, '"Come what may we're here to stay": remembering the Asian Youth Movements', *Tribune Magazine*, 18 December 2020, https://tribunemag.co.uk/2020/12/come-what-may-were-here-to-stay-remembering-the-asian-youth-movements/ [accessed November 2021].
2. K. Puri, 'The pool of blood that changed my life', *BBC News*, 5 August 2015, bbc.com/news/magazine-33725217 [accessed November 2021].
3. Ibid.
4. Interview with Suresh Grover, 2014, Bishopsgate Institute, digital:works collection, DW/6/13.
5. Interview with Balraj Purewal, 2014, Bishopsgate Institute, digital:works collection, DW/6/1; 'Southall: town under siege, June 1979', London Metropolitan Archives, Black Parents Movement Ealing Section: Southall Riots, LMA/4463/B/02/02/044/A.
6. 'Asian Youth Movements in Bradford', *Working Class History*, podcast, 2019, https://workingclasshistory.com/2019/09/18/e28-29-asian-youth-movements-in-bradford/.
7. J. Rose, 'The Southall Asian Youth Movement', *International Socialism* 91 (1976), pp. 5–6.
8. Ibid.
9. C. Foley, 'Police violence and death: an old story', *Guardian*, 26 April 2009, https://www.theguardian.com/commentisfree/2009/apr/26/police-blair-peach [accessed November 2021].
10. L. Mackie, 'Kingsley Read's red-letter day for racialists', *Guardian*, 7 January 1978, p. 17; Standard Reporter, '"Wogs, coons" man is cleared', *Evening Standard*, 6 January 1978, p. 1.
11. B. Bland, 'Gurdip Singh Chaggar, the Southall Youth Movement and the background to April 1979', *Discover Society*, 3 April 2019, https://archive.discoversociety.org/2019/04/03/gurdip-singh-chaggar-the-southall-youth-movement-and-the-background-to-april-1979/ [accessed November 2021].
12. Ibid.
13. A. Ramamurthy, *Black Star: Britain's Asian Youth Movements* (Pluto Press, 2013), p. 27.
14. Interview with Balraj Purewal.
15. Ibid.
16. Ibid.
17. 'Incitement to racial hatred', *Hansard*, Vol. 914, Thursday 8 July 1976, https://hansard.parliament.uk/Commons/1976-07-08/

debates/11f355cb-9138-4646-88f1-00dae4b48061/Incitement
ToRacialHatred?highlight=southall#contribution-4287a1d1-2ba6-
4a04-b002-19074e6b2b53 [accessed September 2021].

18. K. Thapar, 'Asians in Britain: no place like home', *The Times*, 21 June
    1982, p. 10.
19. 'Buzzcocks X-O-Dus (Exodus)', flyer, Alexandra Park 1977,
    Manchester Digital Music Archive, https://www.mdmarchive.co.uk/
    artefact/20080/BUZZCOCKS_X-O-DUS_%28EXODUS%29_
    ALEXANDRA_PARK_FLYER_1977 [accessed September 2021].
20. D. Hencke, 'Scotch fuels the Cuban fiesta', *Guardian*, 26 July 1978,
    p. 3.
21. H. Punja, 'The need for unity: an interview with Vishnu Sharma',
    *Race & Class*, 58:1 (2016), p. 108.
22. D. Renton, *Never Again: Rock Against Racism and the Anti-Nazi
    League 1976–1982* (Routledge, 2018), p. 136.
23. 'IWA Southall, Review – Report (August 1977–August 1979)',
    Institute of Race Relations, 01/04/04/01/12/050.
24. D. Renton, 'On deadly policing and the 1979 Southall Protests',
    *LitHub*, 10 July 2020, https://lithub.com/on-deadly-policing-and-
    the-1979-southall-protests/ [accessed September 2021].
25. D. Renton, '"Between the police and us": Southall and the death of
    Blair Peach', *Discover Society*, 3 April 2019.
26. Asian Youth Movement Bradford, 'Southall on Trial', *Kala Tara*,
    No.1, p. 4, Ahmed Iqbal Ullah Race Relations Archive, Tandana
    Archive: papers of the Bradford and Sheffield Asian Youth
    Movements, GB3228.6/1/1/15.
27. Interview with Balraj Purewal.
28. Asian Youth Movement Bradford.
29. D. Ransom, 'Southall gets a white-wash', *New Statesman*, 5 October
    1979, Ahmed Iqbal Ullah Race Relations Archive, Tandana Archive:
    papers of the Bradford and Sheffield Asian Youth Movements,
    GB3228.6/1/2/10.
30. D. Renton, '"Between the police and us": Southall and the death of
    Blair Peach', *Discover Society*, 3 April 2019.
31. Ibid.
32. Ransom.
33. Foley.
34. Ramamurthy, p. 53.
35. R. Lewis, 'Real Trouble: A study of aspects of the Southall trials',
    1980, Institute of Race Relations, 32HPX.K.
36. Ransom.
37. Ramamurthy, p. 53; *The Day that Changed the Face*, dir. N. Philips
    and T. Hampton, British Film Institute, 1980, https://player.bfi.org.
    uk/free/film/watch-the-day-that-changed-the-face-1980-online
    [accessed February 2023].
38. Interview with Balraj Purewal.
39. *Southall Defence Committee Bulletin*, 1, London Metropolitan
    Archives, Black Parents Movement Ealing Section: Southall Riots,
    LMA/4463/B/02/02/044/A.

40. Ramamurthy, p. 53.

41. Foley.

42. J. Nightingale, 'Bradford named as second least romantic place in country', *Telegraph & Argus*, 8 February 2013, https://www.thetelegraphandargus.co.uk/news/10214942.bradford-named-as-second-least-romantic-place-in-country/ [accessed September 2021].

43. C. Jones, 'Bradford Curry Awards 2022 nominees announced with dozens of restaurants in the running', *YorkshireLive*, 15 July 2022, examinerlive.co.uk/whats-on/food-drink-news/bradford-curry-awards-2022-nominees-24487049 [accessed September 2021].

44. K. Malik, 'Here to stay, here to fight', extract from 'From Fatwa to Jihad', *Pandaemonium*, 28 March 2012, https://kenanmalik.com/2012/03/28/here-to-stay-here-to-fight/ [accessed September 2021].

45. The organisation had previously been the Indian Progressive Youth Association.

46. 'Asian Youth Movements in Bradford'.

47. A. Ramamurthy, 'Families divided: the campaign for Anwar Ditta and her children', *Our Migration Story*, ourmigrationstory.org.uk/oms/families-divided-the-campaign-for-anwar-ditta-and-her-children [accessed September 2021].

48. Ibid.

49. Ibid.

50. Ibid.

51. Ramamurthy, pp. 104, 109.

52. Ibid., p. 109.

53. Ahmed Iqbal Ullah Race Relations Resource Centre, 'Anwar Ditta's Fight for Her Children', 2018, https://soundcloud.com/aiucentre/albums [accessed September 2021].

54. Ahmed Iqbal Ullah Race Relations Resource Centre, 'Anwar Ditta campaign: The extraordinary tale of a mother's courage', 2018, https://www.racearchive.org.uk/download/anwar-ditta-project-booklet/?wpdmdl=3409&refresh=614c790c481a31632401676 [accessed February 2023].

55. P. Valentine, 'The week in view', *Observer*, 15 March 1981, p. 48.

56. Ramamurthy, p. 60.

57. Ibid., p. 61.

58. G. Sharma, 'The British Asians who fought fascism in the seventies', Al Jazeera, 23 April 2019, https://www.aljazeera.com/features/2019/4/23/the-british-asians-who-fought-fascism-in-the-seventies [accessed September 2021]; Malik.

59. 'Free the Bradford 12', *Ufahamu: A Journal of African Studies*, 11:3 (1982).

60. Ramamurthy, p. 124.

61. M. Pithers, 'Asians cleared of petrol bomb charges', *Guardian*, 17 June 1982, p. 24.

62. M. Pithers, 'Judge vets jury for race bias as Asian youths go on trial', *Guardian*, 5 May 1982, p. 4.

63. 'The Bradford 12: reflecting on the trial of the decade', *Race Today*, reprinted in P. Field, R. Bunce, L. Hassan and M. Peacock (eds), *Here to Stay, Here to Fight* (Pluto Press, 2019).

64. M. Nally, 'Law officers' concern over bombs trial', *Observer*, 20 June 1982, p. 3.
65. 'Free the Bradford 12' leaflet, Ahmed Iqbal Ullah Race Relations Archive, Tandana Archive: papers of the Bradford and Sheffield Asian Youth Movements, GB3228.6/1/7/4.
66. Standard Reporter, 'Black gang "in plot to bomb police"', *Evening Standard*, 5 August 1981, p. 5.
67. 'Free the Bradford 12' leaflet.
68. ARAF, *Bradford 12*, 1 (October 1981), Ahmed Iqbal Ullah Race Relations Archive, Tandana Archive: papers of the Bradford and Sheffield Asian Youth Movements, GB3228.6/1/6/2.
69. 'Petrol bombs case man bailed', *Guardian*, 22 August 1981, p. 3.
70. Ramamurthy, p. 129; 'Free the Bradford 12' leaflet.
71. Ramamurthy, p. 136.
72. 'Free the Bradford 12' leaflet.
73. Bradford 12 Defence Fund, *Bradford 12 are freed!*, Ahmed Iqbal Ullah Race Relations Archive, Tandana Archive: papers of the Bradford and Sheffield Asian Youth Movements, GB3228.6/2/3/1.
74. ARAF.
75. Ibid.; E. Clayton, 'Textile Hall blaze put an end to dancing days heyday', *Telegraph & Argus*, 1 March 2020, https://www.thetelegraphandargus.co.uk/news/18270613.textile-hall-blaze-put-end-dancing-days-heyday/ [accessed September 2021].
76. Our Correspondent, 'Solicitor withdraws from petrol bomb case', *The Times*, 2 October 1981, p. 3.
77. Bradford 12 Defence Fund, 'Self defence is no offence', *Campaign News*, Ahmed Iqbal Ullah Race Relations Archive, Tandana Archive: papers of the Bradford and Sheffield Asian Youth Movements, GB3228.6/2/3/1.
78. M. Pithers, 'Defence objects to selection of jury panel', *Guardian*, 27 April 1982, p. 7.
79. Pithers, 'Judge vets jury for race bias'.
80. Ramamurthy, p. 135.
81. M. Nally, '"Free Bradford 12" chants at court', *Observer*, 23 May 1982, p. 2.
82. 'The Bradford 12: reflecting on the trial of the decade'.
83. Ramamurthy, p. 142.
84. 'The Bradford 12: reflecting on the trial of the decade'.
85. Ibid.
86. A. Wilson, 'Victory for the Bradford 12', *Economic and Political Weekly*, 17:28/29 (1982), p. 1141.
87. Ibid.
88. Ibid.
89. Ramamurthy, p. 141.
90. Nally, '"Free Bradford 12" chants at court'.
91. Ramamurthy, p. 142; G. Pierce, 'Revealed: a British community living in terror', *Guardian*, 21 June 1982, p. 11.
92. Wilson.
93. Ramamurthy, p. 142.

94. 'Bradford 12 show trial underway', *FRFI*, 20 June 1982, Ahmed Iqbal Ullah Race Relations Archive, Tandana Archive: papers of the Bradford and Sheffield Asian Youth Movements, GB3228.6/2/3/1.
95. Ramamurthy, p. 139.
96. Bradford 12 Defence Fund, 'Bradford 12 words in court', *Bradford 12 are freed!*, Ahmed Iqbal Ullah Race Relations Archive, Tandana Archive: papers of the Bradford and Sheffield Asian Youth Movements, GB3228.6/2/3/1.
97. Ibid.
98. Pierce.
99. M. Pithers, 'Court told Asian bombs were for self defence', *Guardian*, 28 May 1982, p. 4.
100. Nally, 'Law officers' concern over bombs trial'.
101. 'The Bradford 12: reflecting on the trial of the decade'.
102. Ramamurthy, p. 144.
103. Nally, '"Free Bradford 12" chants at court'.
104. Ramamurthy, p. 139.
105. Pierce.
106. Pierce; Bradford 12 Defence Fund, 'Pig ignorance or state conspiracy?', *Bradford 12 are freed!*, Ahmed Iqbal Ullah Race Relations Archive, Tandana Archive: papers of the Bradford and Sheffield Asian Youth Movements, GB3228.6/2/3/1.
107. Pithers, 'Asians cleared of petrol bomb charges'.
108. Ramamurthy, p. 121.
109. 'All 12 Asians acquitted in Bradford bombs trial', *The Times*, 17 June 1982, p. 2.
110. 'Asian Youth Movements in Bradford'.
111. Thapar.
112. Nally, 'Law officers' concern over bombs trial'.
113. To find out more see: Journey to Justice, 'The Newham 8, police racism and community action', https://jtojhumanrights.org.uk/local-stories/local-stories-posts/the-newham-8-police-racism-and-community-action/.
114. G. Robertson, 'Safeguarding the right to speak from the dock', *Guardian*, 21 October 1982, p. 15.
115. 'Second Report – Death of Blair Peach', Metropolitan Police, 14 September 1979.
116. V. Chaudhary, 'Forty years on, Southall demands justice for the killing of Blair Peach', *Guardian*, 21 April 2019, https://www.theguardian.com/uk-news/2019/apr/21/southall-demands-justice-killing-of-blair-peach-1979?fbclid=IwAR2lvVJMdoKI7wfPvmAkF RiPho9wBLU_NlAQdY3WQ_PItLpqqlZ8EF2qMLI [accessed September 2021].
117. Metropolitan Police, 'Release of the reports and other material relating to the death of Blair Peach', 2010, https://www.met.police.uk/SysSiteAssets/foi-media/metropolitan-police/other_information/corporate/blair-peach---synopsis. All the documents can be seen here: https://www.met.police.uk/foi-ai/af/accessing-information/met/investigation-into-the-death-of-blair-peach/.

118.  Chaudhary.
119.  R. Evans, 'Met spied on partner of Blair Peach for more than two decades, inquiry hears', *Guardian*, 6 May 2021, https://www.theguardian.com/uk-news/2021/may/06/met-spied-on-blair-peach-partner-for-more-than-two-decades-inquiry-hears [accessed September 2021].

## Chapter Eleven: 1981

1.    A. Mohdin, 'How the New Cross fire became a rallying cry for political action', *Guardian*, 15 January 2021, https://www.theguardian.com/uk-news/2021/jan/15/how-the-new-cross-fire-became-a-rallying-cry-for-political-action [accessed December 2021].
2.    Office for National Statistics, 'Unemployment rate (aged 16 and over, seasonally adjusted)', 14 December 2021, https://www.ons.gov.uk/employmentandlabourmarket/peoplenotinwork/unemployment/timeseries/mgsx/lms [accessed December 2021].
3.    'Today in London anti-racist history, 1981: the Black People's Day of Action protests the New Cross Fire', *past tense* blog, 2 March 2020, https://pasttenseblog.wordpress.com/2020/03/02/today-in-london-anti-racist-history-1981-the-black-peoples-day-of-action-protests-the-new-cross-fire/ [accessed December 2021].
4.    E. Byrne, 'St Pauls 1980: This is what happened on a night of chaos and confusion that went down in Bristol's history', *Bristol Post*, 2 April 2020, bristolpost.co.uk/news/Bristol-news/st-pauls-riot-uprising-anniversary-4006101 [accessed December 2021].
5.    'Black People's Day of Action: The Race Today Collective reunite 40 years on, Part 1: Political strategy and organisation', webinar, March 2021, Darcus Howe Legacy Collection, https://www.youtube.com/watch?v=Hfh4cU2wlcM&t=2s [accessed February 2023].
6.    'Black People's Day of Action: The Race Today Collective reunite 40 years on, Part 1: Political strategy and organisation'.
7.    Author interview with Farrukh Dhondy, 31 March 2022.
8.    'Black People's Day of Action: The Race Today Collective reunite 40 years on, Part 1: Political strategy and organisation'.
9.    K. Andrews, 'Forty years on from the New Cross fire, what has changed for black Britons?', *Guardian*, 17 January 2021, https://www.theguardian.com/world/2021/jan/17/forty-years-on-from-the-new-cross-fire-what-has-changed-for-black-britons [accessed December 2021].
10.   'Today in London anti-racist history, 1981: the Black People's Day of Action protests the New Cross Fire'.
11.   Alliance of the Black Parents Movement, Black Youth Movement and the Race Today Collective, *The New Cross Massacre Story: Interviews with John La Rose* (George Padmore Institute, 2020, first edition 1984), p. 12.
12.   *Uprising: Blame*, dir. S. McQueen, BBC, 2021.
13.   New Cross Massacre Action Committee meeting flyer, London Metropolitan Archives, LMA4463/B/08/02.

14. 'Black People's Day of Action: The Race Today Collective reunite 40 years on, Part 1'.
15. Andrews.
16. Letter from National Front organiser Brian Bunting to families of deceased, George Padmore Institute, NCM1/3/1/1/28.
17. 'Black People's Day of Action: The Race Today Collective reunite 40 years on, Part 2: A watershed moment', webinar, March 2021, Darcus Howe Legacy Collection, https://www.youtube.com/watch?v=Zg6xV5VT8ec [accessed February 2023].
18. V. Ware, *The Black People's Day of Action 02.03.1981* (Café Royal Books, 2020), p. 1.
19. Author interview with Farrukh Dhondy.
20. 'Black People's Day of Action: The Race Today Collective reunite 40 years on, Part 2'.
21. Ibid.
22. N. White, 'Black People's Day of Action: Inside the 1981 New Cross Fire march that brought Britain to a standstill', *HuffPost*, 18 January 2021, huffingtonpost.co.uk/entry/new-cross-fire-black-peoples-day-of-action_uk_5e582608c5b6450a30bc0ac3 [accessed December 2021].
23. Alliance of the Black Parents Movement, Black Youth Movement and the Race Today Collective.
24. 'Black People's Day of Action: narrative of events on the day of the protest march through London', George Padmore Institute, NCM1/2/2/2/1.
25. 'Black People's Day of Action: The Race Today Collective reunite 40 years on, Part 2'.
26. P. Brown, D. Budge and K. Deyes, 'Day the Blacks Ran Riot in London', *Sun*, 3 March 1981, pp. 14–15, George Padmore Institute, NCM4/1/1.
27. P. Mason and P. Hardy, 'Rampage of a Mob', *Daily Express*, 3 March 1981, p. 1, George Padmore Institute, NCM4/1/1.
28. S. Cook, 'Police deny that patrol tactics were provocative', *Guardian*, 13 April 1981, p. 2.
29. C. John, 'The legacy of the Brixton riots', *BBC News*, 5 April 2006, http://news.bbc.co.uk/2/hi/uk_news/4854556.stm [accessed April 2022].
30. R. Waters, *Thinking Black: Britain, 1964–1985* (University of California Press, 2019), p. 175.
31. V. Hunter, '"Defend yourself, unity is strength", the Brixton Defence Campaign 1981–1985', Black Cultural Archives, https://www.bcaexhibits.org/brixtondefence/impact [accessed December 2021].
32. Cook.
33. 'How smouldering tension erupted to set Brixton aflame – archive, 1981', *Guardian*, 13 April 1981, https://www.theguardian.com/theguardian/1981/apr/13/fromthearchive [accessed December 2021]; F. Brenton, 'Brixton riots (April 10–12 1981)', Blackpast, 13 June 2010, https://www.blackpast.org/global-african-history/brixton-riots-april-10-12-1981/ [accessed December 2021].
34. *Uprising: The Front Line*, dir. S. McQueen, BBC, 2021.

35.  'How smouldering tension erupted'.
36.  L. Mackie et al., 'Brixton rioting flares again as police move in', *Guardian*, 13 April 1981, p. 1.
37.  R. Ramdin, *Reimaging Britain: 500 years of Black and Asian history* (Pluto Press, 1999), p. 300.
38.  Brenton; C. Brown, 'Whitelaw pressed to expand scope of Scarman inquiry into Brixton riots', *Guardian*, 14 April 1981, p. 4.
39.  Author interview with Farrukh Dhondy.
40.  J. Pierre, 'From Brixton 1981 to BLM 2020: reflections on Black uprisings', Museum of London, 27 October 2020, https://www.museumoflondon.org.uk/discover/brixton-1981-blm-2020-black-uprisings-londons-history [accessed December 2021].
41.  L. Mackie and P. Keel, 'Fears of violence threaten rally', *Guardian*, 15 April 1981, p. 24.
42.  Cook.
43.  'How smouldering tension erupted'.
44.  A. McHardy, 'Injured PCs describe ordeal of bricks, bottles and flames', *Guardian*, 13 April 1981, p. 2.
45.  J. Schneider, 'Ferguson: Riot or rebellion?', *Huffington Post*, 18 February 2015, https://www.huffpost.com/entry/ferguson-race-riots-rebellion_b_6354102 [accessed April 2022].
46.  'Writer to BBC interviewer: "Stop accusing me of being a rioter"', Yahoo!, 9 August 2011, https://news.yahoo.com/news/blogs/cutline/writer-bbc-interviewer-show-respect-old-west-indian-203939047.html?guccounter=1&guce_referrer=aHR0cHM6Ly93d3cuZWNvc2lhLm9yZy8&guce_referrer_sig=AQAAAJLe0DzttAVsEo1Iub7IpQ-i6hnMBY-_5oeWsLny6yuJZYl1S_n98eyiZZZkk__VzwVlrFZgSgaHq1SOXmLbFLvqra_ui_nZT4EZ1qUFt4vvfuoJTEyK4xXrYVTiuxwSoNY2DEBIwbrz6D6EKV7RaU7lsE0UbCWnK0WqsFsZiyj2 [accessed April 2022].
47.  Mackie and Keel.
48.  Ibid.
49.  P. Keel, C. Brown and J. Langdon, 'Scarman will hold Brixton riot inquiry', *Guardian*, 14 April 1981, p. 1.
50.  'The New Cross Fire 1981 Lewisham', flyer from Brixton Black Women's Group, George Padmore Institute, NCM1/3/1/2.
51.  P. Fryer, *Staying Power: The history of black people in Britain* (Pluto Press, reprint 2018, original 1984), p. 402.
52.  '"Halt Brixton inquiry" fails', *Evening Standard*, 9 July 1981, p. 2.
53.  S. V. Rattner, 'New violence hits 10 English cities but is less serious', *New York Times*, 12 July 1981, https://www.nytimes.com/1981/07/12/world/new-violence-hits-10-english-cities-but-is-less-serious.html [accessed December 2021].
54.  K. White, '4-Skins manager boasted of being a thug for Nazis', *Observer*, 12 July 1981, p. 3.
55.  G. Sharma, 'The British Asians who fought fascism in the seventies', Al Jazeera, 23 April 2019, https://www.aljazeera.com/features/2019/4/23/the-british-asians-who-fought-fascism-in-the-seventies [accessed December 2021].

56. P. Deeley et al., 'Portrait of an urban village', *Observer*, 5 July 1981, p. 13.
57. C. Foley, 'Police violence and death: an old story', *Guardian*, 26 April 2009, https://www.theguardian.com/commentisfree/2009/apr/26/police-blair-peach [accessed December 2021].
58. Interview with Balraj Purewal, 2014, Bishopsgate Institute, digital:works collection, DW/6/1.
59. *Brixton Defence Campaign Bulletin*, 2 (1981), p. 5, Ahmed Iqbal Ullah Race Relations Archive, Tandana Archive: papers of the Bradford and Sheffield Asian Youth Movements, GB3228.6/1/7/6.
60. Interview with Suresh Grover, 2014, Bishopsgate Institute, digital:works collection, DW/6/13.
61. The Monitoring Group, 'Our history', https://tmg-uk.org/historyoftmg [accessed December 2021].
62. A. Beckett, 'Toxteth, 1981: the summer Liverpool burned – by the rioter and economist on opposite sides', *Guardian*, 14 September 2015, https://www.theguardian.com/cities/2015/sep/14/toxteth-riots-1981-summer-liverpool-burned-patrick-minford-jimi-jagne [accessed December 2021]; *Brixton Defence Campaign Bulletin*, 2 (1981), p. 2.
63. E. Vulliamy, 'Toxteth revisited, 30 years after the riots', *Guardian*, 3 July 2011, https://www.theguardian.com/uk/2011/jul/03/toxteth-liverpool-riot-30-years [accessed December 2021].
64. Beckett; 'Britain: the cities erupt', *Newsweek*, 20 July 1981, Ahmed Iqbal Ullah Race Relations Archive, Institute of Race Relations newspaper cuttings, GB3228.1/46.
65. 'Police chief defends use of CS gas in Toxteth riots', *Birmingham Post*, 18 September 1981, Ahmed Iqbal Ullah Race Relations Archive, Institute of Race Relations newspaper cuttings, GB3228.1/48.
66. T. Sharratt, 'Police cleared of manslaughter in Toxteth riot', *Guardian*, 6 May 1982, p. 4.
67. *Brixton Defence Campaign Bulletin*, 2 (1981), p. 3.
68. Vulliamy.
69. F. Ridley, 'Will it take an away match to waken Downing Street?', *Guardian*, 13 July 1981, p. 7.
70. M. Morris et al., '1,000 on rampage in Moss Side', *Guardian*, 9 July 1981, p. 1.
71. G. John, *Moss Side 1981: More than just a riot* (Gus John Books, 2011), p. 54.
72. 'Moss Side 1981 – riot or uprising?', *The Meteor*, 28 February 2021, themeteor.org/2021/02/28/moss-side-1981-riot-or-uprising [accessed December 2021].
73. R. Thornber et al., 'Anderton takes off the kid gloves', *Guardian*, 10 July 1981, pp. 1 and 24.
74. A. Elliott-Cooper, *Black Resistance to British Policing* (Manchester University Press, 2021), p. 42.
75. John, p. 20.
76. Ibid., p. 14.

77. Ibid., p. 60.
78. *Brixton Defence Campaign Bulletin*, 2 (1981), p. 6.
79. M. Morris et al., 'Renewed violence flares up in Moss Side', *Guardian*, 9 July 1981, p. 26.
80. *Brixton Defence Campaign Bulletin*, 2 (1981), p. 6.
81. 'Editor's Comment, Let's make sure it doesn't happen here', *Edgware & Mill Hill Times*, 9 July 1981; A. Trimingham, 'Could the riots happen here?', *Evening Argus*, 22 July 1981, Ahmed Iqbal Ullah Race Relations Archive, Institute of Race Relations newspaper cuttings, GB3228.1/46.
82. A. Butler, 'Toxic Toxteth: Understanding press stigmatization of Toxteth during the 1981 uprising', *Journalism*, 21:4 (2020), p. 542.
83. A. Rusbridger, 'We weren't looking for trouble . . .', *Guardian*, 10 July 1981, p. 13.
84. P. Bishop, 'When Brixton went up in flames', *Observer*, 10 April 2011, https://www.theguardian.com/uk/2011/apr/10/brixton-riot-april-1981-feature [accessed December 2021].
85. Lord Scarman, *The Scarman Report: The Brixton Disorders 10–12 April 1981* (Penguin, 1982), p. 209.
86. Ibid., p. 119.
87. Ibid., p. 198.
88. *Uprising: The Front Line*; Alliance of the Black Parents Movement, Black Youth Movement and the Race Today Collective, p. 27.
89. 'Margaret Thatcher's criticism of Brixton riot response revealed', *BBC News*, 30 December 2014, https://www.bbc.com/news/uk-30600064 [accessed December 2021].
90. Alliance of the Black Parents Movement, Black Youth Movement and the Race Today Collective, p. 51.
91. Scarman, p. 205.
92. Elliott-Cooper, p. 43.
93. Ibid., p. 45.
94. 'Thatcher urged "let Liverpool decline" after 1981 riots', *BBC News*, 30 December 2011, https://www.bbc.com/news/uk-16361170 [accessed December 2021].
95. J. Carpenter, 'Regeneration and the legacy of Thatcherism', *Metropolitics*, 15 October 2014, https://metropolitics.org/IMG/pdf/met-carpenter.pdf [accessed December 2021].
96. O. Saumarez Smith, 'Action for cities: the Thatcher government and inner city policy', *Urban History*, 47:2 (2019), p. 12.
97. S. Rogers, 'How Britain changed under Margaret Thatcher. In fifteen charts', *Guardian*, 8 April 2013, https://www.theguardian.com/politics/datablog/2013/apr/08/britain-changed-margaret-thatcher-charts [accessed December 2021].
98. Saumarez Smith.
99. 'The Thatcher years in statistics', *BBC News*, 9 April 2013, https://www.bbc.com/news/uk-politics-22070491 [accessed December 2021].
100. 'Youth training scheme a failure and a disgrace, Labour says', *Independent*, 13 February 1995, https://www.independent.co.uk/

news/youth-training-scheme-a-failure-and-a-disgrace-labour-says-1572820.html?r=34586 [accessed December 2021].

101.   S. Johns, 'The UK school students' strike, 1985', LibCom, 19 October 2015, https://libcom.org/history/uk-school-students-strike-1985-steven-johns [accessed December 2021].

102.   E. Ogbonna and M. Noon, 'Experiencing inequality: Ethnic minorities and the Employment Training scheme', *Work, Employment & Society*, 9:3 (September 1995), p. 538.

103.   'Youth training scheme a failure and a disgrace'.

104.   G. Younge, 'In these bleak times, imagine a world where you can thrive', *Guardian*, 10 January 2020, https://www.theguardian.com/commentisfree/2020/jan/10/bleak-times-thrive-last-column-guardian [accessed December 2021].

105.   *Uprising: Blame.*

**Conclusion: So, What Happened Next?**

1.   G. Younge, 'Ambalavaner Sivanandan obituary', *Guardian*, 7 February 2018, https://www.theguardian.com/world/2018/feb/07/ambalavaner-sivanandan [accessed January 2021].

2.   K. Shukra, *The Changing Pattern of Black Politics in Britain* (Pluto Press, 1998), p. 59.

3.   For example, academic Anandi Ramamurthy thinks it was government strategy, while Stella Dadzie, one of the founders of OWAAD, says that given the inability of the government to organise anything, it is unlikely this was a conscious choice. G. Sharma, 'The British Asians who fought fascism in the seventies', Al Jazeera, 23 April 2019, https://www.aljazeera.com/features/2019/4/23/the-british-asians-who-fought-fascism-in-the-seventies [accessed September 2021]; author interview with Stella Dadzie, 20 April 2022.

4.   Data Journalism Team, 'Election 2019: Britain's most diverse parliament', *BBC News*, 17 December 2019, https://www.bbc.com/news/election-2019-50808536 [accessed December 2021].

5.   Office for National Statistics, 'Population of England and Wales', 7 August 2020, https://www.ethnicity-facts-figures.service.gov.uk/uk-population-by-ethnicity/national-and-regional-populations/population-of-england-and-wales/latest.

6.   Commission on Race and Ethnic Disparities, 'Commission on Race and Ethnic Disparities: The Report', March 2021, p. 8.

7.   Home Office, 'Hate Crime, England and Wales, 2019 to 2020', 28 October 2020, https://www.gov.uk/government/statistics/hate-crime-england-and-wales-2019-to-2020/hate-crime-england-and-wales-2019-to-2020 [accessed December 2021].

8.   Author interview with Farrukh Dhondy, 31 March 2022.

9.   Z. Masani, 'We'll take care of it ourselves', *Time Out*, 8–14 June 1979, p. 8, Tower Hamlets Local History Library and Archives, LCX00002 Class 300.2 Folder 2.

10.   Home Office, 'Police, Crime, Sentencing and Courts Bill 2021: protest powers factsheet', 7 July 2021, https://www.gov.uk/

government/publications/police-crime-sentencing-and-courts-bill-2021-factsheets/police-crime-sentencing-and-courts-bill-2021-protest-powers-factsheet [accessed December 2021].

Bringing a book from manuscript to what you are reading is a team effort.

Dialogue Books would like to thank everyone who helped to publish *The Shoulders We Stand On* in the UK.

**Editorial**
Sharmaine Lovegrove
Maisie Lawrence
Amy Baxter
Zoe Carroll

**Contracts**
Megan Phillips
Bryony Hall
Amy Patrick
Sasha Duszynska Lewis
Anne Goddard

**Sales**
Caitriona Row
Dominic Smith
Frances Doyle
Hannah Methuen
Lucy Hine
Toluwalope Ayo-Ajala

**Design**
Charlotte Stroomer

**Production**
Narges Nojoumi

**Publicity**
Millie Seaward

**Marketing**
Emily Moran

**Operations**
Kellie Barnfield
Millie Gibson
Sanjeev Braich

**Finance**
Andrew Smith
Ellie Barry

**Copy-Editor**
Howard Watson

**Proofreader**
Kim Bishop